INTERPRETING THE SELF

INTERPRETING THE

Two Hundred Years of American Autobiography

ELF

DIANE BJORKLUND

The University of Chicago Press

Chicago & London

DIANE BJORKLUND is an assistant professor in the
Department of Sociology and Anthropology at Illinois
State University. This is her first book.

The University of Chicago Press, Chicago 60637
The University of Chicago Press, Ltd., London
© 1998 by The University of Chicago
All rights reserved. Published 1998
Printed in the United States of America
07 06 05 04 03 02 01 00 99 98   1 2 3 4 5
ISBN: 0-226-05447-0 (cloth)

Library of Congress Cataloging-in-Publication Data

Bjorklund, Diane.
    Interpreting the self : two hundred years of American
autobiography / Diane Bjorklund.
        p.   cm.
    Includes bibliographical references and index.
    ISBN: 0-226-05447-0 (cloth)
    1. Autobiography.   2. United States—Biography—
History and criticism.   I. Title.
CT25.B58   1998
920'.073—dc21
    [B]   98-23914
                                                  CIP

⊗The paper used in this production meets the minimum
requirements of the American National Standard for
Information Sciences—Permanence of Paper for Printed
Library Materials, ANSI z39.48-1992.

FOR DAVID & THOMAS

Contents

Prologue

When I was a child, one thing I seldom brought home from the library was an autobiography. During summers in particular, I would read many books, but I always skipped over biographies and autobiographies. At the time, I thought they would be boring; I assumed they were nothing more than a collection of dull facts about historical figures—full of details that I probably would have to study at school anyway. It wasn't until much later that I began to appreciate autobiographies on both a personal and a theoretical level. I came to see that autobiographies can help us make sense of our lives and give voice to thoughts and feelings that we also may have had. We may be reassured to learn what we share with others, while also getting a glimpse of the compass of human experience yet unknown to us. With autobiographies, as literary theorist J. Hillis Miller (1995, p. 69) has observed about stories in general, "We investigate, perhaps invent, the meaning of human life."

Moreover, autobiographies, as a record of how people have interpreted and explained their lives, are full of rich material for theorists. They are much more than straightforward attempts at personal histories; they are an amalgam of cultural ideas, scruples, art, imagination, rhetoric, and self-presentation. As literary scholars in the last half of the twentieth century have increasingly recognized this complexity, they have shifted from their former neglect of autobiography as "an artless literature of fact," as Paul John Eakin (1992, p. 30) has pointed out, to an appreciation of autobiography as "imaginative art." Since the 1950s, literary critics such as Roy Pascal have explored the nature of truth in autobiography, and they have recast it as both creative act and literary genre. The subjectivity of autobiography has become a topic for analysis, particularly the fine line between fact and fiction when persons tell their life stories. Critics now recognize that an autobiographer faces complex and intriguing problems of self-interpretation and self-construction. Furthermore, in conjunction with the contemporary interest in narrative, literary scholars have become engaged by the question of how the textual requirements of fitting one's life into an intelligible and recognizable story transform autobiographies. In their studies of autobiographies, these scholars have based much of their work on the careful analysis of a small number of well-crafted, classic autobiographies— works that are to be appreciated on an individual basis and evaluated as art.

As a sociologist, however, I am interested in autobiographies as both cultural product and social act. They are texts in which the authors reflect as well as respond to their culture. The self-interpretations of autobiographers can tell us about changing ways of thinking and talking about the self. Their stories are not strictly personal and unique; they consider their own lives and organize their experiences in the light of general ideas they have learned about what it means to be human. Like all of us, their ideas about themselves have been significantly shaped by their culture and era. They articulate even their most private self-understandings to themselves using the social medium of language, and their understandings cannot escape the influence of what they have learned as participants in a shared social world. Thus we are able to ask these sociological questions: How does historical location shape the stories persons tell about themselves and the ways in which they think about themselves? And how have ways of thinking about self changed over time? There has been considerable interest among social scientists in the concept of the self, but they have generally left aside questions of historical and cultural differences in how people have interpreted and explained the self.

Furthermore, autobiographers' attempts at self-interpretation are even more complicated because they are simultaneously engaged in a performance—that is, they are trying to place themselves in a good light for their readers. By writing an autobiography, they are engaging in a social act. Because they expose their personal lives to criticism, they attempt to give not only meaning to their lives but also value. We can see how they use rhetoric (sometimes adeptly, sometimes awkwardly) to persuade their readers that they have admirable traits and have made important choices in their lives for acceptable reasons. What traits they claim to possess and how they justify the choices they have made can tell us about extant values and ideas during the eras in which they wrote.

Autobiographies, therefore, are a good resource for investigating changing ideas about the self. They are historical records that have been steadily produced and preserved over a lengthy time period. Autobiographers show us how people have made sense of their lives and experiences as they answered the question, "Who am I?" They also offer many clues (implicitly and explicitly) as to how they have conceived the self and what they have considered to be a good life. We can see, for example, whether they think of human beings as creatures who cannot control their "passions" without divine assistance, or whether they see them as beings with great potential to be cultivated. We can find them answering questions such as the following: What part do others play in their lives? What do all human beings share, and conversely, what distinctions can be made between them? How difficult is it for individuals to know themselves? Has society shaped who they are and how they act? How much control do they have over the direction of their lives? Accordingly, autobiographies offer researchers a way of looking into the storehouse of ideas about the self. We can use autobiographies, in the spirit of C. Wright Mills (1959), to draw the connection between history and individual biography.

In this book, my objective has been to explore these social aspects of autobiographies—their use of shared cultural ideas about the self as well as the social situational constraints of impression management and the conventions and requirements of form when turning one's life history into a narrative. I read more than one hundred American autobiographies from the last two centuries—including not only the famous but also the obscure. By choosing autobiographers from every decade since 1800, I was able to compare ideas they used to interpret and explain the self and look for changes over time. From these comparisons, I have outlined four models of the self used by these American autobiographers during different time periods. Such models make it possible to gain analytical focus within the complexity of social life and see patterns in the ideas that autobiographers use. Autobiographers usually do not explicitly and systematically lay out a coherent theory of the self, but they do reveal their assumptions about human nature and selfhood as they explain their own lives.

As part of the generalizing that accompanies a sociological study of many autobiographers, what we admittedly lose is the fullness and distinctiveness of each autobiographer's self-portrait. Although our own contemporary (Western) preference is to stress the singularity of individual lives, what we gain in abstracting from these autobiographies and looking for similarities is a bigger picture—the cultural and historical background of ideas about the self. The autobiographer, no matter how exceptional, uses shared vocabularies of the self to communicate with others and to think about self. We cannot easily detect such commonalities by reading just a few autobiographies or focusing on individual stories. But with a perspective gained by comparisons, we can then return to specific autobiographers and enhance our understanding of them by seeing how they reflect, affirm, modify, reject, evaluate, or weave together the ideas common in their own eras to create personal meaning for their own lives. We can discover what they are taking for granted, and we can see more clearly how each autobiographer is unique.

Autobiographers also wrestle with the question of how much emphasis to give to their individuality as opposed to universal feelings, thoughts, and experiences that will resonate with readers. They, too, must gloss over the complexity of their own views and abstract from the myriad details of their lives for the sake of putting together a story of manageable length. In a memoir of a person's life, as André Gide (1935, p. 234) expressed it simply, "Everything is always more complicated than one makes out." They try to reconcile the particular with the universal, the idiosyncratic with shared cultural understandings, and the subjective with the objective. In the words of literary scholar Marjorie Smelstor (1984, pp. 245–46), autobiographers must contend with the "tension between the family and the Family, the mother and the Mother, the self and the Self." They are seeking to be recognized as singular human beings, but they also aspire to speak beyond their personal experience to contribute, in at least some small way, to an understanding of the human condition—answering the question of what they have learned about life.

Acknowledgments

Samuel Johnson once commented that "the greatest part of a writer's time is spent in reading . . . a man will turn over half a library to make one book." But he also could have acknowledged the importance of conversations. While preparing this book, I found discussions with friends and colleagues to be invaluable. I wish to thank Ralph Turner, Robert Perinbanayagam, Sam Heilman, Harry Levine, Pyong Gap Min, Bernadette Tarallo, Beverly Lozano, and Conrad Miller. Special thanks to Lyn Lofland, who has always stood as a model scholar for me, and to Gary Hamilton, who invariably can, with a few perspicacious questions, lead me to see things more clearly. I'm also grateful to Lauren Seiler for his careful reading of the manuscript; to Bob Kapsis for his encouragement and assistance; to my editor, Doug Mitchell, for his patience and graciousness; and to the two anonymous readers for the Press for their astute suggestions and criticism. And, of course, I'm indebted to Paul Blumberg, my companion and colleague, whose support and never-failing sense of humor have carried me through.

Chapter One $\mathcal{I}$NTRODUCTION

Consider what immense forces society brings to play upon each of us, how that society changes from decade to decade; and also from class to class; well, if we cannot analyze these invisible presences, we know very little of the subject of the memoir; and . . . how futile life-writing becomes. VIRGINIA WOOLF

"I only put in all that self stuff," Erving Goffman once remarked about his analyses of social interaction, "because people like to read about it."[1] Goffman was joking, but he was right, of course, that most of us find the topic of self to be fascinating. As human beings, we are self-reflective creatures. We ponder not only our own qualities and traits but also the nature of self-hood—trying to make sense of what it means to be human. Researchers, too, have shown considerable zeal for "all that self stuff" in recent decades. As the clinical psychologist Louis Sass (1988, p. 551) observed, "The 'self' . . . seems to have returned with a vengeance." Sass was referring to the revitalized significance of the concept of self for psychologists and psychoanalysts, but his comment applies to the burgeoning discussions of the self by anthropologists, sociologists, and literary scholars as well.[2] In this chapter, I want to place my own interest in ideas about the self in American autobiographies into this larger story about changes in scholarly theorizing about the self.

Much of this academic attention has focused on the self as a concept used by persons in everyday life. Researchers have generally turned aside from questions about the nature of the self (i.e., as some essence or entity with attributes) to an examination of how people talk about the self.[3] This view of the self as a linguistic concept, in turn, is part of a widespread scholarly interest in the more general question of how people make sense of and talk about their worlds and everyday experience. How do people categorize and organize their experience? What do their customs, rituals, and institutions mean to them? How do they account for their behavior and that of others? Examining how human beings give meaning to the world springs from a reflexive trend in the humanities and social sciences that involves asking epistemological questions about the nature and limitations of knowledge and reason. The question becomes not only how accurately human beings can know and represent the world using language, but also how they (including scientists and scholars) do explain the world and what influences these explanations.

Such questions contrast with the approach of those scientists earlier in the twentieth century who found inquiry into the human mind (including how human beings interpret their worlds) unworthy of pursuit since it involved the study of what was going on "inside" people's heads and was unreliably subjective. Behaviorists, for example, who were prominent in psychology from the 1920s into the 1940s, opted instead to investigate the readily observable behavior of people—a choice that led the philosopher and social psychologist George Herbert Mead (1934, p. 3) to comment that their attitude toward the mind reminded him of the Queen of Hearts in *Alice in Wonderland:* "Off with their heads!" But now researchers with an interpretive orientation stress that, to understand human beings, we must do more than observe their actions; we must interpret the meanings communicated by their actions (words, gestures, and acts) and, more generally, the meanings and import they attach to self, others, and world.

Theorists who adopt such an outlook generally base their approach on the sociological and anthropological assumption that persons' ideas about the world are profoundly influenced by social context: place, time, and social situation. The ways in which individuals construe their world and their experiences are not simply arbitrary but are influenced by their cultural and historical vantage points. In the words of the anthropologist Clifford Geertz (1973, p. 360), "Human thought is consummately social: social in its origins, social in its functions, social in its forms, social in its applications." The research goal, therefore, becomes what Geertz (1983, p. 154) has called "the ethnography of thinking": not universals about human behavior or a generic explanation of the functioning of the human mind, but the examination of beliefs and practices within a social context ("local knowledge")—looking at the diversity of historical, cultural, and situational differences.

In anthropology, where ethnographers have done much to establish the proposition that culture influences human behavior, the interest in meaning is illustrated by the development of cognitive anthropology in the late 1950s and the interpretive or symbolic anthropology of Clifford Geertz, Victor Turner, and David Schneider since the 1960s. Geertz (1973, p. 89), in particular, has promulgated the idea that culture is a shared system of meanings and symbols that persons use to "communicate, perpetuate, and develop their knowledge about and attitudes toward life." The task, then, for interpretive anthropologists has been to offer an in-depth explication of the "native's point of view." Rather than focusing on political and economic determinants of human behavior, they look to the influence of culture on how people think, feel, and act upon the world (Ortner 1984). Even those anthropologists who argue that this view of culture, with its implications of homogeneity, overlooks important differences, conflicting "discourses" (accounts of the world), and power relations, still look to socially situated or contextualized ideas as important in elucidating human behavior.

Similarly, by many reports, a "cognitive revolution" occurred in psychology during the 1950s and 1960s. Rather than sidestepping questions about the human thought process as did the behaviorists, cognitive psychologists legitimized the study of mental processes and cognitive representations of the world—including how people explain human behavior (e.g., causal attribution theory). Their approach, however, has generally been universalistic (looking for invariants of mental processes) rather than cross-cultural, and many have turned to a study of the mental processing of information in the mind using the computer as a model. Nevertheless, some researchers such as Jerome Bruner, a pioneer in cognitive psychology, continue to urge their colleagues to study collectively constructed meanings within specific social settings in order to understand human behavior. Kenneth Gergen and John Shotter, strong advocates within psychology for a social constructionist approach, also call for an investigation of the way people make sense of the world in terms of their culture and era (and how Western psychology itself can be viewed in these terms).

In sociology, there has been considerable interest in the construction of meaning in everyday life. In symbolic interactionism, ethnomethodology, conversation analysis, sociolinguistics, cognitive sociology, cultural studies, interpretive social science, and Berger and Luckmann's (1966) influential discussion of the social construction of reality, we can find a recognition of the importance of what the sociologist William I. Thomas (1923) had earlier called "the definition of the situation." Thomas, along with Florian Znaniecki, was influential in turning sociological attention to "attitudes" and values in order to understand human action (Fleming 1967). Sociologists generally assume that there is a shared set of ideas (norms, beliefs, values, and meanings) within a culture that makes it possible for persons to communicate with one another and conduct a shared social life; these have been variously called background expectancies (Garfinkel 1967), shared understandings (Becker 1982), social presuppositions (Goffman 1983), and so forth.

This enthusiasm for investigating the construction of meaning extends beyond the social sciences to the humanities, where there has been particular interest in how people "do things with words" (following the work of Wittgenstein, Ryle, Austin, and Searle). A consideration of how people comprehend the world and communicate with others necessarily includes an examination of language as a tool that both enables and restricts these processes. In philosophy and literary criticism, the increased attention to the social nature of language and its relationship to human thought is part of what prognosticators have deemed a "linguistic turn" or an "interpretive turn."[4] Philosophers and literary theorists look to the "predicaments" of having to use language to think about and represent the world as well as the socially situated nature of such representations. Among those literary critics who study discourse, rhetoric, or narrative, some have adopted Berger and Luckmann's notion of the social construction of reality, although they often combine it with a study of how the asymmetries of social power relate to the dominance of particular ideas. The work of Michel Foucault has also been influential in directing attention to the uses of discourse, in particular how power and authority are interwoven with the promulgation and maintenance of ideas.

As scholars have turned to the question of how human beings interpret the world, it is not surprising that they have also asked questions about self-interpretation as well. A crucial part of giving meaning to the world is giving meaning to one's self—how we reflect about ourselves and our experiences and, more generally, what we think about the nature of human beings. In many disciplines, accordingly, scholars have converged upon the idea that the self is a concept that is socially created (Johnson 1985). From this perspective, we should examine how people comprehend and describe the self instead of trying to investigate the self as some hypothetical set of traits or internal center of conscious action.[5]

Studying how people use the concept of self in everyday life leads us to the question of cultural and historical variations in ways of understanding the self. Do other groups understand the self as we do? How have our (and their) constructions of the self changed over time? Since the 1950s, anthropologists have developed Marcel Mauss's ([1938] 1979) argument, following Emile Durkheim's ([1912] 1961) discussion of collective representations, that the self has assumed different meanings in different places.[6] They study how people in different cultures explain emotions, the life cycle, the nature and capabilities of human beings, and so on. And they ask how such persons make use of such interpretations of the self to explain and account for their actions in everyday life.

In contrast, however, there has been little extended empirical work into historical changes in understandings of the self.[7] This has been true for both psychology and sociology. In American psychology, the concept of the self was out of favor when behaviorism was dominant from the 1920s into the 1940s. B. F. Skinner (1974, p. 184), for example, had jettisoned the self as "a vestige of animism, a doctrine which in its crudest form held that the body was moved by one or more indwelling spirits." In the 1940s, however, psychologists such as Gardner Murphy and Gordon Allport helped restore an appreciation of the self as indispensable in explaining human behavior. Since then, psychologists have done abundant empirical research on the self-concept, particularly the idea of self-esteem.[8] In addition, cognitive psychologists in the mid-1970s began to view the self as an "organization of knowledge" that helps to systematize a person's experience cognitively, and they began researching mental representations of the self.[9] Much of this research, however, like studies of the self-concept, has been predicated upon psychology's traditional goal of explaining the generic human being independent of historical or cultural influences. More recently, psychologists who take a social constructionist approach have argued for an interpretive psychology that studies historical and cultural differences in how persons conceptualize the self.[10]

Within sociology, the idea that the self is a social creation has been well established since Charles H. Cooley's ([1902] 1956) and George Herbert Mead's (1934) influential discussions of the social nature of self-awareness—a trait that they believed distinguishes human beings from other animals. Mead argued that a person's self-awareness and concept of self are not given, but emerge only through social interaction and hence are social creations. That is, persons learn to reflect about themselves and their own actions in light of the responses of others. Mead's position, therefore, contrasts with the belief of idealistic philosophers and psychologists, as A. R. Luria (1976, p. 144) has explained, that "self-awareness is a primary and irreducible property of mental life, with no history in and of itself."

In particular, the sociologists known as symbolic interactionists have developed this interest in the reflexivity of the actor and the importance of the self as a construct. They have examined the ways in which social interaction, based on shared symbols, shapes the meaning that human beings give to the self. To avoid a determinist cast, however, many symbolic interactionists have emphasized the inventiveness of individuals in creating meaning. Hence they have focused on the process of face-to-face interaction rather than the specifics of the "normative background" or shared cultural ideas about the self.

Erving Goffman was particularly important in extending the notion of the self as a social creation by stressing its situational nature. He emphasized that the self is not something internal that is continuous and persists over time, but instead that its meaning is established dramaturgically during social interaction in particular situations. Thus Goffman (1959, pp. 252–53) defined the self as "a *product* of a scene that comes off, and . . . not a *cause* of it" (his emphasis). Although he noted that the presentation of self will vary both historically and culturally, his purpose was to detail the process of staging appearances and not to do comparative work in cultural or historical variations in this process.

Sociologists, like psychologists, have also done many empirical studies of the self-concept.[11] In the 1950s, Manford Kuhn and Thomas McPartland recognized the influence of self-attitudes on human action, and they set out to develop empirical measures of the self-concept such as the Twenty Statements Test. Following in this vein, Morris Rosenberg (1979) and others have related self-concept and self-esteem to social determinants such as education and social class. But the empirical focus of this research has been individuals' specific self-concepts, leaving aside a consideration of changing cultural ideas about the self as a social factor in the formation of self-concept.

In the mid-1970s, however, Ralph Turner helped pave the way for sociological research on historical variations in how people use the concept of self by publishing an influential article on shifts in the meaning of the phrase "the real self."[12] His findings from the administration of the Twenty Statements Test and his own "True Self" questionnaire, however, were necessarily limited to recent decades. Additionally, some sociologists such as Robert Perinbanayagam (1991) have begun to connect Mead's argument that the self is a social creation to the flourishing interest in the humanities in the topics of discourse and narrative. Such an alliance leads to the question of how persons have conceptualized and talked about the self in everyday discourse, and how people make sense of their experiences through stories.[13]

Continuing in this general direction of examining the self as a concept that varies culturally and historically will help us develop a comprehensive theory of self-understanding. Socially shared ideas about the self are an integral part of our self-concepts. We all make observations and develop hypotheses about what motivates human beings (be it love, innate drives, self-esteem, desire for wealth, or transcendental forces) and how human beings ought to act. We learn such theories of the self through social interaction, and they frame the processes of developing a self-concept and self-esteem. As part of our socialization, we learn *vocabularies of self* to think about and assess our experiences and behavior.[14] We use these vocabularies to describe ourselves and explain our actions to others (and to ourselves) in the course of everyday life. Such vocabularies of self are not strictly personal; we enter into an ongoing conversation. Shared understandings about selfhood include beliefs about the extent to which human beings are in control of their lives, the traits shared by all human beings, the role of emotion in human actions, the ability of human beings to explain their own actions, what kind of change (if any) is to be expected in one's self over a lifetime, and what qualities are admirable in human beings.

As Mead (1934) argued, we learn to see ourselves as others do by "taking the role of the other." We begin to conceptualize our own self—a reflexive process enabled by communication with others.[15] Once we become self-aware, we can then begin to render our own history. Mead (1934, p. 158) also observed that through social interaction we learn shared cultural ideas—what he called the "generalized other." He added that "these social or group attitudes . . . are included as elements in the structure or constitution of his self, in the same way that the attitudes of particular other individuals are." Mead's analytic interest, however, was in the *process* of developing self-awareness, and he was not as directly concerned with the specifics of the varying standards, beliefs, and values that constitute the generalized other.[16] The self, however, arises not only out of the interaction process with specific others but also by using ideas available for constructing a viewpoint of the self. Selves are culturally as well as socially constructed.

When, in our role as researchers, we ask people to tell us about themselves, we are not accruing "raw" data uninfluenced by history, culture, or situation. We have no direct access to lives as actually lived; what we get are interpretations of experience.[17] When people produce such self-reports, they draw from what they have learned from participation in a culture. As Mead (1936, p. 375) argued, "The human self arises through its ability to take the attitude of the group to which he belongs—because he can talk to himself in terms of the community to which he belongs." But I would add that persons can also talk *of* themselves for this reason. Moreover, such self-conceptions are mediated by a language that is public and not private.

These shared understandings about the nature of selfhood should be an essential part of a comprehensive theory of the self. As sociologist Philip Corrigan (1975, p. 219) noted in a more general context: "What is left out of accounting are the collective and historical practices which provide *resources:* the *range* of possible ideas from which 'thoughts' may be taken; the *sum* of sentiments which may be used to evaluate people and things; and the '*dictionaries*' of grammar and vocabulary, which make talk possible" (his emphasis). We can enrich our understanding by fully investigating how self-theories vary between (and within) different cultures, from one historical period to another, and from situation to situation. Furthermore, we can examine how persons actively use these ideas for their own purposes. To pursue such questions empirically, we can ask people about their ideas, or we can interpret the meaning of ideas as they are publicly expressed (and thus observable) in the social world—through conversation, writings, rituals, institutions, and ideology. One way to study vocabularies of the self over time is through autobiographies.

Autobiographies as a Source of Data

Autobiographies are a bountiful source of information about vocabularies of the self, and they allow us to study changes in self-understandings over time. We can see how people from different eras interpret and portray their lives for an audience of readers. As autobiographers put together their life histories, they must reflect about themselves and develop an overarching perspective on their lives to a greater extent than most of us have the inclination to do. To write such a sustained story of self, as the literary scholar Paul John Eakin (1985, p. 9) commented, requires "a special, heightened form of that reflexive consciousness which is the distinctive feature of our human nature."

Despite the abundance of autobiographies (over 11,000 have been published in the United States alone), researchers in the social and behavioral sciences have made little use of them. A prominent early exception was William James ([1902] 1939) in *The Varieties of Religious Experience*. In the following decade, W. I. Thomas and Florian Znaniecki ([1918–20] 1958) included autobiographical material in *The Polish Peasant in Europe and America,* and they proclaimed that personal life records are the "perfect type of sociological material" (pp. 1832–33). Not everyone, however, has been so enthusiastic about such records, and criticism of the use of personal documents has been common since Thomas and Znaniecki's classic work.[18] In sociology, it was not until the late 1970s, as part of the increased concern with how people give meaning to the world, that there has been significant renewed interest in personal documents and in the act of reporting and writing about oneself.[19]

Critics of personal documents have questioned the reliability of such introspective accounts, which they assume to be intermixed with emotion and imagination. Sociologists Howard Schwartz and Jerry Jacobs (1979, p. 70), for example, commented that life histories must be, "if possible, corroborated by another in order to ensure against distortions in memory, selective perceptions, and the like." This concern over the unreliability and subjectivity of autobiographies is well-advised for those who would use them for factual data on topics such as criminal behavior or historical events. But as a record of prevailing ideas about self, the subjectivity of autobiographies is precisely what is interesting. As Herbert Blumer (1969) argued, we ought to study human action from the perspective of the persons involved.

Autobiographies also cannot tell us if there are historical changes in how people act in their everyday lives. It makes sense that persons' beliefs about self will affect their action—as we can see, for instance, in studies relating a poor self-concept to behavior. As William I. Thomas and Dorothy S. Thomas (1928, p. 572) observed, "If men define situations as real, they are real in their consequences." If persons believe, for example, that human actions are caused by external forces, then such a belief about self must significantly influence their decision-making processes and feelings of responsibility (Smith 1981). Furthermore, as the sociologist Pierre Bourdieu (1977, p. 15) has observed, an idea such as honor can even be found "embedded . . . in the form of bodily postures and stances, ways of standing, sitting, looking, speaking, or walking." In autobiographies, however, we can see how people describe themselves and their actions, but we cannot determine the linkage between what people say and how they act or what they privately believe.

Critics also point out that autobiographers do not represent a random sample of the general population. We cannot use autobiographical evidence to determine how widely shared these vocabularies of self have been among people living in the United States in different eras. Despite William Dean Howells's (1909, p. 798) claim that autobiography is the "most democratic province" of literature, such a province does not contain a true cross-section of the population. In recognition of this problem, some scholars are actively gathering the life stories (including diaries, journals, letters, and oral histories) of a wide range of persons—particularly those whose stories have previously been excluded.[20] The literary scholars Sidonie Smith and Julia Watson (1996, p. 17), for example, advocate "backyard ethnography"—looking at how people in general tell stories about their experiences—in contrast to what they call "'the high culture' of published, 'artful' autobiography."

The universe of published autobiographies, however, has not been limited to "high culture" or autobiographies of the famous or rich.[21] Particularly in the first few decades of the nineteenth century, but later as well, autobiographers could find local printers to publish their books (Charvat 1959; Cremin 1980). More than a dozen of the autobiographers in my sample had their life stories produced in such a manner. It was possible, for example, for someone obscure but with an interesting story such as the disabled sailor Samuel Patterson ([1817] 1825, p. 1), to publish an autobiography in an effort to "obtain some alleviation of . . . misfortunes from a generous publick." Furthermore, an autobiographer need not be well-educated; an editor or acquaintance could correct the grammatical and spelling errors if this was required. Thus, as the literary scholar Laura Marcus (1994) has pointed out, it became a matter of concern for nineteenth-century critics that too many ordinary persons were publishing their autobiographies. In 1826, for example, a critic in the *Quarterly Review* complained that "England expects every driveller to do his Memorabilia" (Vincent 1981, p. 30). Today, those who can't interest a publisher in their life stories can turn to vanity presses if they have the means to fund the publication. Hence, those who have published their life stories over the years include miners, school superintendents, nurses, salesmen, auctioneers, church elders, beekeepers, insurance underwriters, waiters, bus drivers, and cub scout leaders, among many others. Many of these narratives, however, have not been included in any canon of autobiographical literature or even preserved in public libraries.

Furthermore, the interpretation and explanation of selves in autobiographies is not a novel view to be found only among those who publish their life histories.[22] Autobiographers write with the intention of making sense to a general readership. To "make sense," they use shared ideas—the vocabularies of self that they have learned.[23] In addition, as I argue in Chapter 2, autobiographers are concerned with being viewed by readers as admirable persons, and they usually tailor their life stories to try to meet the general standards for such a designation. And most of them must comply with editors and publishers who, as gatekeepers, want the work to be intelligible and interesting to a general readership. Thus, although autobiographers do not represent a random sample of the population, their stories do teach us about the available vocabularies of the self.

Because of concerns about the reliability of autobiographies, social scientists have generally left it to literary scholars to lead the way in using autobiographies as a source of information about human self-understanding and self-explanation. Literary critics, too, had once shown little interest in autobiographies. During the first half of this century, when many social scientists found autobiographies too subjective and cast them, in effect, into the category of fiction, many literary critics thought of them as too fact-laden to qualify as art and placed them in the category of historical nonfiction. At midcentury, Wayne Shumaker (1954, p. 1), who undertook a historical study of English autobiographies, could compare autobiographies to an untouched abundant feast waiting in a room while the researchers stood at the door "inviting each other, by gestures and smiles of encouragement, to go first." But this situation has changed significantly among literary scholars as they have come to view autobiography as a literary genre rather than a pedestrian category of history (Sheringham 1993; Marcus 1994).

In the 1950s, this newfound interest in autobiography was represented by an influential essay by Georges Gusdorf, in which he suggested that concepts of self found in autobiographies are culturally variable (Olney 1980). Then, in 1960, the literary scholar Roy Pascal's *Design and Truth in Autobiography* kindled further interest by raising the question of whether we can distinguish between fact and fiction in autobiography. A year later, Louis Kaplan (1961) made the first bibliography of American autobiographies available, and, later in the decade, American studies theorists such as William Spengemann and L. R. Lundquist (1965) began to discuss autobiography and its relationship to American concepts of self (Hazlett 1990). Despite such developments, however, the literary critic James Olney (1972, p. ix) could still write in 1972 that "surprisingly little has been written about autobiography at all, and virtually nothing about its philosophical and psychological implications."

Since the 1970s, however, literary scholars have published over 250 books in English on the topic of autobiography (Bloom and Yu 1994). They have increasingly turned to the subject of self-construction in autobiography as they have come to appreciate the interesting self-definitional problems of autobiographers (Eakin 1985). Accordingly, as the literary critic Thomas Couser (1989, p. 17) observed, an "attack on the common-sense conception of the self as an essence preceding or transcending context and language . . . has been even more aggressive in the study of literature than in the social sciences." The contemporary attention in the humanities to the subjects of narrative, rhetoric, and discourse has also augmented the notice given to autobiography (Martin 1986; Raval 1987). Some of these critics take the notion of a self to be a fiction.[24] They find it useful to deconstruct the terms that we use to think about the self, by pointing out, for example, how our Western concept of the self connotes continuity, coherence, stability, and individuality while disregarding change, fragmentation, and inconsistency. They question the culturally ordained dichotomies we use to consider the self such as self/society and inner/outer. Some theorists, following the ideas of Michel Foucault, prefer the term "subject" over that of "self" to emphasize that notions of the self are not independent constructions but are determined by language, culture, historical era, social groups, and ideological concerns. Such a viewpoint has led to an assault on the idea of the coherent, stable, executive self as it appears in autobiographies.

Literary scholars who discuss the construction of the self in autobiographies, however, have generally based their work on the in-depth analysis of a few autobiographies. As Laura Marcus (1994) has pointed out, they have usually limited their interest to "literary" autobiographies. Some, however, like Paul John Eakin (1985, 1992), have begun to emphasize the role of cultural "models of identity" in autobiographies, but they have done relatively little empirical work as of yet in examining historical changes in ideas about the self in autobiographies. As Eakin (1991, p. 5) acknowledges, literary scholars have made little use of the bibliographies of American autobiographies. What we need to expand their careful studies of individual autobiographers is empirical work on a larger number and wider range of autobiographies. We need extended work on the development of autobiography as the psychologist Jerome Bruner (1987, p. 15) has called for: "I cannot imagine a more important psychological research project than one that addresses itself to the 'development of autobiography'—how our way of telling about ourselves changes, and how these accounts come to take control of our ways of life. Yet I know of not a single comprehensive study on this subject." I believe a good starting place is an analysis of historical changes in ideas about self in American autobiographies.

Organization of This Study

As the basis for this work, I read and analyzed 110 American autobiographies published since 1800. I chose a minimum of four males and one female from each decade, and I included autobiographers from different social classes and ethnic groups.[25] For data, I used the comments that autobiographers make on many topics, such as human nature, the self, parents, religion, spouse, emotions, the writing of an autobiography, and psychological or sociological ideas. I also noted any omission of these subjects, and I paid attention to how the autobiographies were constructed.

To understand autobiographical depictions of the self, we should consider the social situation of writing an autobiography as well as the historical context. In Chapter 2, therefore, I discuss how autobiographers also use vocabularies of the self in their attempts to impress readers that they are persons to be admired by contemporary standards. What autobiographers write about themselves is not heedless of the reactions of their readers. They are trying to persuade their audience that they are a particular kind of self—a self worthy of dignity. And they manage to do so while also responding to the social conventions of narrative.

In the following chapters, I outline four models of the self in American autobiographies. I make no claim, however, that all American autobiographies fit neatly into these models, or that these models are the only ones we could discern. Such models can neither be comprehensive nor encompass the diversity found among autobiographies. They are ideal-typical in the sense that Max Weber (1949, p. 90) described: "This conceptual pattern brings together certain relationships and events of historical life into a complex, which is conceived as an internally consistent system. Substantively, this construct in itself is like a *utopia* which has been arrived at by the analytical accentuation of certain elements of reality." These models represent purer and more coherent patterns of ideas than occur in the vast majority of autobiographies.

Such models allow us to make analytic comparisons, to observe patterns of interrelated ideas, and to make sense of what autobiographers are doing. For the purposes of analysis or even description, we must unavoidably abstract from the complexity of social life. As the writer Jorge Luis Borges (1964a, p. 66) has commented, "To think is to forget differences, generalize, make abstractions." Thus, as Weber (1949, pp. 95–96) made clear, "Those 'ideas' which govern the behavior of the population of a certain epoch . . . can . . . be formulated precisely only in the form of an ideal type, since empirically it exists in the minds of an indefinite and constantly changing mass of individuals and assumes in their minds the most multifarious nuances of form and content, clarity and meaning." Once we have created such models, however, we can add to our understanding of individual autobiographers by comparing how they correspond to or diverge from the model.

Autobiographers often do not have a coherent, clearly formulated theory of self, for this is not their purpose in writing their stories. Their conjectures may be inconsistent or ambiguous. They may blend ideas, or they may reject contemporary ideas in favor of long-standing ideas such as those from the Bible. Vocabularies of self are extensive and people put them to situational use. A turn-of-the-century autobiographer like the banker Roeliff Brinkerhoff (1900), for example, wove together contradictory ideas about religion and self-culture. Others combined ideas gleaned from psychology, sociology, and the philosophy of self-development. No one autobiographer, therefore, can perfectly represent a particular model, since these models do not precisely describe any individual case. Historically, there are no convenient dividing lines where the use of one model ceases and another begins. One set of ideas is not simply replaced by another but may coexist as a rival—although often with some accommodations.

The autobiographers do not simply duplicate the ideas of their era. Meanings, as Herbert Blumer (1969) emphasized, are modified by the individual. In making their life stories public, autobiographers contribute to vocabularies of the self by evaluating, adapting, and sometimes rejecting ideas. To focus on general patterns, however, we must gloss over this diversity and complexity to be found among individual autobiographers. Furthermore, even the most creative thinkers cannot liberate themselves from the constraints of language or escape entirely from their sociohistorical context. They use conventional concepts to communicate, and they are immersed in intersubjective understandings from the moment of their first use of language. Even if they are rebellious, they must push off from a knowledge of these shared ideas and conventions. But we cannot clearly see these shared understandings if we read just a few autobiographies.

Finally, in outlining these models, I have tried to avoid presenting them as an illustration of progress toward a sophisticated understanding of the self, or as evidence for the evolution of the human mind, or as steps indicative of the emergence of individualism.[26] To do so would invoke the subjective bias of "presentism"—described metaphorically by David Hackett Fischer (1970, p. 135) as "the mistaken idea that the proper way to do history is to prune away the dead branches of the past, and to preserve the green buds and twigs which have grown into the dark forest of our contemporary world." It is tempting, of course, to believe that our current conceptions of the self are more sophisticated because they must be the result of cumulated knowledge. But earlier ways of thinking about the self are not necessarily the preliminary steps (or errors) on the path to our own understanding, nor do changing ideas about the self represent some inexorable developmental process. As the historian Herbert Butterfield (1965, pp. 16–17) argued, "[Real historical understanding] is only reached by fully accepting the fact that their generation was as valid as our generation, their issues as momentous as our issues and their day as full and as vital to them as our day is to us." Instead, it is an illuminating exercise to juxtapose the various ways in which autobiographers have responded to and adapted extant vocabularies of the self.

For each of these models of the self, I begin by discussing the historical background of ideas relating to self-interpretation. I also examine how each model represents a different approach to questions about human nature, components of the self, changes in the self, the importance of society and other persons in the autobiographer's life, and the construction of the life story.[27] In Chapter 3, I discuss the religious autobiographies that were prevalent throughout the nineteenth century in the United States. In such autobiographies, the authors' agreement that human nature is innately corrupt was an essential part of their explanations of self. Their tales were to stand as examples of religious conversions. In contrast, a competing model of the self in the nineteenth century, which related to evolutionary theory, promoted the optimistic idea of self-development. This model of the self, the subject of Chapter 4, highlights character, willpower, and the importance of taking control of one's own fate. In Chapter 5, I discuss an autobiographical model of the self related to the development of psychology as a science. Psychology, with its goal of explaining human behavior, offered autobiographers (beginning in the late nineteenth century) additional concepts and theories to explain their own actions. Such a model focuses on motivation and the role of emotions, instincts, and drives in explaining human action. Beginning also in the latter half of the nineteenth century, sociologists and others began to promulgate a point of view that emphasized society's effects on the self. In Chapter 6, I discuss a model of the self that takes this possibility into account and responds to its deterministic implications.

Autobiographers sometimes worry openly that their stories are not interesting enough to merit the attention of their readers. Arthur Koestler ([1952] 1969, p. 13), for example, felt it necessary to apologize to the readers of his autobiography for the egocentric focus on himself. He offered a simple line from Tolstoy: "And he went on talking about himself, not realizing that this was not as interesting to the others as it was to him." By considering autobiographies, however, as resourceful "dialogues with history," we can find any life story to be intriguing, no matter how uncomplicated or even mundane it appears at first glance.

Chapter Two ℋUTOBIOGRAPHY AS A SOCIAL SITUATION

To expose myself to others, but to do so in a narrative which I hoped would be well-written and well-constructed, perceptive and moving was an attempt to seduce my public into being indulgent. MICHEL LEIRIS

"It would, indeed, be a nice problem in the descriptive geometry of narrative," the minstrel Ralph Keeler (1870, p. 11) mused in his autobiography, "to determine the exact point where the lines of the two interests meet, that of the narrator and that of the people who have to endure the narration." With such a comment, Keeler informed his readers that he was well aware of the social nature of writing and publishing an autobiography. To analyze vocabularies of self in autobiographies, we should consider how the writing of an autobiography constitutes a social situation. Unless autobiographers intend their life stories to be private documents only for themselves, they are communicating with a future audience of readers. Autobiographers are not only construct-ing the stories of their lives, they are also strategically presenting the self. We can usefully apply Erving Goffman's (1959) analysis of impression manage-ment to autobiographers since they are attempting to persuade readers that they are, in some crucial way, admirable persons.[1]

In addition, putting together an autobiography is not simply a matter of recalling and recording the facts of one's personal history. As an act of com-munication, it entails problems of composition and rhetoric—something openly acknowledged by many autobiographers.[2] Autobiographers select "events" and "facts" from their lives that fit into a comprehensible narra-tive.[3] Thus, as the anthropologist Edward Bruner (1984, p. 7) also has ob-served, "Life histories are accounts, representations of lives, not lives as actually lived." The definition of self in autobiography is shaped not only by historical changes in the available vocabularies of self (as I discuss in later chapters), but also by the constraints, complexities, and opportunities of the social situation of presenting an autobiography. The autobiographer considers the composition of the intended audience, the current "climate of opinion" concerning what is an acceptable self, and the conventions of storytelling and autobiography. The writing of an autobiography is a social act—both as a part of a "community of discourse" and as a type of social in-teraction in which one tries to influence others (Barbour 1992).[4]

Interaction with an Audience

Although the audience is not physically present and there is usually no face-to-face interaction between autobiographers and readers (allowing no immediate feedback as in a conversation), the autobiographers do take into account the reactions of the expected audience.[5] They must present a portrait of self that cannot, in the sociologist Robert Perinbanayagam's (1991, p. 12) words, be "altered, enriched, impoverished, beclouded, and qualified" as it could be in a direct dialogue. The story told in an autobiog-raphy will depend, in part, on whom the author assumes will be in the au-dience.[6] This consideration of the eventual readers affects matters such as the thoroughness of explanations, what events are relevant to the telling of a life story, and the presentation of self in the autobiography.[7] If the auto-biography is to be published for a general audience, its author will not know who specifically will be among the readers. As the autobiographer Richard Rodriguez (1982, p. 182) explained, "I write today for a reader who exists in my mind only phantasmagorically." The audience is likely to be conceived, in George Herbert Mead's (1934) terms, as the "generalized other," that is, the community whose "organized social attitudes" are important to the person.

If the audience will be composed of friends and relatives only, then autobiographers need not elaborate as extensively as would be necessary to be comprehensible to a broad audience. If they write the autobiography for immediate family members only, it would be obvious, for example, who "Bob" is. Moreover, autobiographers may find it unnecessary to polish their prose as diligently for their families as for a general audience. Benjamin Franklin ([1793] 1923, p. 15), when he noticed that he was rambling in the first part of his memoir that he was writing originally for his son only, made this observation: "One does not dress for private company as for a publick ball."[8] Knowing that family members will read the autobiography, however, also can place significant constraints on what may be disclosed. As the novelist Arthur Koestler ([1952] 1969, p. 32) remarked in his autobiography, "The awareness that [my mother] is going to read this passage in print has the same paralyzing effect which prevented me as a child from keeping a diary."

If the audience is potentially large, the descriptions of events must be more thorough so that most readers are not puzzled by the references. Autobiographers must then clarify and elaborate more than they would need to do otherwise. Richard Rodriguez (1982, p. 186) commented in his autobiography, "I write very slowly because I write under the obligation to make myself clear to someone who knows nothing about me." Thus the publisher Ebenezer Thomas (1840, p. 140) did not simply mention friends in his autobiography, he also graciously introduced them to his readers: "I must digress here for a moment, to make the reader acquainted with my travelling companions." Even for a general audience, however, autobiographers should not tediously explain what "everyone knows." William Alcott (1839, p. 50), prominent in his day as an educational reformer, made this comment in his autobiography about his classroom system, "I need not describe the system of 'going up,' for it is probably well known to nearly every individual in New England." As we can see, however, this can cause problems for readers from future eras who are unfamiliar with such terms.[9]

An extensive audience also may include readers able to contest the stories presented in an autobiography. "I am forced to be veracious," Ralph Keeler (1870, pp. 12–13) forthrightly told his readers about his account of his youthful vagabond days as a "cork-face" minstrel, "by the fact that there are scores of people yet in the prime of life who are cognizant of the main events of the ensuing narrative."[10] Among family members, an autobiographer might get away with exaggerating, for example, his accomplishments as a

Civil War soldier, but if readers included fellow soldiers, this would likely temper his remarks.

An autobiographer also must consider general standards of taste, since a diverse audience increases the risk of offending some readers. Material that is amusing to some readers, such as the ridicule of certain persons or groups, is distasteful to others. Autobiographers with an extensive audience of readers are not able to engage in what Erving Goffman (1959) has called "audience segregation." Their stories must be suitable for all their readers. Ebenezer Fox (1838, p. 87), for example, felt compelled in his memoir of the Revolutionary War to defend his use of the phrase "damned rebel": "My apology for occasionally repeating such profane expressions is, that the young readers may know to what insulting and contemptuous language their forefathers were exposed while contending, with a haughty foe, for liberty and independence." And John Binns (1854, pp. v–vi), known in his day as the controversial publisher of the *Democratic Press* in Philadelphia, included this pledge in his preface: "I can assure my female readers that, in these Recollections, there is nothing to wound their feelings, or tint their cheeks." What is acceptable material in an autobiography, of course, varies historically and culturally. In 1822, the gambler Robert Bailey could blithely tell a joke in his autobiography that many today would find racist. In contrast, profanity and discussions of sexuality are far more acceptable today than in nineteenth-century autobiographies.

The audience, too, and the publishers are likely to have definite opinions about what an autobiography ought to include.[11] As I discuss in later chapters, many nineteenth-century American autobiographers presumed that an autobiography should be a story of a model life or at least contain a moral. More recently, however, a journalist summed up contemporary readers' expectations for autobiographies: "The fact is, if you ask readers to pay $22 for a book, you have to reveal new material. Ironically, the better known the person the more they must reveal" (Smilgis 1989, p. 82).[12] Publishers with marketability concerns will require that the autobiography be interesting and in "good taste" as they define these qualities.

Autobiographers often make it clear that they are taking the audience into account. The literary scholar Wayne Booth's (1983, p. 138) comment about fiction is also appropriate for autobiography: "The author creates, in short, an image of himself and another image of his reader." Autobiographers may directly comment on this matter, as did Richard Rodriguez (1982, p. 177): "It is to those whom my mother refers to as the *gringos* that I write." They also may give clues that suggest whom they imagine will be in the audience—clues such as the choice of vocabulary, the subtlety of humor, the formality of their language, and the qualifications they make.[13] Or they may engage in direct address: "Dear reader" or "Gentle reader."

The image that autobiographers create of their audience, in turn, may be part of their efforts to curry favor with the readers.[14] The use of literary allusions, for example, often carries an assumption that the readers are knowledgeable persons who would recognize the source (Alter 1989). As George Dillon (1986, p. 24) observed in his book on rhetoric, "By assuming a piece of specialized knowledge, the Writer moves toward solidarity with the Reader, and a reader may respond to that gesture by pretending to know the presupposed information." H. L. Mencken ([1940] 1955, p. 167), in his memoir of childhood, flattered the perceptive reader directly—using the phrase, "As smarties will have guessed by now."

The assumed presence of an audience, therefore, complicates the stories of self told by autobiographers. There must be a balance between the interests of the readers and the autobiographers' aspirations to find personal meaning in their own stories. Although some autobiographers may believe they write only for themselves and that deferring to the readers would detract from their own integrity, they cannot disregard the audience for, at a minimum, they must make their writing understandable.

The Presentation of Self

The autobiographical self-portrait is responsive to shared understandings about how "good" or "normal" persons should act and what commands respect from others. Autobiographers generally use rhetorical strategies to compare themselves to normative standards and persuade readers that they embody at least some virtues or "human excellences": wit, intelligence, modesty, sensitivity, practicality, generosity, truthfulness, insight, and so forth.[15] The autobiography serves as a tool to accomplish such an end even if this is not its author's conscious intention. Autobiographers' stories of self will differ in this regard from those told by biographers who have less reason for putting the subject in a good light and who view the subject from a different vantage point. Furthermore, even those autobiographies written in collaboration with a ghostwriter will be tailored to help the subject come across favorably to the readers. Such a relationship with the readers has led the writer and playwright Frank Chin (1985, p. 124) to assert that "autobiographies can only be written on your hands and knees in a kowtow, begging any passing reader to like you, love you, want to be like you, laugh at your wit, gurgle at your cleverness, lick your dirty car clean with their tongues in appreciation of your dashing sleight of verb or noun."

It is possible to portray oneself as emotional, witty, introspective, acceptably masculine or feminine, insightful, virtuous, and so on, through the construction of the autobiography and through the inclusion of illustrative events, thoughts, and feelings. What particular merits autobiographers choose to display is dependent, in part, on the qualities valued in a particular society at that time. Even if they argue that they do not care about the judgments of readers, they are likely to want, at a minimum, to be appreciated for their "independent" stance (Pratt 1977). In some cases, they may have reason to acknowledge traits that are not generally valued, such as weakness of will, but it will probably be for the greater gain of excusing untoward behavior. Or they may explain the circumstances that justify an action (Bruner 1990). The autobiographers may reveal misgivings about past conduct, but they can frame such accounts in the context of an "I'm older now and wiser" argument that attempts to rectify their reputation.

Autobiographers seek to persuade readers that they possess desirable characteristics through either the content or, less obviously, through the construction of the narrative. Favorable comments about self, however, should not be blatant, since they can be construed as bragging. Autobiographers are not able to use the extraverbal means of communication available to speakers during face-to-face interaction, such as facial expressions, body language, gestures, and the vocal effects that constitute paralanguage. But they can use such things as choice of vocabulary, irony, informality, parenthetical comments, punctuation marks, italics for emphasis, and the coherence of their stories to communicate additional information about themselves (Booth 1983; Dillon 1986).

If autobiographers wish to show, for example, that they are well educated, they will mention universities attended or degrees obtained. Or they may detail the amount of "serious" reading they have done—making their intellectual interests apparent to the audience (although preferably not too ostentatiously). The actor Anthony Quinn (1972, p. 186), for example, wrote, "I began to haunt second-hand bookstores and buy volumes on every subject—philosophy, science, literature. I read Fielding and Smollett, Baudelaire and Balzac, Dante and D'Annunzio. I read Ford Maddox [sic] Ford, Sinclair Lewis, Scott Fitzgerald, Wolfe, Hemingway." In general, I found that many of my autobiographers treated reading as a virtuous activity. As the writer Sherwood Anderson ([1924] 1969, p. 156) observed in his autobiography, "The owning of books has become in most American families a kind of moral necessity." Thus autobiographers may proudly say, as did the publisher John Binns (1854, p. 18), "I have continued a great reader all my life." They also may provide evidence of their education by using quotations from literary sources, an extensive vocabulary, foreign phrases, correct grammar and punctuation (at least in unedited autobiographies), and informed discussions of contemporary ideas.

Some autobiographers who have not been well educated give an account for their lack of education. Peter Cartwright (1856, p. 6), an itinerant Methodist preacher, apologized to readers for the ways in which his autobiography revealed his inadequate schooling: "I . . . send [my autobiography] out with all its imperfections, hoping that it may in some way . . . do more than merely gratify an idle curiosity, or offend the fastidious taste of some of our more highly favored and better educated ministers, who enjoy the many glorious advantages of books, a better education, and improved state of society, from which we as early pioneers were almost wholly excluded." Even autobiographers who ridicule formal education make it clear that they are aware that readers are likely to be judgmental about this particular merit.

Another quality that autobiographers can display is a sense of humor or the ability to recognize irony. Some autobiographers apparently believe that the way to accomplish this is with a joke, even if they find it difficult to work such a demonstration of their sense of humor into a coherent narrative. They may have to interject an aside such as "That reminds me of a story."[16] Robert Bailey (1822, p. 37), for example, apologized for straying from his story line: "Digressions are odious to me, but I must again beg the forgiveness of my readers for the liberty of introducing another anecdote." Freud ([1905] 1960, p. 15), in his analysis of humor, found the inclusion of jokes in autobiographies to be noteworthy: "Even men of eminence who have thought it worth while to tell the story of their origins . . . are not ashamed in their autobiographies to report their having heard some excellent joke."

Virtues also include having felt commendable emotions such as love and compassion. As Aristotle (1962, p. 43) argued, moral goodness includes having the right feelings "at the right time, toward the right objects, toward the right people, for the right reason, and in the right manner." Chester Harding (1866, p. 18), a popular portrait painter, employed sentimentality to recall his feelings when parting from his mother: "I started with all the firmness and resolution I could call to my aid; yet if my mother could have looked into my eyes, she would have seen them filled with big tears." Autobiographers also may have reason to declare their feelings to be above reproach, as did the newspaper publisher John Binns (1854, p. 161), who led a fight against Andrew Jackson's election: "I never knew what envy was, nor have I ever cherished personal ill-will or unkindly feelings."

Among the virtues, however, three qualities have been particularly germane for American autobiographers: modesty, honesty, and a life that has been interesting. These are all virtues that relate to interaction with the readers. The need to be attentive to these qualities depends on the sociohistorical context. Yet, because they relate to moral issues, I found a general concern with them among autobiographers over the entire nineteenth and twentieth centuries. The display of these particular virtues is a challenging rhetorical task because they can place conflicting demands upon the autobiographer.

Modesty

Demonstrating educational credentials or otherwise impressing the reader is likely to be counterbalanced by the desire of many American autobiographers to meet norms of civility that expect persons to be properly modest and keep their egos in check. Many autobiographers, male as well as female, appear to agree (at least in principle) with the belief that "custom has made it a fault to speak of oneself, and obstinately forbids it, in hatred of the boasting which always seem to attach to self-testimony."[17] Thus the gambler Robert Bailey (1822, p. 77), after detailing his aid to the indigent, inserted this note into his memoir and followed it by a justification for his apparent boasting: "I think I hear my reader say 'Charity is always silent.'" The issue of modesty looms large for autobiographers who, by the nature of their task, devote many pages to speaking of themselves. They face what the critic Wilfrid Sheed (1987, p. 5) has called "the self-importance problem endemic to all autobiography." As Lindley Murray (1827, p. 2), known in his day for his widely used *English Reader*, acknowledged, "It is always a delicate point to speak, or to write, properly, concerning one's self." Furthermore, among religious autobiographers who saw vanity as the chief sin, modesty was a crucial quality.

Particularly in the nineteenth century, we can find many autobiographers directly accounting for the apparent vanity involved in publishing their life stories, which implied that their lives were more important, interesting, or exemplary than others. They often placed a disclaimer to this effect in a preface to the autobiography. Lindley Murray (1827, p. 2) implored his readers to understand that "being at once the subject and the narrator, it will not be possible to prevent a very frequent recurrence of the obnoxious pronoun." Annie Dumond (1868, p. vi), a traveling book peddler, tried to disarm critics who would charge that she was egotistical: "I . . . entreat them not to condemn the work until they have tried, and ascertained from their own experience, how difficult it is to write one's own life without speaking of one's self." And John Moody ([1933] 1946, p. vii), publisher of a manual of industrial securities, asked this rhetorical question in his autobiography: "The question may well be asked, why should I, a man of no importance outside my little world, indulge in such insufferable conceit as to write a story about myself, and flaunt it before the public?"

Some autobiographers have dealt with this issue of vanity by specifying that there was a compelling reason (other than conceit) for publishing their life stories. Lucy Richards (1842, p. 7), in her religious memoir, asserted she had "no other apology to offer for writing the following, than a sense of duty and a desire to be useful." Likewise, Elihu Shepard (1869, p. 5), headmaster of a private school, explained why he wrote his autobiography: "The exhibition of an autobiography to a reader naturally suggests the object of the author in writing and publishing it . . . The author of this commenced it at the earnest request of his daughter . . . that she might preserve an accurate genealogy of her ancestry as far as possible." In these instances, the explanations function as disclaimers by presenting the argument that "I realize that this appears egotistical, but . . . " (Hewitt and Stokes 1975).

Another method that autobiographers have used in dealing with the accusation of vanity is to confront this issue head-on and admit it—but only as an all-too-human trait shared by all.[18] Alexander Graydon (1811, p. 1), a Revolutionary War soldier, began his lively memoir by scoffing at other autobiographers' declarations of humility: "The dealers in self-biography, ever sedulous to ward off the imputation of egotism, seldom fail to find apologies for their undertakings. Some, indeed, endeavor to persuade themselves that they design their labors merely for their scrutoires; while others, less self-deceived, admit they have an eye to the public." Yet Graydon then insisted that the focus of his memoir was not himself but "the character, spirit, and more minute occurrences of his time" (p. 2). A more scientific version of this "all-too-human" argument was offered by Andrew Jackson Davis (1857, p. 20), a well-known spiritualist, when he commented that "this instinct for autobiography is implanted in the nature of all men."

"Modest" autobiographers must be discreet in displaying their merits. If they openly commend themselves or mention their admirable qualities or deeds, they may appear self-serving, and readers may doubt their ability to be objective about their own lives. Rather than saying directly, "I have been a success," autobiographers may try to let the facts speak for themselves while mentioning a few inconsequential failures as well.[19] Plutarch (1905, p. 317), in his essay "How a Man May Inoffensively Praise Himself without Being Liable to Envy," once gave just such advice: "For the most part it is a good antidote against envy, to mix amongst our praises those faults that are not altogether ungenerous and base." Similarly, Dr. Samuel Johnson once commented that "all censure of a man's self is oblique praise. It is in order to shew how much he can spare" (Boswell 1934, p. 323). Discussing a few of one's failures or difficulties in life may win the sympathy of the reader, but mentioning many faults and failures may miscarry. An important consideration in this regard is what the audience already knows. Psychologists Barry Schlenker and Mark Leary (1982), in a study of self-enhancement in social interaction, found that persons present themselves modestly when they assume the audience is aware of their successes, but they present themselves self-enhancingly if they think the audience is uninformed about their accomplishments. Thus, in Schlenker and Leary's words, "Successful self-presentation involves maintaining a delicate balance among self-enhancement, accuracy, and humility" (p. 89).

For the sake of modesty, autobiographers may attribute career success to luck, good fortune, or Divine Providence. Once again, in Plutarch's (1905, p. 314) words: "Now those who are forced upon their own praises are the more excusable, if they arrogate not the causes wholly to themselves, but ascribe them in part to Fortune and in part to God." Chester Harding (1866, p. 92), a portrait painter of many notables in the 1800s, used such an attribution when recalling his social success in England: "What freak of fortune is this which has raised me from the hut in my native wilds to the table of a duke of the realm of Great Britain!" More recently, the writer Paul Monette (1992, p. 135) offered a similar explanation in his autobiography: "I had a second stroke of good fortune that spring. I won a summer traveling fellowship from the college." Ascribing one's good fortune to Divine Providence also carries the implication that one was favored by God, while managing to maintain a semblance of modesty.[20]

Autobiographers may explain particular talents as "gifts" (perhaps from God) or inherited. "I had a natural gift for nursing," wrote the governess and teacher Georgiana Kirby (1887, p. 315). Likewise, Andrew Carnegie (1920, p. 4) downplayed his own writing ability by referring casually to his "scribbling propensities" as a matter of inheritance. These attributions, although they may be sincere beliefs of the autobiographers, serve as evidence for readers that the authors do not consider themselves superior since such talents are the result of simple blind fortune. Devereux Jarratt (1806, p. 19), an Episcopal minister, made just such a defense after telling his readers about his remarkable memory: "As what I have here said respecting my memory . . . relate merely to gifts of nature, which I had no hand in acquiring, there can be no vanity in writing them down."

Modest autobiographers may carefully present testimonials from others, as did John D. Rockefeller (1913, p. 101): "I have no wish to reprint the complimentary allusion to myself in Mr. Backus's letter, but have feared to omit a word of it lest some misunderstanding ensue." Likewise, the businessman Edward Hewitt (1943, p. 284), when discussing his own love of fishing, managed to highlight his fame as an angler by humbly asking the reader's permission to repeat another's words regarding his ability: "Perhaps I may be allowed to quote here some excerpts from Mr. Geoffrey T. Hellman's 'Profile,' which appeared in the *New Yorker.*" Mentioning famous people one has known also may bolster one's worth indirectly by association, although readers may scorn this proclivity as "name-dropping." Clarence Darrow (1932, p. 317), well-known in his own right as a lawyer, anticipated such a reaction: "Of course we met and knew many other interesting people, but, why brag about it here?" Similarly, the illustrator, television host, and raconteur Alexander King (1958, p. 373) let it be known he fraternized with the rich and famous while repudiating just such a boast: "I have hardly mentioned the endless numbers of very famous people whom I have come to know in the course of my life. They don't appear in this book simply because I don't see any particular reason why I should try to aggrandize myself at the expense of their distinguished reputations." Even a description of one's travels, as Clarence Darrow (1932, p. 313) pointed out, presents a problem for the tactful author: "It is no distinction to have visited Europe, but it is rather a condescension to tell about it, for it carries the assumption that the reader has not been there."

Modesty also is intertwined with another essential quality to be displayed in an autobiography—honesty. Modesty can help support autobiographers' claims that they are being truthful and sincere by showing that they are capable of objective appraisals of self and not given to exaggeration. Yet, at the same time, the understatement that accompanies modesty can make autobiographers appear deceptive. Too much modesty can be seen as disingenuous—particularly if the audience is aware of the author's successes. Readers also may interpret excessive modesty as self-deprecation and a lack of proper self-regard. Thus the bibliophile Wilmarth Lewis (1967, p. xi) complained in his autobiography, "The difficulties of writing one's life are intimidating . . . You mustn't praise yourself; you mustn't run yourself down." As the psychologist James Averill (1986, p. 107) has remarked about the challenge of being modest, "The trick . . . is to be proud without being boastful, arrogant, pompous or conceited; but also without donning a false mask of humility. There are heuristics for pride; and from every indication, they are as difficult to master as the heuristics for chess." From such a perspective, we can appreciate Lindley Murray's (1827, p. 87) attempt to balance modesty and pride in alluding to the success of his English grammar books: "I am sensible it is difficult to write with proper delicacy, concerning publications which have been made by one's self; especially if they have been attended with any demonstrations of public favor and respect." Or the actress Ilka Chase's (1941, p. 49) seemingly casual account of her social class background: "Owing to my mother, I apparently belonged socially to the upper stratum." Or Bishop Fulton Sheen's (1980, p. 232) reference to his audience with the Pope: "Humility forbids me to reveal all that he said about my being a 'prophet of the times' and that 'you will have a high place in Heaven.'"

Honesty

Many people see truthfulness as an important trait in social interaction because it underpins trust. This value placed on honesty is supported by studies such as that of the psychologist Norman Anderson (1968), who found that subjects rating 555 personality-trait words included "sincere," "honest," and "truthful" among the five most likable traits, and "untruthful," "dishonest," "phony," and "liar" among the least likable traits. Truthfulness has been an important virtue for autobiographers, as the minister R. G. Williams (1896, p. 5) recognized when he vowed he was writing "the history of a life, honest and truthful, without any exaggeration, paint or varnish." Readers generally assume the writer of an autobiography, by definition, has attempted to tell a true story. Philippe Lejeune (1989, pp. 22–23), a prominent student of autobiography, has referred to this assumption as the "referential pact"—the author intends to restrict himself or herself to the truth—"making allowances for lapses of memory, errors, involuntary distortions, etc."

Although autobiographers and critics alike have increasingly acknowledged the difficulties and complexities of telling the "truth" in an autobiography, I believe it safe to say most readers still expect autobiographers to be making a good faith effort to tell the truth as they see it.[21] Hence autobiographers try to establish moral credentials of sincerity and truthfulness through rhetorical strategies—making it clear they are not intentionally falsifying or embellishing the story even though it may be to their benefit to do so. Such rhetorical attempts, as I discuss later, depend on whether the autobiographers see their task as a simple matter of recollection or as a creative act, for in the latter case they feel freer to take greater license with the facts.[22]

Autobiographers usually do not document their accounts with footnotes and a bibliography—even when recounting historical events. Instead, they may vow that their life stories are true. Nineteenth-century autobiographers often did so in a preface. "I do pledge myself upon the honor of a soldier, an officer, and a gentleman," promised the gambler Robert Bailey (1822, p. 7), "to give a true and literal account of every act or transaction relating thereto." Mrs. Rachel Watson (1871, p. i) pointed out that her memoir of domestic life included "no sickly attempt at rhetorical embellishment." And George Train (1902, p. viii), a wealthy merchant who claimed that his own trip around the world in eighty days was the model for Jules Verne's story, declared, "Thanks to my early Methodist training, I have never knowingly told a lie; and I shall not begin at this time of life." In contrast, those who wrote their autobiographies from a presumably moral high ground (such as members of the clergy) usually did not feel it necessary to make such a declaration.

Some autobiographers have handled the question of credibility by directly confronting the readers' potential doubts about the veracity of the account. Joseph Martin (1830, p. iv), for instance, began by declaring that the thought of embellishing his memoir of Revolutionary War experiences was repugnant: "I wish to have a better opinion of my readers . . . than ever to think that any of them would wish me to stretch the truth to furnish them with wonders that I never saw, or acts or deeds I never performed." Martin encouraged his readers to view themselves as superior to any such imputed reader who desired an exaggerated story, and he was bolstering his own avowal of truthfulness. Autobiographers also may employ this tactic of directly anticipating the readers' skepticism if a particular event in the story appears farfetched.[23] They may offer a disclaimer to the effect that "I know this is hard to believe, but . . . " Stephen Burroughs ([1804] 1924, p. 169), who told of his adventures as a rogue, summoned up his emotions to help allay his readers' likely reservations: "Are these matters painted to you, sir, in colors too high for the simple statement of facts? No, sir, indeed they are truths, the force of which I must feel while I set [sic] poring over the scenes."

Another way that autobiographers have enhanced their claims of truthfulness has been to attest to the reliability of their faculties of memory. Robert Bailey (1822, p. 7) gave this assurance to the readers of his autobiography: "My recollection of past events makes me confident that no circumstance, with reference to myself, will be forgotten. I can now repeat a sermon almost word for word, or any narrative of not more than one hour's duration." In her spiritual memoir, Lucy Richards (1842, p. 7), too, found the remembrance of things past to be a simple process: "When I have thought of writing, my mind has been fruitful, and past occurrences, which I had not thought of for years, have been as fresh in my remembrance as if they had but just taken place." If such autobiographers acknowledged problems of memory, it was from the perspective that they could no longer retrieve such memories, not that memory could be distorted. These nineteenth-century autobiographers viewed the act of remembrance as a simple matter of "searching the store-house of memory for those facts then laid up in it for future use" (Thomas 1840, p. 252). Later

American autobiographers, as I will discuss, began to worry about the subjectivity of memory and the relation between memory, emotion, and imagination.

Yet another way for autobiographers to show they are being truthful is by being frank, that is, willing to admit things that might not redound to their credit in the reader's eye.[24] The use of frankness by autobiographers relates to the prevailing standards for what can or should be admitted, the importance of being honest, and the stress placed on telling an interesting story.[25] As the literary scholar Laura Marcus (1994) has discussed, such frankness is also based on what the autobiographers see as the purpose of recording their life histories. If their memoirs are to stand, in effect, as the lasting records of the achievements of notable persons, then candor and descriptions of their personal lives may not be advisable. But if they are to serve as records of the experiences of a wide range of persons, then frankness and descriptions of "private" life may be acceptable or even obligatory. What autobiographers consider to be frank may be discussions of misdeeds, sexual behavior, family conflicts, unseemly emotions, failures, and so forth.

Frankness in the form of admitting a fault can be viewed as truthfulness (as well as modesty), and autobiographers may feel virtuous for having done so. As one turn-of-the-century commentator, W. A. Gill (1907, p. 76), advised in his article on autobiography: "Confess a crime, and you will be believed. Palliate your share in it, and your pleas, though true, will be rejected." Readers may assume there is nothing to be gained by a confession of faults (unless it be part of a religious narrative), and so such a disclosure, which the autobiographer "blushes to tell," suggests honesty.[26] Perhaps readers may feel a sympathetic bond with an autobiographer who appears vulnerable—associating the sharing of such information with that of intimate friendship. Such frankness is not to be dismissed, however, as only a rhetorical technique, for autobiographers who genuinely desire self-knowledge will want to confront their faults as well as their virtues, yet we may still ask: Why do it publicly?

When considered as a strategy, frankness can be tricky since autobiographers may be admitting things that undercut the image of themselves that they are constructing. Alexander Graydon (1811, p. 87) recognized this problem when he commented on the difficulties of being an autobiographer: "To expose his follies, though but his early ones, is far from a pleasant task; and yet it is in some degree, imposed upon him by the obligation he is under to represent himself truly." Furthermore, such frankness might be seen as pandering to the prurient interests of the public for the sake of book sales by persons whose lives might interest an audience only if they reveal titillating details. As a result, autobiographers may remind the readers, after a frank admission, that they are doing so for the higher value of truthfulness. Robert Bailey (1822, pp. 74–75), following a description of his participation in a fight, noted that "I have set out agreeable to my prospectus to write a true history of my life, and occurrences like these, however disagreeable they may be, I must encounter." Another tactic is to make it clear that they are making such admissions about former behavior from an older-but-wiser perspective. Or, as the literary scholar Stephen Shapiro (1968) has observed, some autobiographers, such as Rousseau, may carefully juxtapose an admission of an undesirable action or trait between discussions of actions that are clearly commendable.

Autobiographers also may try to manage the potential repercussions of such frankness. Mark Twain (1924, 1:305) wrote forthrightly of a candid remark he once made that he later regretted. He then added this further confession to his declaration of remorse: "Possibly when I said that about regret, I was doing what people so often unconsciously do, trying to place myself in a favorable light after having made a confession that makes such a thing more or less difficult. No, I think it quite likely that I never regretted it at all." Such an admission works to establish Twain's own truthfulness in the eyes of his readers.

Critics have not failed to see that frankness may be a rhetorical strategy on the part of the autobiographer. Rousseau ([1781] 1953, pp. 478–79), for example, ridiculed Montaigne's efforts at being frank in his essays: "I had always been amused at Montaigne's false ingenuousness, and his pretense of confessing his faults while taking good care only to admit to likable ones." About his own life, Rousseau asserted that "it is the ridiculous and the shameful, not one's criminal actions, that it is hardest to confess" (p. 28). George Orwell is also said to have scoffed at the possibility of frankness when writing about oneself. As Tom Wolfe (1986, p. 28) reported, "He never read autobiographies because their writers confessed to rakish vices and passed that off as candor. A true confession, he maintained, would be a chronicle of the humiliations that make up 75 percent of every human being's emotional life." Such problems are probably what led Freud (1975, p. 391) to conclude that "what makes all autobiographies worthless is, after all, their mendacity." Philip Roth (1988, p. 175), too, has argued that the guise of fiction allows a writer to speak more frankly about private thoughts, feelings, and embarrassments than in an autobiography where there is a "human, if artistically fatal, concern for one's vulnerable self."

Autobiographers do discuss the problem of truly being frank about their own lives. In the eighteenth century, Rousseau ([1781] 1953, p. 169) had confidently claimed he could avoid deceiving himself and the reader by "relating . . . all that had happened to me, all that I have done, all that I have felt."

But later we find autobiographers who were not so certain that it was possible to be this candid or this thorough. As Ralph Keeler (1870, p. 12) jocularly remarked (in the style of his friend Mark Twain): "I should like to be allowed to add that I have never known or conceived of a person—except probably the reader and writer of these pages—who could talk five minutes about himself without—lying." Twain (1924) also had insisted it was possible to be frank only in an autobiography published posthumously.

Finally, a "tell-all" autobiography would conceivably include the author's candid opinions of others. But circumventing the truth in such a situation can be construed as tact and discretion. As Twain (1935, p. 345) summed it up in his *Notebooks*, "Good breeding consists in concealing how much we think of ourselves and how little we think of the other person." The autobiographer must choose between telling the "whole truth" or avoiding the distress to others that such revelations might bring. Freud (1975, p. 391) wrote in a letter that he rejected the idea of writing his own "psychologically complete and honest confession of life" because it "would require so much indiscretion (on my part as well as on that of others) about family, friends, and enemies, most of them still alive, that it is simply out of the question." Some autobiographers, however, have tried to handle this problem by changing names to protect others or candidly discussing only those already dead. As John Binns (1854, p. 13) pointed out, there is an advantage in writing an autobiography late in life: "It insures a more full and frank disclosure of facts than would, probably, have been given at an earlier period. Nearly all the persons I shall name . . . have been called hence, and their remains consigned to their silent graves."

The Importance of Being Interesting

Another issue for autobiographers has been the question of whether they have led interesting lives.[27] For if this were not the case, who would want to read their autobiographies? Persons who talk extensively about themselves (just the task of the autobiographer) run the risk of being perceived as bores. Thus Ward McAllister (1890, p. v), a socialite most notable for giving the name *The Four Hundred* to the exclusive New York social set, asked in his autobiography, "How then does a man, be he good or bad, big or little, make his Memoirs interesting?"[28] As Mary Louise Pratt (1977) observed in her study of literary discourse, a person who tells a story is asking audience members, in effect, to suspend the normal turntaking rights to the floor that are part of conversation. In return, a voluntary audience raises their expectations that the story should be engaging and worth their time.

The problem of being interesting also relates to the expectation that autobiographers be modest, since the egoism implied in the act of publishing a life story may seem more flagrant if the autobiographer led an uneventful life. Those who have achieved celebrity or notoriety may assume this automatically lends interest to the stories of their lives, but for those who have not achieved fame, their stories must be worthwhile. On the other hand, too much modesty may make the story uninteresting. As Arthur Koestler ([1952] 1969, p. 39) noticed, humility can result in what he called the "dull dog fallacy" in autobiographies, which "requires that the first person singular in an autobiography should always appear as a shy, restrained, reserved, colorless individual."

What autobiographers categorize as "interesting" varies both historically and culturally. They may view the events of childhood as worth relating, for example, if they see this stage of life as having formative importance. Beginning in the latter half of the nineteenth century, some autobiographers in the United States produced memoirs focusing exclusively on childhood—memoirs that particularly raise the question of what makes an interesting story, since these accounts usually conclude before the advent of the author's career (Coe 1984). In contrast, an early nineteenth-century autobiographer, Stephen Burroughs ([1804] 1924, p. 4), felt it necessary to apologize for mentioning "the insipid anecdotes of my childish years." To qualify as interesting, autobiographers may present unusual lives, model lives, or, on the other hand, ordinary lives—but so perceptively analyzed or well-written that they strike a "responsive chord" with readers who have experienced and felt similar things.[29] An autobiographer who can take an ordinary life and make it fascinating encourages readers to see how events in their own lives (such as a first love) can be equally interesting.

Some autobiographers make it clear that they worry about the obligation of being interesting by directly bringing up the question of whether their lives have been too prosaic to merit an autobiography. Discussing their uneasiness may in itself enhance their claims of modesty. Ebenezer Fox (1838, p. vi), in his recollections of life as a Revolutionary War soldier, directed a comment to both issues—telling an interesting story and appearing to be modest: "Should it be thought that my simple narrative does not contain matters of importance sufficient to interest the reader, I can only say, that the partial judgment of friends, and my belief that any circumstances relating to the most interesting period of our history would prove entertaining to the young, must be my excuse for presenting it to the public." Joseph Martin (1830, p. iv) also confronted his readers directly on the topic of whether his account of Revolutionary War experiences was worth their while: "But, says the reader, this is low, the author gives us nothing but everyday occurrences. I could tell as good a story myself. Very true,

Mr. Reader, every one can tell what he has done in his lifetime, but everyone has not been a soldier." These memoirists maintained that their personal lives might not have deserved an autobiography, but the events to which they were eyewitnesses would engage readers.

Another tack employed by some autobiographers is the contention that anyone's life is interesting—a democratic argument I found increasingly used among autobiographers in the late nineteenth century.[30] The financial publisher John Moody ([1933] 1946, p. ix), for example, declared, "There is a story worth the telling in the life of every man, could it but be fully told." Similarly, Andrew Carnegie (1920, p. 1) embraced this reasoning (which also buttressed his claim of modesty): "If the story of any man's life, truly told, must be interesting, as some sage avers, those of my relatives and immediate friends who have insisted upon having an account of mine may not be unduly disappointed with this result."

The issue of what is interesting to readers also pertains to the question of what specific details and events should be included in an autobiography. For many American autobiographers over the last two centuries, this has meant that they eschewed the prosaic details of daily life as boring or irrelevant unless an analysis of such particulars somehow offered a key to understanding their behavior.[31] The physician Faye Lewis (1971, p. vii), for example, explained in her autobiography, "There is seldom much glamour in the everydayness of living, especially to the young." Autobiographers do not typically discuss mundane events like sleeping, bathing, and eating—except, perhaps, to mention memorable meals or engage in nostalgic recollections of favorite foods if it is acceptable to speak of such worldly pleasures.[32] Descriptions of how autobiographers acted in everyday life could disclose much about them, but, as readers, we only have access to what they have chosen to tell us. As Mark Twain (1924, 1:288) said, "An autobiography that leaves out the little things and enumerates only the big ones is no proper picture of the man's life at all." Autobiographers, however, look for the drama in their lives—the conflicts, the milestones, the transformations, the contrasts between past and present viewpoints. The philosopher Herbert Spencer (1904, 2:384) astutely commented on this aspect of autobiography: "A biographer, or autobiographer, is obliged to omit from his narrative the common-places of daily life, and to limit himself almost exclusively to salient events, actions, and traits . . . But by leaving out the humdrum part of the life, forming that immensely larger part which it had in common with other lives, and by setting forth only the striking things, he produces the impression that it differed from other lives more than it really did."

To include routine details about one's everyday life may appear conceited by its implication that readers must find every particular about one's life to be interesting. On the other hand, if the autobiographer wishes to appear natural and artless, then the inclusion of some everyday details may be effective. To capture the voice of baseball player Yogi Berra (Berra and Fitzgerald 1961, p. 224), for example, the ghostwriter of his autobiography included such comments as "I like things like pork chops and lamb chops as much as steak and roast beef, and I still love ravioli and lasagna and spaghetti." Additionally, as the literary scholar John Sturrock (1993) has pointed out, mundane details can be used effectively if an autobiographer wishes to provide a contrast to highlight the drama of a moment such as an epiphany or a miracle.

Some autobiographers explain or apologize for the inclusion of details that the audience may find trivial or unnecessary.[33] Stephen Burroughs ([1804] 1924, pp. 171–72) did so by justifying the inclusion of a minor detail in his memoir: "This circumstance, you may think, was of too small consequence to find a place in this narration, but the reason why I relate it, is the disagreeable effect it had upon my mind." Or they may explain that they are inserting particular details for the express purpose of engaging the reader. Henry Ossian Flipper ([1878] 1968, p. 49), the first African American graduate at West Point, pointed out that he included "the cant lingo" of the cadets in order to avoid a "dry and uninteresting" narrative. Autobiographers make it clear, with such comments, that they do not ignore the reactions of their readers.

Disregard of everyday life in an autobiography may mean little discussion of immediate family members or close friends. Autobiographers differ in how they distinguish between what is to be made public and what is to remain private. Particularly in the nineteenth century, the autobiographers in my sample usually did not even mention the names of their spouses or children. Thus the gambler Robert Bailey (1822, p. 11), who did refer to his brothers and sisters, believed it necessary to apologize since "the degression [sic] may appear to be unwarrantable as having little or no connection with a history of my own life." In a similar manner, Calvin Fairbank (1890, p. 181), who spent more than a dozen years in prison for his abolitionist activities, concluded his autobiography with the comment: "My private sorrows and joys cannot interest the world." And John D. Rockefeller (1913, p. vii) commented that "a long account of [my daily and intimate companionship] would not interest the reader." Whether autobiographers discuss family relationships depends partly on the focus of the autobiography as well as extant ideas about the significance of relationships in a person's life. If the main interest in an autobiography is the understanding of self, then details of relationships may be important. But if the primary focus is a person's career or spiritual life, then family life may not be pertinent (Shumaker 1954). Lee Iacocca (1984), for example, in recounting his executive career in the auto industry, told his readers little about his family.

Some twentieth-century autobiographers, in contrast, have worried that readers might interpret a failure to discuss family life as cold and unfeeling. In the case of Iacocca, lest readers wonder about his relative silence about his family, he (and his ghostwriter) added this disclaimer: "Yes, I've had a wonderful and successful career. But next to my family, it really hasn't mattered at all" (p. 305). Decades earlier, the railroad signalman James Fagan (1912, p. 196) offered this apology to his readers: "I am sorry that I am obliged to crowd out this inner circle of my life-story with the simple statement that I look upon my married life as an ample and happy reward for all the disappointments and difficulties contained in the rest of my experience." Lincoln Steffens (1931, p. 153) also justified his failure to discuss his marriage extensively in his autobiography, and he added an amusing story of how a fellow autobiographer was even worse by neglecting even to mention his wife in his life story:

> When [Frederick C. Howe] had laid the finished manuscript of his autobiography proudly before his wife and she had read it, she looked up at him with the humor that is all hers and said, "But, Fred, weren't you ever married?"
> "Oh, yes," he answered. "I forgot that. I'll put it in."

The expectation that autobiographers tell an "interesting" story also may conflict with the requirement that they be truthful. William James ([1890] 1950, 1:373–74) observed that when people tell others about their experiences, they "almost always make [the stories] more simple and more interesting than the truth." To write an engaging life story may induce autobiographers to embellish, dramatize, and craft an unrealistically coherent account of their lives. In a memoir of life in the U.S. Navy, James Bruell (1886, pp. 3–4) recognized this temptation when he defensively insisted, "The facts I have given without exaggeration, and told them in a style . . . without rhetorical flourishes or nay aim to set off the truth with artificial coloring." Yet he went on to add (referring to himself in the third person) that "if the 'old salt' has succeeded in interesting his readers, his object has been gained." As Philippe Lejeune has recognized, "A paradox of autobiography is that the autobiographer must carry out this project of impossible sincerity using all the usual tools of fiction."[34] Henry Adams, after his attempt at autobiography, wrote to a friend that he learned that "narrative and didactic purpose and style" could not be successfully mixed in an autobiography.[35]

Despite their aspirations to be interesting, autobiographers may feel it is in their interest to add the disclaimer that this does not mean that they have embellished the story. The prize-fighter Joseph Hess (1888, p. 137), even with a subtitle of *A Book of Thrilling Experiences,* included this disavowal: "I have not endeavored to put before the public a volume containing beautiful figures of speech and diction; for in this I would undoubtedly have failed. My aim has been to relate in plain and simple language an account of my life." The Revolutionary War soldier Joseph Martin (1830, p. iii) offered the disclaimer, "No alpine wonders thunder through my tale." In a study of eighteenth-century English biography, Donald Stauffer (1941, p. 16) also found autobiographers who denied the taking of rhetorical liberties—often rewording a line from Shakespeare's *Othello* to make this avowal: "I have borrowed nothing from the wardrobe of fiction, I have extenuated nought, nor set down aught in malice." Here, then, we can see autobiographers' recognition of the conflict between the necessity to be truthful and the desire to tell a good story.

By the twentieth century, however, some autobiographers such as Sherwood Anderson ([1924] 1969, p. 19) began to admit that, as writers of a narrative, they become "the tale-teller, the man who sits by the fire waiting for listeners." As actress and radio talk show host Ilka Chase (1941, p. 219) mused, "The more I write the more I find literary integrity a problem. Should you recount exactly what happened, or should you be interesting?"[36] The American autobiographer, according to the critic and literary editor Wendy Lesser (1988, p. 3), now deals with the issue of truth by "purposely allying his autobiographical venture with fiction." In effect, as Lesser noted, the autobiographer says, "'I'm an *artist* . . . so don't expect unvarnished truth from me! What you get here is *better* than truth!'"[37] Some autobiographers choose to be candid about the difficulties in telling the truth in their autobiographies, and they may ask for any fictionalizing to be taken as art or a deeper truth. "I have perhaps lied now and then regarding the facts of [my father's] life," Sherwood Anderson ([1924] 1969, p. 383) told his readers, "but have not lied about the essence of it." And Ernest Hemingway (1964, p. i), in the preface to his memoir of life in Paris in the 1920s, offered this option to his readers: "If the reader prefers, this book may be regarded as fiction. But there is always the chance that such a book of fiction may throw some light on what has been written as fact." Such discussions of the problem of truth being at cross-purposes with art serve as disclaimers that anticipate criticism by the readers.[38] Autobiographers can, in effect, argue that readers should not regard such a failure to tell the truth as a moral problem but rather as the result of the subjectivity of an individual's viewpoint. In other words, they have not intentionally deceived the readers.

Finally, autobiographers may have other motives as well that add to the complexity of the portrayal of self. They might, for example, anticipate that the audience will include those who have an unfavorable impression of them, so they design the autobiography to rectify such views. Or, they may write their autobiographies with the sole intention of making money. Robert Bailey (1822, pp. 330–31), who offered his life story as a warning to others about the wages of sin, lamented he was "without property and without money" and wrote his memoir to "get something to live upon, and some little clothing for myself and my family." To tell a life story to earn money, as Bailey did, surely must mean a selection of events certain to interest readers.

Telling a Story

Most American autobiographers construct their life stories by weaving together selected experiences into an intelligible story.[39] This act of putting together a narrative, using the conventions of storytelling and autobiography, places further constraints on the self-interpretation presented in an autobiography. Although it is commonsensical to think that "the content of a life shapes the form of its story," we can also argue the reverse (Howarth 1974, p. 363). As Paul de Man (1979, p. 920) contended in his discussion of autobiography, "Whatever the writer *does* is in fact governed by the technical demands of self-portraiture and thus determined, in all its aspects, by the resources of his medium."[40] The novelist Ludwig Lewisohn (1922, p. 1) recognized this in his autobiography when he lamented that "an artistic pattern comes between the teller of the tale and his reality."

An autobiography, as a story, needs a beginning, middle, and an end.[41] As Wallace Martin (1986) commented in his summary of theories of narrative, this may seem like a trifling observation until we recognize that time itself has no such confines, and boundaries have to be artificially imposed.[42] Such a requirement is not as simple a matter as explained by the King of Hearts to the White Rabbit in Lewis Carroll's (1866, p. 182) *Alice in Wonderland:*

> "Where shall I begin, please your Majesty?" he asked.
> "Begin at the beginning," the King said, gravely, "and go on till you come to the end: then stop."

The autobiographer must choose some event or observation that will qualify as a beginning. For many, birth appears to be the logical opening for a chronological story.[43] Or perhaps a brief inventory of immediate ancestors.[44] These are such customary openings that some autobiographers have chosen to poke fun at them. "A 'respectable family,'" wrote Ralph Keeler (1870, p. 15), "has long since become the acknowledged starting-point . . . of your conventional autobiography." And Ilka Chase (1941, p. 2) remarked in her life story that "if this is to be an autobiographical treatise, I suppose it would be more orderly if I got myself born." But birth need not be the starting point for a story of one's life.[45] Autobiographers may begin in the present and employ flashbacks, or they may first describe a relevant historical event. They may recount their first memories, describe their home towns, or perhaps pick the most significant event in their lives. And these possibilities, of course, do not exhaust the options. What choice they make depends, in part, on the themes they wish to pursue.

They may then proceed with a chronological telling, which is easier, as Paul John Eakin (1992, pp. 192–93) has pointed out, than "the strenuous creativity that would exploit the possibilities of structure as a primary means of self-expression." A chronological account, by presumably paralleling the life course, may seem to be the most objective.[46] Some autobiographers, therefore, have even apologized for straying from a strict chronology. Lindley Murray (1827, p. 35), for instance, made this comment to his readers: "This tribute to the merit of an old friend, will not, I believe, be deemed an impertinent digréssion from the work in which I am engaged.—To the regular progress of that work, I now return."

How to end a life story presents an even greater problem for the autobiographer. A character in Cervantes's ([1604] 1950, pp. 176–77) *Don Quixote* expressed this predicament:

> "If you want to know about [my life], I am Gines de Pasamonte, and I have written my life with these very fingers . . . "
> "And what is the title of the book?" asked Don Quixote.
> *"The Life of Gines de Pasamonte,"* replied that hero.
> "Is it finished?" asked Don Quixote.
> "How can it be finished," replied the other, "if my life isn't?"[47]

A common procedure for autobiographers has been to proceed through a chronological accounting of important events and then bring the story to a close when reaching the present. Such a conclusion, if written after retirement, can seem like an anticlimax. Worden McDonald (1978, p. 154) ended his self-published autobiography of a "free-spirited working man" with these words: "Thanks for reading my story. I hope there's something in it that you can use." Similarly, the novelist Gertrude Atherton (1932, p. 578), despite her experience from writing more than forty-five books, concluded her autobiography abruptly with a simple sentence: "And that brings these reminiscences to date." For autobiographers who have developed a theme in telling their life stories, the ending may be some type of closure of that theme—perhaps the distillation of wisdom gained in a lifetime or a philosophy of life. In the final paragraph of his autobiography, Lincoln Steffens (1931, pp. 872–73) offered this summation: "My life was worth my living. And as for the world in general, all that was or is or ever will be wrong with that is my—our thinking about it." As another example, Hannah Solomon ([1946] 1974, p. 263), a founder of the National Council of Jewish Women, concluded her life story by returning to the metaphor she chose for life: "The fabric of my life is now spread out . . . the threads uncut . . . the spindle not yet stilled."[48]

Since it is unlikely that readers could be found who would be fascinated by an account of everything another person remembers, an autobiographer must be selective in what events to include from the flow of life. And, of course, to record everything would be an impossible task.[49] So here is a place where the creative element of finding meaning in one's life enters. Autobiographers emphasize some time periods; they abbreviate or skip over others. Robert Louis Stevenson's ([1884] 1948, p. 92) comment about literature is also appropriate for autobiography: "Life is monstrous, infinite, illogical, abrupt, and poignant; a work of art, in comparison, is neat, finite, self-contained, rational, flowing, and emasculate."[50] The autobiographer may end up with a unified life story with no inconsistencies or gaps. It is tempting, as Mary McCarthy (1957, p. 164) observed in her memories of childhood, to have "arranged actual events so as to make 'a good story' out of them."

To give substance to faded or incomplete memories, autobiographers may fill in details they cannot clearly remember—thereby raising the issue of truth. Or they may not recall the exact sequence of events, but they need to order them to create a narrative. McCarthy discussed this desire to paint a complete picture for the readers of her autobiography: "The temptation to invent has been very strong, particularly where recollection is hazy and I remember the substance of an event but not the details—the color of a dress, the pattern of a carpet, the placing of a picture. Sometimes I have yielded, as in the case of the conversations. My memory is good, but obviously I cannot recall whole passages of dialogue that took place years ago" (p. 3). As McCarthy also discussed, autobiographers may decide to include extended dialogue—overcoming their qualms about the impossibility of actually recalling extensive conversations word for word. One of the great limitations of biography (and autobiography), according to Leon Edel (1984, p. 23), is that "the world does a great deal of talking—but rarely in biographies." Autobiographers, therefore, may try to make their stories more "life-like" by including dialogue. They may even declare that they can remember such conversations or at least the gist of them.

The story told in an autobiography, moreover, is not a simple excavation of events from the past since persons determine the meaning of their lives in light of later events. As Mead (1932, p. 12) argued, "The past . . . is as hypothetical as the future." And nowhere is this more likely to be so than in the autobiography where a person attempts to develop an overarching perspective on his or her life. "The act of remembering," as the autobiographer Richard Rodriguez (1982, pp. 175–76) acknowledged, "is an act of the present." We can see how such perspectives change when we can find autobiographers making subsequent comments about their previously published life stories. Arthur Koestler ([1952] 1969, p. 11), for example, included this disclosure in a preface to the second edition of his *Arrow in the Blue*: "I wrote this autobiographical account when I was forty-six. Now, at sixty-four, I would of course write it differently . . . Reading through the proofs of this new edition after so many years, I often sweated with embarrassment."

Writing an autobiography, as Jean-Paul Sartre (1964, p. 125) explained, is like reading one's life backward: "The end is regarded as the truth of the beginning."[51] When we recall the past, we do so with knowledge of the consequences of our actions. We are likely to forget our uncertainties and hesitations at junctures in our lives. Richard Rodriguez (1982, p. 28), for example, wrote in his autobiography, "The day I raised my hand in class and spoke loudly to an entire roomful of faces, my childhood started to end." But his designation of this moment as a turning point probably was not so clearly perceived at that time. For autobiographies to be similar to life, as Sartre noted about novels, they would have to "restore to the event its brutal freshness, its ambiguity, its unforeseeability."[52] Instead, autobiographers may end up with stories of lives free of failures, mistakes, discontinuities, contradictions, and hesitations.

It is also unlikely that autobiographers can fully capture their own outlooks as children since they recall these earlier viewpoints overlaid with later interpretations and emotions. The physician Faye Lewis (1971, p. vii) found the understanding gained by such distance to be useful: "It is the looking backward after a lapse of time that gives one perspective, enables one to assess the meanings and values of what he has lived through." Likewise, the spiritualist Andrew Jackson Davis (1857, p. 83) remarked that "the blooming Eden of childhood is known only to the full-grown, healthy man; that is, 'tis a pure maturity alone which can truly appreciate the good, the romantic, and the beautiful." But others such as Sherwood Anderson ([1924]

1969, p. 123) realized how an adult perspective could misrepresent the story of one's childhood: "I again find myself plunging forward into a more advanced and sophisticated point of view than could have been held by the boy, beginning to remake his own life more to his own liking by plunging into a fanciful life." Or, as Koestler ([1952] 1969, p. 96) noticed, autobiographers may recall the incidents of childhood in "a patronizing, anecdotical style"—unsympathetically treating what they once experienced as "the agonies of youth" from an adult perspective that finds such suffering to be amusing. Autobiographers may, in fact, use a dramatic contrast of present perspective with that of a past one to structure their life stories (Marcus 1994).

For narrative continuity, the autobiographer must make meaningful transitions from one event to another despite any jumps in time. Chapter divisions (even short chapters if necessary) can help smooth over passages in time by allowing breaks in the narration (Shapiro 1968). But within the chapters, linking experiences and creating transitions are not always easy tasks. The autobiographer Robert Stevenson Coffin (1825, p. 7), for example, used a self-conscious transition: "I shall now throw a forward somerset [somersault] over several years of my earthly pilgrimage, which will bring me to the age of twelve years." The portrait painter Chester Harding (1866, p. 147) simply noted, "Little of interest occurred in my life for several years." And Andrew Jackson Davis (1857, p. 163) awkwardly ended one chapter in his autobiography with this statement: "Remembering nothing more in my history for several months of any psychological interest to the reader— I will close this chapter." The British novelist Julian Barnes's (1984, p. 31) description of biography is appropriate in this regard—"a collection of holes tied together with string."

Because of the alterations that autobiographers make to fit the events of their lives into a story from a present perspective and because of their dependence upon memory, we may question the extent to which the result is a "true" life history.[53] As the literary critic Elizabeth Bruss (1976, p. 18) asserted, "No autobiographer ought to depict himself without first becoming aware of how much fiction is implicit in the idea of a 'self.'" In response, some autobiographers, aware of these problems of ascertaining the "truth" about the self, have openly employed techniques from fiction such as the use of flashbacks and fictional characters (Shumaker 1954).

This is not to argue, however, that all autobiographers consciously attempt an artistic rendering of their life stories. Mark Twain contended that "autobiography is not literature since it need not be pruned and shaped as other works are" (Smelstor 1984, p. 243). In this spirit, he dictated his autobiographical material, although it should be added that he did rehearse before the dictation. We also can find autobiographers in the nineteenth century who showed little concern for crafting their stories by writing apparently only one draft. Robert Bailey (1822, p. 134), for example, chose to correct an error of fact made earlier in his autobiography by simply mentioning it many pages later: "Here I will take an opportunity of correcting an error, inadvertantly [sic] made, in the preceeding [sic] part of this book." The educator William A. Alcott (1839, p. 18), after detailing an event, returned to the subject later with the phrase, "I forgot to say . . ." Although this introduces a charming informality and spontaneity to the story, I suspect this was not Alcott's intent. For those autobiographies produced by ghostwriters, being too well-written, in fact, may detract from its authenticity. William Novak, the writer hired for Lee Iacocca's (1984) autobiography, disclosed that the publisher rejected his first submission. "They said, 'Well this is wrong, this is too well-written . . . It doesn't sound like Lee Iacocca talking to you, it sounds like a writer writing.'"[54]

Telling a good story, making a good impression—these are the requirements of the social situation of writing an autobiography. The act of self-interpretation in an autobiography is a resourceful act of public self-interpretation. Not only have autobiographers learned what it means to be a self, they also are well aware of the standards by which persons evaluate selves, and they are positioning themselves in relation to these standards. I do not wish to argue, however, that autobiographers are exclusively engaged in the task of impression management, for this would not give them proper credit for their conscientious attempts also to understand themselves and make sense of their lives. But impression management does complicate and make even more interesting what they are accomplishing.

The production of the autobiography as a public story also is tied to changing assumptions about the self. Just as the constraints of storytelling shape the autobiography, contemporary answers to questions about the self also influence the story. For example, what are admirable human qualities? What changes, if any, are noteworthy about the self? What makes a life interesting? Autobiographers work with contemporary solutions to these debates about the self—perhaps sustaining them, perhaps modifying or challenging them. And the answers they give to these questions affect not only their self-interpretations but also their self-presentations.

Chapter Three THE ELF AS MORALITY PLAY

Fear not enemies without, but yourselves at home.   THOMAS SHEPARD

William Dean Howells (1909, p. 796) once declared that autobiography is "supremely the Christian contribution to the forms
of literaturing." Given the contemporary proliferation of celebrity
autobiographies focusing on the worldly aspects of life, we might
initially find his characterization to be puzzling. But if we examine
the history of American autobiographies, we will find Howells's
description to be apt. Conversion narratives and the life histories
of Protestant clergymen compose the largest single category of
autobiographies from 1800 to the 1930s.[1] Moreover, some commentators even trace the development of the genre of autobiography in the West directly from religious narratives—often St.
Augustine's *Confessions* in A.D.400.[2]

In this chapter, I examine how the self is depicted in this

prominent type of American autobiography. Similar to medieval English morality plays, which personified the conflict between virtue and vice, these religious autobiographies concentrated on the struggle between good and evil, but they portrayed the battle as occurring within the individual. A crucial question for them was how to gain control over the passions or appetites that impel people toward sin.

Historical Background

Many commentators have noted the centrality of religion in nineteenth-century America.[3] Alexis de Tocqueville ([1835] 1966, p. 268), for example, was initially struck by the religious atmosphere in the United States in the early 1830s, and he described it as "the place where the Christian religion has kept the greatest real power over men's souls." The historian Perry Miller (1965, p. 10) also concluded that the United States in the early nineteenth century was "a society where a general consent to the principles of Protestant Christianity was taken for granted." During the years from approximately 1800–1835, designated by some historians as the "Second Great Awakening," many religious revivals in the United States swelled church membership.[4] This awakening involved a shift in Protestant religious doctrine from the Calvinist belief in predestination—in which only the elect achieve salvation—to the doctrine of Arminianism in which salvation was available to all who have faith (McLoughlin 1968; Mathews 1978). By placing value on good works and allowing for a self-initiated seeking of salvation, this doctrinal change meant all persons theoretically could benefit from religious revivals. In the United States, the ascension of Methodism furthered evangelical Arminianism as it grew from a small group in America in 1776 to the largest single denomination by 1850, accounting for more than one-third of all American church members (Cremin 1980; Finke and Stark 1992).

Such an evangelical climate fostered the publication of conversion narratives in the United States.[5] These narratives, of course, were well established before this period.[6] Some commentators take the first conversion narrative to be the biblical story of the transformation of St. Paul on the road to Damascus (Delany 1969). Other influential religious narratives have been St. Augustine's *Confessions* and John Bunyan's *Grace Abounding to the Chief of Sinners* (1666). In America, beginning in the seventeenth century and for about two centuries thereafter, New England Puritans, as well as later evangelical Protestants, were generally expected to give a public account of their conversion experience to qualify for church membership.[7]

During the nineteenth century, the number of religious autobiographies increased from a little more than a dozen published in America during the first decade of the 1800s to more than ten times that number published in the 1890s.[8] Rising literacy in the nineteenth century had helped create a larger market for books, and technological improvements in publishing made it possible to mass-produce books at a reduced cost. For evangelical Protestants, published accounts of religious conversion provided moral lessons and commendable reading matter—in contrast to fiction, which they believed could "overexcite" the emotions and "seduce mortals from the path of virtue" (Harding 1866, p. 30).[9] Furthermore, this type of autobiography could be written by almost anyone who had gone through an exemplary religious conversion. One need not be famous, well-educated, or wealthy.[10]

Even secular autobiographers in the 1800s, who discussed mundane matters or historical events, often acknowledged the religious ideas and moral issues of their time by referring to sin, the power of Satan, the weakness of human nature, Divine Providence, and so on. For instance, Ebenezer Fox (1838), in his recollections of life as a Revolutionary War soldier, blamed the devil's influence when he meditated on his own failings. And when it came to explaining his own good fortune in surviving the war, he thanked God ("by whose goodness we have been preserved") and Divine Providence (p. 195). Rogues and criminals, too, who made up the second largest category of autobiographers in the United States in the first half of the nineteenth century, used religious ideas.[11] By framing their exploits as moral lessons on the wages of sin, such picaresque autobiographers were able to make titillating material into acceptable reading matter in the early nineteenth century.[12] The prizefighter Joseph Hess (1888, p. v), for example, wrote of his battle with "the demon alcohol," and he suggested that "some who are now in sin and darkness, who are slaves to appetite and passion, may profit by my sad and bitter experience." Authors like Hess could structure their memoirs as a struggle (albeit an unsuccessful one) against the temptations of the flesh. The tavern owner Robert Bailey (1822, pp. 13–14), in this manner, told his readers how he regretted his gambling and his dalliances with two thousand women, but he added in his defense that he was neither "a reviler or scoffer of religion" nor "a cheat or defrauder of any neighbor on earth."

Such a religious viewpoint, therefore, contributed to a distinct model of the self. For these nineteenth-century autobiographers, their ways of understanding the self, recounting changes in the self, thinking about the relationship between self and others, and narrating their life stories were influenced by their view of human nature. In the balance of this chapter, I outline such a model of the self.

Theory of the Self

The theory of the self in early nineteenth-century religious autobiographies (and other autobiographies of this period as well) is built upon a clearly articulated idea of human nature as sinful and weak.[13] This view of human nature involved a characterization of the "passions" (the term used in particular for emotions that impel us to action), reason, and will as components of the self; a notion of change occurring in the self only through God's grace; and a lack of concern about the relationship between self and society. They did not explicitly and systematically develop such ideas into a coherent theory of the self, but more typically revealed their understandings by their assumptions about human nature and selfhood as they interpreted their own lives. In addition, they used the long-standing term "soul" rather than "self," and it is likely that the latter term carried more individualistic connotations than their religious humility would allow.

Human Nature

These nineteenth-century autobiographers treated human nature—those traits and capacities common to all human beings—as the key to understanding a person's life.[14] They conceived of human nature as an immutable and universal limitation for all human beings regardless of social station—"the awful state of all men, by nature" (Alden 1827, p. 35). We do not hear from them the opinion as expressed by Hamlet: "What a piece of work is a man! how noble in reason! how infinite in faculty!" Human beings could be considered the epitome of God's handiwork, but instead we find pessimistic remarks such as those of the tavern owner and gambler Robert Bailey (1822, p. 66) who, with good personal reason, observed: "As a man is a human, he acts in conformity to the dictates of his nature, which is weak and fallacious."

This view of human nature is often attributed to the biblical account of Adam and Eve's expulsion from the Garden of Eden.[15] As a result of Adam's disobedience, human beings were fated to be weak and sinful creatures condemned to suffer and die—"the sad lot of human kind" (Graydon 1811, p. 127). Furthermore, as John Gano (1806, p. 47), a Baptist chaplain for the Continental army, reasoned in his autobiography, this weakness of human nature explains suffering: "As we saw infants, from their birth were subjects of pain, anguish, and death, it was unreasonable to suppose a being, infinitely good, would inflict this great penalty on beings perfectly innocent, pure, and blameless." Because these religious autobiographers (particularly during the early nineteenth century) believed sinfulness to be a fundamental part of human nature, they perceived even newborn infants as depraved. As the prominent Presbyterian clergyman Lyman Beecher (1865, p. 473), father of thirteen children, commented in his autobiography, "The child does . . . very early show signs of anger and selfishness."

In this explanation of human nature, human beings are characterized as pursuing their passions beyond what are acceptable limits: "There is a native selfishness in human nature" (Bailey 1822, p. 214). Such an explanation of human nature gave an answer to the important question, as Socrates once phrased it, "How is it that men know what is good, but do what is bad?"[16] These self-interested passions must be curbed for the sake of life with others, and control of the passions is a key aspect of morality. But since human nature is weak, self-control is a fundamental problem. The evangelical Protestant autobiographers envisioned a battle within each human being to subdue the passions that lead a person to commit the "seven deadly sins": pride, lust, envy, wrath, avarice, gluttony, and sloth.[17] Such sins, which arise from "the baseness of the human heart" (Burroughs [1804] 1924, p. 198), are evident in actions and thoughts like the gambling, drinking, and swearing reported by males, and the dancing, lying, willful disobedience, and pride reported by females. As Maggie Van Cott (1883, pp. 47–48), who claimed to be the first woman licensed to preach in the Methodist Episcopal Church, recalled about her own conversion, "Often . . . did she hear the Spirit say, 'Sister spirit, come away from the world of gayety and fashion.'" Likewise, Peter Cartwright (1856, p. 75), a popular Methodist itinerant preacher whose conversion narrative comes close to epitomizing this religious view of the self, referred to the vanity of wearing rings, ruffles, and ornamental dress as the "superfluity of naughtiness."

The Components of the Self

In their discussions of human nature, these nineteenth-century religious autobiographers usually made reference to reason, will, and the passions. Their understanding of these components of the self was consonant with the faculty psychology dominant in the United States for much of the nineteenth century.[18] Faculty psychology explained the human mind in terms of faculties or "powers of the mind"—usually reason, emotion, and will.[19] As the psychologist Theodore Sarbin (1986a, p. 85) has commented, faculty psychology served as "a simple classificatory scheme which was invented to talk about and to study the human condition." It is a means of discussing the human capacities of feeling, thinking, and willing.

PASSIONS. These autobiographers commonly lumped together both emotions and desires into the ambiguous category of *passions*—forces that impel a person in a spontaneous manner.[20] They contrasted such passions with will and reason, which also impel a person, but involve control and consideration of consequences as well. In this type of nineteenth-century autobiography, the authors described passions and feelings as dynamic and able to "take possession" of a person.[21] Here we can see the relation of the word *passion* to *passive* in the sense of being acted upon. The compulsory nature of such passions, these autobiographers argued, make human beings appear to be no more than beasts. They did not characterize passions as something that represented one's "true self," as some later autobiographers have done, but saw them as something that must be checked. The counterfeiter and imposter Stephen Burroughs ([1804] 1924, p. 2), for example, discussed both passions and feelings as in need of being "properly regulated." And what must be particularly curbed are the "animal passions" that lead one to sin (Cartwright 1856, p. 509). "The usual depravity of the human heart" (Bailey 1815, p. 13) is a problem for all human beings.

These autobiographers' beliefs about the passions, however, were complex. As the prominent nineteenth-century Presbyterian revivalist Charles G. Finney taught, not only sin but also holiness are located in the "heart" (Miller 1965). Some emotions, particularly socially beneficial ones, are desirable. Coexistent with the concern about controlling passions and unbridled emotion was the conviction that the motivational force of strong feelings (such as fear, regret, love, and joy) must be an essential part of religious faith, such that faith should come from the heart rather than from the head.[22] Martin Marty (1972, p. 46) summed up this idea in his study of Protestantism: "Once again a pendulum was to swing back to the experiential and emotive elements in Protestantism, with a reappearance of Methodism, or *evangelicalism*, in England and America—out of Puritan roots . . . The warmed heart was again elevated over the informed head in the hierarchy of Christian values." They recognized that emotion, as a powerful motivating force, can both enrich and disrupt individuals' lives, which leads to the seeming contradiction that the historian E. P. Thompson (1966, p. 368) pointed out, "It is the paradox of a 'religion of the heart' that it should be notorious for the inhibition of all spontaneity."

Among evangelical Protestants, an ardent display of feelings was an essential part of a conversion. Powerful emotions were expected to be a part of one's relationship with God; a passionate embrace of religion was an indicator that one was doing so "wholeheartedly" and sincerely rather than with reluctance. At some of the revivals during the early decades of the nineteenth century, emotions reached a frenetic level.[23] Peter Cartwright (1857, p. 51) commented in his autobiography on the "jerks" and other "strange and wild exercises into which the subjects of [a] revival fell; such . . . as the running, jumping, barking exercise."

These autobiographers freely used stereotypical descriptions of praiseworthy emotions experienced during religious conversions and in some aspects of everyday life such as a reunion with a family member. They used phrases common also to sentimental novels: heaving chests, trembling or melting hearts, quivering lips, and hearts leaping for joy. They did not, however, describe flashes of anger or pangs of jealousy except as an illustration of their sinful preconversion selves. Furthermore, females were not the only ones to use such effusive descriptions of emotions. The tavern owner Robert Bailey (1822, p. 18), for example, described how he would "alleviate [his] aching heart by venting a torrent of tears." Such tears, regardless of gender, were to be taken as a sign of sincerity. Additionally, some autobiographers, to underscore the intensity of their emotions, declared that they could not adequately express their feelings in words.[24] For example, Stephen Burroughs ([1804] 1924, p. 101) asserted that "there is a language of the heart which we cannot express, it so far exceeds the descriptive powers of speech."

Some of these religious autobiographers also experimented with using the idea of a "moral sense" or an innate moral faculty within human beings based on sentiment and serving as an internal guide to moral behavior.[25] The emotion of sympathy, therefore, might be the foundation of moral behavior. This idea, however, which locates the source of morality within the individual, was precariously close to vanity for these religious autobiographers.

REASON. A second component of the self, reason, was viewed by many of these autobiographers (particularly in the first half of the nineteenth century) as not much more than a weak advisor to the will. They had little of the Enlightenment faith in reason and learning. Since human beings are weak and imperfect creatures, so, too, are their faculties of reason.[26] As an autobiographer recalled hearing in a sermon, "Reason is carnal and surely delusive" (Davis 1857, p. 162). Stephen Burroughs ([1804] 1924, p. 80) also explained that "the feelings of the human heart, the weaknesses of nature, and the errors of judgment, all set themselves in array against us, when we attempt to listen to the dictates of wisdom in our practice." Reason, as a frail faculty, led to "many errors in judgment and practice" (Cartwright 1856,

p. 509), and it was not sufficient to provide persons with "right estimates of the various effects which will follow the measures [they] pursue" (Burroughs [1804] 1924, p. 226). Furthermore, controlling impulses and passions required much more than the use of reason and will. There was little chance for the impotent faculty of reason to gain control during an outpouring of intense feelings or passions.

As many persons observed, the human faculty of reason was not even able to comprehend or explain life and its joys and suffering adequately. God's plan for the universe was beyond the comprehension of human beings, and they could only explain sorrow and tragedies as the workings of Divine Providence. As Mrs. K. White (1809, p. 27) exclaimed in her memoir of her abduction by Indians, "The ways of Providence are awful and mysterious!" As a consequence, as Peter Cartwright (1856, p. 438) earnestly preached, believers must trust in God's designs: "I am devoutly glad that there is an overruling Providence, where we may place our hope and confidence . . . though we cannot see through or comprehend the permissive providences of God." For the evangelical Protestants, therefore, reason surely could not stand alone as the basis for religious faith.[27] Itinerant ministers such as Cartwright ardently taught a "religion of the heart," not of the mind. Or, as the evangelical minister Calvin Pease declared, "A production which originates in the head is, as such, artificial and arbitrary; while one which originates in the heart, is spontaneous and vital" (Miller 1965, p. 65).

Additionally, too much faith in reason was dangerous because it could lead to the sin of intellectual pride and an exaggerated sense of human self-importance. On this subject, Andrew Jackson Davis (1857, p. 110), a spiritualist and author of more than two dozen books, wrote: "In sailing from the continent of Superstition to the harbor of true Religion, there is a strait that may be called Skepticism; in which the person is beset by tempestial gales from the shores of both hemispheres, but feels none of that beautiful repose which . . . faith sometimes so graciously bestows upon its faithful follower." Reason could lead to disbelief, and it could be seen as a tool of Satan. As Victor Hugo (1937) once commented, the serpent in the Garden of Eden can be taken to symbolize the intellect. Such a perspective casts doubt on the idea that reason could be the foundation for morality.

Later in the nineteenth century, however, some of these religious autobiographers appeared to be more ambivalent about the role of reason in their lives. They discussed the possibility that reason plays a part in moral conduct and can help a person determine right from wrong. Such a modification was in line with the Arminian belief that salvation is available to all who have faith. From this standpoint, it was possible to ascribe greater importance to self-willed actions (such as piety and good works) as a means, along with faith, to receive God's grace and achieve salvation. Even though they still emphasized the importance of emotions in religion and the need for God's grace, they allowed that reason could play a role in good works.[28]

During the Second Great Awakening, preachers began to use methods that were "calculated to cause the hearers to make a decision and to make it right" (Hudson 1973, p. 136). Although this usually meant appealing to the emotions of the audience, it could also include "moral suasion," that is, a rational appeal to the moral sense to convince persons of their sins and their need to become Christians (Kett 1977). As Perry Miller (1965, p. 34) expressed it, "There is . . . at the heart of [the revival] a resolution to escape from the trammels of 'inability.'" The writer Rebecca Harding Davis (1904, p. 96), recalling the 1840s, commented on this change in belief and its effect on childrearing: "There were heard at first timorous suggestions of 'moral suasion.' Was the soul really reached by a rawhide on the back? Why not appeal to the higher nature of the child? Why not give up thrashing and lure him to virtue by his reason?" Lyman Beecher (1865, p. 473), who promoted revivalism and played a prominent role in doctrinal shifts, insisted that reason should be the guide in morally responsible choices: "There must be a knowledge of duty, or the power of distinguishing between right and wrong. Without such perception of rule, I do not see how blame could exist." Beecher raised the question of accountability: If human beings are sinful by nature and equipped with impotent reason and will, how can they be held responsible for their actions?

WILL. This third component of the self—the capacity of human beings to control their own actions—raises a key moral issue for these religious autobiographers. As the anthropologist Louis Dumont (1985) has observed, the will is a crucial concern throughout the history of Christianity. The nature of the will, however, is a troubling and complex problem.[29] In a state of sin, willfulness meant contrariness and arrogance. Being too self-willed can lead to the sin of vanity as well as rebellion against God as it did in the story of Adam and Eve.[30] In addition, even "good works," which involve will, could easily cause pride, and they were not sufficient to achieve salvation. In the words of E. P. Thompson (1966, p. 364), "Works were the snares of pride and the best works were mingled with the dross of sin; although—by another opportunistic feint—works might be a *sign* of grace." Will, however, could also be viewed as the means by which human beings can liberate themselves from the determinism of the body—that is, to do other than what the passions impel them to do and not remain "deeply bound by the chains of appetite" (Morgan 1874, p. 84). To be able to choose to do otherwise means that persons can be held morally responsible for their actions.

Nevertheless, many Protestant autobiographers in the early part of the nineteenth century took the position that the will, as a human faculty, is exceptionally limited.[31] As the literary historian Perry Westbrook (1979, p. 35) has emphasized, "The central paradox of Puritanism [is] the paradox of a drastically proscribed liberty of will existing with full responsibility for one's actions."[32] Thus Rachel Watson (1871, p. 64) could write in her memoir of domestic life that her children "could not understand the full resignation of will to the will of God; and who does?" For those who believed in predestination, salvation was not a matter of one's own will but rather God's will. The schoolmaster and preacher Henry Morgan (1874, p. 187) made such a point in one of his sermons: "No good works will save thee . . . Without the Spirit you may vainly struggle for a lifetime. Man may make a bird, and give it eyes and feathers and wings, but he can never make one that can breathe or fly . . . The Spirit from a higher source must nerve the wings of thy faith; the Spirit must make thee free." To achieve control of the passions and to be virtuous required nothing less than the divine assistance of God. The will must be dramatically transformed by God's grace. But once this conversion had occurred and individuals had become instruments of God, they would find it easier to regulate the passions. Thus these autobiographers would not have considered the phrase "self-control" to be the most apt description for the control of the passions. Furthermore, they could not easily reconcile the notion of self-control with the deterministic idea of Divine Providence.

The Methodists, however, did begin to argue that human beings could become sinless through their own individual efforts, albeit with the help of God and the support of fellow Methodists. The idea that a revival could inspire persons to seek salvation is premised on such a concept of the nature of human beings. Thus, for Methodists, as the historian Bernard Semmel (1973, pp. 12–13) concluded, "Wesley appealed to both the Puritan sense of man's degenerate state, with its passionate plea for God's grace so essential to salvation, as well as to the Arminian insistence on personal responsibility, on free will and good works." The controversial Baptist minister John Leland ([1838] 1845, p. 39) lamented this change in doctrine: "I have been preaching sixty years to convince men that human powers were too degenerate to effect a change of heart by self-exertion . . . But now a host of preachers and people have risen up, who ground salvation on the foundation that I have sought to demolish."

Most of the early nineteenth-century autobiographers in my sample used only indirect references to will. Lucy Richards (1842, p. 38), a missionary school teacher among the Oneida Indians, asserted that the battle was between grace and nature, not will and nature, although she still admonished her readers to follow the biblical advice to "watch and pray, lest ye enter into temptation." In the latter half of the nineteenth century, however, religious autobiographers used more straightforward descriptions of will and an active striving for salvation.[33] At mid-century, the controversial theologian Horace Bushnell ([1847] 1975, pp. 20–21) criticized the idea that one could not battle the passions successfully until after a conversion: "The supposition that [a person] becomes, at some certain moment, a complete moral agent, which a moment before he was not, is clumsy and has no agreement with observation." Bushnell, who developed the idea that Christian character can be the result of nurture, countered that "depravity is best rectified . . . before it is stiffened into habit" (Fleming ([1933] 1969, p. 198). Ministers like Lyman Beecher (1865, p. 473) contended that "voluntary agency seems . . . indispensable to accountability." And the preacher Henry Morgan (1874, pp. 29, 340), who asserted in his autobiography that one cannot be saved without the Spirit, nevertheless also counseled that when we find ourselves launched on the "sea of temptation" with "dangerous reefs" in our course, we should heed this advice: "Plant thy feet, pull on the oar of prayer! ARMS, *do your best!* SINEWS, *test your strength!*"

Taken together, the discussion of the passions, reason, and will revolved around these questions: What is it that impels a person to act? What is intentional, and what is involuntary? Religious autobiographers generally stressed the importance of human nature in answering this question. Will and reason may prompt a person to act in a virtuous manner, but these faculties are weak by nature. As the tavern owner Robert Bailey (1822, p. 216) commented to his readers, "[Man] is a creature endowed with faculties which dictate to him right and wrong, yet [he is] totally incompetent to act the first." If we adopt this perspective, we are then led to the question of how human beings can change.

Changes in the Self

Can a person innately endowed with a sinful human nature develop or change? The answer to this question depended upon the extent to which these autobiographers accepted the concepts of predestination and original sin. For those who believed in such ideas, true change in the self occurs only through the divine intervention of God. They described such a metamorphosis of the self as occurring as part of a three-stage process during a religious conversion.[34] The age at which persons experienced a conversion, the intensity of emotions they felt, the length of the conversion, the number of its stages, and the abruptness of its onset were all things that could vary during such a transformation.[35]

The first stage was the preconversion period of wickedness. A child, "no matter how sweet or fair," as the writer Rebecca Harding Davis (1904, pp. 93–94) wrote in her memoir of life in the 1800s, "was held to be a vessel of wrath and a servant of the devil." Although some theologians were challenging the idea of infant depravity by the 1830s (Wishy 1968), religious autobiographers in my sample continued to use the notion of childhood as sinful. They stressed the wicked deeds and impious thoughts of childhood—recollections that, inadvertently or not, added spice to their narratives.[36] Peter Cartwright (1856, p. 27) admitted he was "naturally a wild, wicked boy, and delighted in horse-racing, card-playing, and dancing." The Methodist missionary teacher Lucy Richards (1842) confessed that, as a child, she disobeyed her parents, wore frivolous dresses, and went dancing. And the spiritualist Andrew Jackson Davis (1857, p. 98) employed this confessional style when he admitted that he once (but only once) swore at his father: "I'll be dod darn to dod darnation if that hain't too thundering dam bad, any how!" None of these religious autobiographers, however, described youthful sexual desire or any shocking transgressions during the preconversion period—lesser sins sufficed to characterize the sinful self.

This depiction of sinful childhoods before conversion illustrated the common "fallen" natures of the autobiographers and provided a dramatic contrast case to highlight their strengthened postconversion ability to resist temptations. By recalling a reasonable number of sins from this period, they showed that they had scrutinized their own lives and thoughts diligently and, furthermore, that they were humble enough to confess such sinfulness publicly. Since all human beings are by nature corrupt, autobiographers could not, in theory, be held individually responsible for this early sinfulness, and it is possible that this idea of a common human nature assuaged some of their feelings of guilt and self-hatred. They knew they could silently say to the reader, "Let him who is without sin among you be the first to throw a stone." During this first stage of the conversion, they were to come to the realization they could not, by their own efforts, be saved, and hence they needed to submit unconditionally to the will of God. In the memoirs of criminals, their stories did not advance beyond this first period of wickedness except for the "mature" reflection that their lives had been sinful.

The next stage was the crucial conversion—the miraculous metamorphosis from the old vile self to a new self. "The great change that took place in my heart and life," wrote the evangelist R. G. Williams (1896, p. 96), formerly a gambler and alcoholic, "from my human nature's darkness into the marvelous light of the gospel of Christ, that now fills my soul, I call the transformation scene." God's grace, that is, God's effort in one's behalf, was a critical element in such a conversion. What was being accomplished was a transformation of a sinner, subject to the passions, to a person forgiven by God, humbly aware of his or her own past depravity and able to battle the passions with greater effectiveness. A person was "reborn."

The conversion process was much like the description of other identity transformations—it was a difficult and necessarily emotional experience that could last for months. Like St. Augustine, persons undergoing a conversion had to experience remorse for their former sinfulness.[37] For some, this process involved "emotion work" to work up the proper emotions of contrition and grief.[38] During his conversion, the Baptist minister Peter Young (1817, p. 17), for instance, worried that he had "not had distress of mind enough, to receive comfort yet, as Christians do." John Leland ([1838] 1845, p. 13) also recalled, "But as I had never passed through stages of distress equal to some others, nor equal to what I supposed an essential pre-requisite to conversion, I could not believe for myself." It was necessary to reach the point of despising the self and giving up all hope of effecting the transformation without divine assistance.

Such a conversion involved an exhaustive examination of one's actions, feelings, thoughts, and bestial "appetites." Although this could mean an immoderate amount of attention to be concentrated on the self, it was necessary to avoid self-deception. "Shew me the worst of my case," cried Peter Young (1817, p. 11) to God, "and bring me to see more and more of my evil heart." Similarly, Lucy Richards (1842, p. 27) found what she was looking for through such intense self-scrutiny: "The depravity that reigned within,—pride, obstinacy, unbelief, the love of the world." It is this requirement of introspection that has led some commentators to argue that Protestantism has played an important role in the history of autobiography.[39]

Soul-searching, nevertheless, was not sufficient. The acknowledgment of one's sinfulness also involved casting off unworthy friends. "I could not go with my old companions," testified Peter Young (1817, p. 11), "for they were no company for me: I could not feel willing to join with them in folly." Peter Cartwright (1856, p. 35), too, began to treat his friends differently: "Soon it was noised abroad that I was distracted, and many of my associates in wickedness came to see me to try and divert my mind from those gloomy thoughts of my wretchedness; but all in vain. I exhorted them to desist from the course of wickedness which we had been guilty of together." Cartwright recounted how he then flung his playing cards into the fire and relinquished his prized racehorse.

At the moment of conversion, these autobiographers report a feeling of acceptance by God, forgiveness of their sins, and measureless joy. Although some religious narratives depict a conversion as a "series of awakenings interspersed with periods of despair and melancholy" (Dorsey 1993, p. 34), I found that my evangelical autobiographers described an abrupt transfiguration. For Cartwright (1856, p. 37), this event came at a public sacramental meeting after three months of feelings of remorse: "In the midst of a solemn struggle of soul, an impression was made on my mind, as though a voice said to me, 'Thy sins are all forgiven thee.' Divine light flashed all round me, unspeakable joy sprung up in my soul." Peter Young (1817, p. 60) proclaimed that at the moment of his conversion he "could only prostrate [himself], wonder and admire [God's] goodness, and praise him in an extacy [sic] of joy."

These autobiographers did not stress the importance of interaction with other persons during the conversion since God's grace was the key element. But after the conversion, they found support for their transformed identities among new friends.[40] As Lucy Richards (1842, p. 29) exclaimed, "O, to be raised from such a depth of sin and misery into the favor and image of God, and into the fellowship of his saints! . . . It now appeared to me that I had ten friends, where before I had only one." Likewise, Cartwright (1856, p. 38) recalled that immediately after his conversion "[m]y Christian friends crowded around me and joined me in praising God."

In the postconversion stage, the struggle to conquer temptation was not over. There remained the continuous possibility of "backsliding" or discovering one had been deluded about the conversion. As the Baptist minister Ariel Kendrick (1847, p. 6) commented in his autobiography, "A large number sadly evinced that the work of grace in their hearts was superficial." Cartwright (1856, p. 468) also noted that the Methodist church took members initially for a six-month trial period to see if they might "fall away" from the church. In describing their lives after conversion, these autobiographers told of trials of their faith and how they were now able to resist many temptations. Yet, for them to assert they were now without sin would have opened them up to the charge that they were succumbing to the sin of pride. The historian Edmund Morgan (1963, p. 70) pithily summarized this dilemma in his study of the earlier Puritan preachers: "In order to be sure one must be unsure." A sinless life, therefore, remained a difficult ideal. Cartwright (1856, p. 525) concluded his autobiography with the comment that, throughout his life, his "shortcomings and imperfections have been without number." Even after giving evidence of his own success as a preacher, he tried to wrap it in modest terms: "Hundreds [have] claimed me as the humble and unworthy instrument of their salvation" (p. 244).

These autobiographers, therefore, do not describe biological stages or claim self-willed changes. Their story is of a transformation wrought by

God. Their objective was not to develop their unique capabilities or discover their "true" selves; it was rather to be among those who had been saved by God and who had greater success in curbing the passions. One's "natural" self for them was something to be cast off, not developed. The appropriate metaphors were transformation and subjugation, not growth.

The Role of Society and Significant Others

The observation in 1660 by the Puritan theologian Thomas Shepard to "fear not enemies without, but your selves at home" continued to be good advice for these religious autobiographers a century and a half later.[41] They worried about the dangers within, and they gave relatively little attention to the influence of other persons in their lives or the deterministic influence of society. They stressed what Alexander Solzhenitsyn (1975, p. 615) has summarized as "the truth of all the religions of the world: They struggle with the *evil inside a human being*" (his emphasis). They did not entertain a notion of the self as decisively shaped by external social influences.

We might argue that they did believe that others (who share a sinful human nature) played a detrimental role in their lives by encouraging them to submit to temptations. Peter Cartwright (1856, p. 34) did condemn his "associates in wickedness," and Henry Morgan (1874, p. 329) scorned his former "pestiferous load of evil associates." Nevertheless, even though other persons might exacerbate one's sinfulness, they were not the cause of such evil. Human beings, from this perspective, are depraved creatures before any contact with others. Furthermore, these autobiographers could interpret the harmful influences of others as the machinations of Satan. The evangelist R. G. Williams (1896, p. 34), for example, commented that one of his erstwhile friends had "acted as agent and guide for the devil."

Significant persons in their lives such as parents and spouses also did not receive credit for playing much of a role in the autobiographer's conversion. If anyone might be given an acknowledgment, it would be the autobiographer's mother. But they made it clear that, while mothers could serve as exemplars, they were not strong formative influences. Some of them used the maxim "Example is more powerful than precept" in reference to mothers. For those who believed strictly in predestination, parents could have no formative influence on a child whose future was already determined. The grace of God (rather than an effective socialization by parents) was the cause of the "saving" of a young person. Such autobiographers might argue in the abstract for the value of a good upbringing, using commonsense ideas such as Alexander Pope's well-known saying, "Just as the twig is bent, the tree's inclined," but they did not use this metaphor to explain their own transformation. They might allow, however, following the model of St. Augustine, that their mothers' love and grief over their sinfulness intensified their wish to cast off the sinful self. As Cartwright (1856, p. 27) sentimentally recalled from his youthful preconversion stage, "My mother often talked to me, wept over me, and prayed for me, and often drew tears from my eyes."

Accordingly, many autobiographers in the nineteenth century (whether religious or not) painted similar portraits of their mothers as models of virtue to emulate.[42] Mothers were never hateful, petulant, selfish, or immoral; they were pious, selfless, pure, helpful to the needy, and of saintly character.[43] Lyman Beecher (1865, p. 21) described his mother, who died shortly after his birth, as "a joyous, sparkling, hopeful temperament." And Henry Morgan (1874, p. 27) commented, "I never shall forget the angelic expression of my dear mother's countenance. Her finely-chiselled features, though paled by deepest sorrow, shone with heavenly love."

As for fathers, these autobiographers tell us little beyond their occupations and their ability to provide for their families.[44] Mrs. K. White (1809, p. 10), for example, describes her father in this manner: "My father, whose mind was already afflicted with misfortunes, was a merchant, and whose endeavors to gain a fortune had been repeatedly frustrated." The publisher Ebenezer Thomas (1840, p. 30) did likewise: "My father's means were limited, but sufficient to furnish all the comforts of life to his small family." Fathers were not as likely as mothers to be described as moral exemplars. Peter Cartwright (1865, p. 27), for example, lamented that his father actually encouraged him to engage in horse racing and cardplaying.

Based on the number of lines devoted to the discussion of intimate relationships during adulthood, readers might conclude that other persons such as spouses and friends played insignificant roles in these autobiographers' lives. If male autobiographers discussed their wives at all, they characterized them as faithful companions and exemplars of virtue for the children. Often they did not find it necessary to mention their wives' names. The autobiographers' children, similarly, were generally treated as superfluous in the telling of a religious conversion. It is likely that others played only a marginal role in accounts of salvation because these were stories of individual struggle, and the subject of such exemplary tales was the conversion, not private life. Moreover, to speak of the delights of relationships would be highlighting a worldly pleasure. As Abigail Bailey (1815, p. 27) confessed, "I found I loved my family with too much creature fondness." And Nancy Towle (1832, p. 50), an evangelist, discussed her fear of "setting [my female traveling companion] up as an idol in my affections."

These autobiographers likewise did not regard society as a formative influence in their lives.[45] Self against society was not a theme for them as it would be for some later autobiographers. Society was not something that constrained the self or threatened one's individuality. None of these autobiographers from the first half of the nineteenth century used the concept of society in this sense. Society, customs, norms—these were things of "this world" and not a source of real concern. Such a world (particularly the "city") might offer tempting opportunities, but the cause of sin ultimately lay within the person. As an earlier Puritan preacher said, "Yet wee must know it is not the *World* simply that draws our heart from God and goodness, but the *love* of the world."[46] Society was nothing more than a backdrop or stage for the self as a morality play.

There also were no arguments from these religious autobiographers that the reason for morally correct behavior is to produce an orderly society. They may have recognized that such behavior is good for a group of interdependent people, but they did not use an encompassing term like *society.* Such a concept, as the cultural critic Raymond Williams (1983) has detailed, was not commonly used until the late eighteenth century in its abstract sense, and these autobiographers in the nineteenth century apparently saw no need for this term. For these writers, morality entailed the commandments issued by God.

I also found little interest in the idea of "social problems" among these early nineteenth-century autobiographers. The writer Rebecca Harding Davis (1904, p. 106) recalled about her childhood in the 1830s that the chief business of a person was to "save his own soul" and not that of his neighbor's. The focus for these believers was on the afterlife. To support the idea of social reform, one must assume that human beings are able to change the world or at least themselves. When evangelical Protestants began to consider salvation as possible for anyone, many did play a role in what could be deemed as social reform. But for them, what needed to be reformed was the individual. They treated social problems as the consequence of individual sin. The historian David Brion Davis (1967, p. 6) has written, "The great object of American revivalists from Jonathan Edwards to Billy Graham has not been to perfect society but to save men's souls by arousing them to a full awareness of their involvement in sin." Even in prominent antebellum reform movements such as abolition and temperance, religious leaders such as Charles G. Finney insisted that the individual must be reformed in order to eliminate these problems. From this perspective, slavery, for example, must be recognized as a sin. As the evangelist Henry Morgan (1874, p. 381) exclaimed, "Take the Bible, and the Bible alone, to reform the world!"

One of the institutions of society, formal education, also was treated as a human—and thus imperfect—institution by these autobiographers. Schooling centered on the deficient faculty of reason. "It is a melancholy consideration," asserted the counterfeiter Stephen Burroughs ([1804] 1924, p. 30), "that our youth should spend so much time in acquiring that knowledge, which is of no use to themselves." Education was neither necessary nor sufficient for salvation. It might be useful in teaching a person to read the Bible or in providing some skills for daily living. And for those who believed salvation was possible for all, Bible reading could help prepare persons for conversion. Nonetheless, as Lucy Richards (1842, pp. 212–13) asked, "What is a knowledge of letters, of the arts and sciences, without a knowledge of sins forgiven? A mere empty pageant." Worse yet, education could lead to unjustified pride, or it might encourage a person to be a "free" thinker and skeptical of religion. Peter Cartwright (1856, p. 405) expressed such an outlook when he made this lament: "But O, how have things changed for the worse in the educational age of the world!" Learning to read meant persons could read the Bible, but it also enabled them to read "unsavory" materials. Thus the Baptist minister Ariel Kendrick (1847, p. 73) warned, "You ought to be quite as cautious of bad books as of bad company."

Some of the early nineteenth-century revivalists railed against any efforts to intellectualize Christianity (Miller 1965). The itinerant Methodist preachers usually were not educated men, and Cartwright (1856, p. 409), for example, defensively pointed out that "Christ had no literary college or university, no theological school or Biblical institute." The stress on emotions in the revivals meant that these men could preach fervidly from the heart. Some of them ridiculed what they believed to be the sterile and detached rhetoric of the educated clergy. Henry Morgan (1874, p. 274), for instance, chose to parody the schooled preachers who would ruin the simple biblical passage, "God said, 'Let there be light'; and there was light," by recasting it as "the Omnipotent commanded: and forthwith coruscations of effulgence descended upon the sable brow of Erebus." As Protestant doctrine shifted toward Arminianism, however, more began to see the importance of Christian learning.

Although social influences were not important in shaping the self, other "external" influences did play significant roles: God and the devil. Some of these autobiographers maintained that the "devil" was an external (or internal) influence acting as a stimulus to the passions.[47] Peter Cartwright (1856, p. 298) described temptation as feeling "the power of the devil, physically and mentally." And the tavern owner Robert Bailey (1822, p. 12) recalled his mother's warning that "there was a great black ugly clubfooted man called the Devil, that would take me and all bad boys and put them in hell and burn them up."

To explain significant (but not mundane) events in their lives, many nineteenth-century autobiographers (including secular ones) used Divine Providence—meaning God's determination of a person's fate. Several autobiographers, including the publisher Ebenezer Thomas (1840, pp. 82–83), approvingly quoted the same line from *Hamlet* to refer to Providence: "There is a Divinity that shapes our ends, / Rough-hew them how we will." Rather than interpreting important happenings in their lives as self-determined or as a matter of chance, they seemed to accept the idea of God's personal direction of the course of these events. Many a man, as Rebecca Harding Davis (1904, pp. 98–99) commented in her autobiography, "held that this Supreme Power took a personal interest in his crops, his rheumatism, and his choice of a wife." Roeliff Brinkerhoff (1900, p. 88), a banker whose autobiography otherwise corresponds more closely with the model of self-development described in the next chapter, employed this idea of Providence: "My own experience has been that my career has been ordered from without, and not from within, and whatever good I have accomplished has been as an instrument and not as a designer." Likewise, Joseph Martin (1830, p. 67) described how he might have been killed in the Revolutionary War, but it was "otherwise ordered by Divine Providence."

Providence also was useful to account for errors and lack of foresight. As Mark Twain (1935, p. 347) said sarcastically, "There are many scapegoats for our blunders, but the most popular one is Providence." In his autobiographical writings, Twain also satirized the vanity implied in the idea of Providence when he explained how, as a child, he interpreted several tragic deaths as warnings from Providence to him: "It sounds curiously innocent and conceited . . . It would not have surprised me, nor even overflattered me, if Providence had killed off that whole community in trying to save an asset like me . . . *Why* Providence should take such an anxious interest in such a property, that idea never entered my head" (1924, 1:133–34).

On the other hand, those autobiographers who believed that their own thoughts and deeds could affect their fate responded to misfortunes (including natural catastrophes) by relentlessly scrutinizing their thoughts and deeds for wrongs for which God must be demanding retribution. Furthermore, this personal notice that God took of their lives meant that God vigilantly observed not only actions but private thoughts and feelings as well. "To [God's] piercing eyes," Ariel Kendrick (1847, p. 14) wrote, "my wicked heart was transparent." Even for those who saw a greater role for reason and will in their lives, arguing that their fates were primarily in their own hands would have been egotistical and forgetful of the role of God's grace. Thus Lyman Beecher (1865, p. 89), who espoused taking greater responsibility for one's own actions, nevertheless accounted for his first ministerial position at the Presbyterian church in East Hampton, Long Island, with this reasoning: "You see I had no plan. It was unexpected entirely. I felt as if it were ordered for me by Providence."

Telling the Story

In telling a story of a religious conversion, these autobiographers, in accord with the principle that "example is more powerful than precept," presented their readers with moral examples to emulate. They appeared to agree, in part, with Dr. Samuel Johnson's ([1750] 1953, p. 132) observation that "no species of writing seems more worthy of cultivation than biography." Even rogues declared a didactic value for their tales. "I will guard youth," asserted the gambler Robert Bailey (1822, p. 14), "against the course I have travelled through life." They did not design their stories to tell their readers of the diversity of human experience; they were to provide examples of lives that demonstrated the importance of certain values.

Since the religious autobiographers concentrated on their transformations, they chose events that would fit into the pattern of a conventional conversion narrative (Shea 1968). Their life stories were to parallel and validate the traditional stories of conversion. The Methodist missionary teacher Lucy Richards (1842, p. 10) made it clear what her criterion for selection of events was to be: "The first thing I can remember of a religious nature." This meant childhood had little importance in itself except to establish the autobiographers' preconversion sinfulness. Childhood, as part of the history of the former self, was not relevant for understanding the transformed self. They did not emphasize their individuality (although by implication they were distinct by virtue of being favored by God). They ostensibly wrote their stories for others and not for self, and their stories carried the implication that it could be anyone's story.[48]

The religious autobiographers' interest in "knowing thyself" was not to discover and celebrate their "true selves"; it was to recognize the full extent of their sinful natures and the necessity for change. Before his religious awakening, for example, Lyman Beecher (1865, p. 45) described himself as "ignorant as a beast of the state of my heart." He, like others, believed it was imperative to scrutinize his own thoughts and actions assiduously for signs of sin and self-deception, while, at the same time, avoiding excessive self-absorption.[49] The details of such a self-scrutiny in the form of a confession confirmed that a person had gone through the requisite stages of the conversion. They had to be careful, however, not to boast of the thoroughness of their self-examination or describe their former sins too enthusiastically lest they be guilty of the sin of pride (Barbour 1992). Even John Bunyan had been reproached for designating himself the "chief of sinners" in his *Grace Abounding to the Chief of Sinners.*

These religious autobiographers, like other autobiographers, aspired for a "proper" self-presentation in their life histories. A particularly important virtue for them was modesty. They wished to restrain self-regard, yet a confession required that they discuss and analyze the self at length. Readers could easily interpret the prolonged attention to self as an exercise in the sin of pride, so these authors took particular pains to include the disclaimer that they were "reluctantly yield[ing] to the many solicitations of [their] friends" who believed that they led exemplary lives (Cartwright 1856, pp. 4–5). Moreover, to affirm that they had received God's grace was not necessarily boastful, since being one of the elect did not mean for them that they had deserved this gift.

When it came to questions of honesty, some religious autobiographers apparently felt they need not make explicit claims about the truth of the story; perhaps they reasoned that readers would not doubt the honesty of a person who had gone through a genuine conversion. Some did offer the disclaimer, however, that a faulty memory accounted for any inaccurate recollections. Peter Cartwright (1856, pp. 7–8), for instance, confessed he had qualms about his ability to recall the past: "My memory is greatly at fault; ten thousand interesting facts have escaped my recollection . . . and I fear that many scenes and incidents, as they now occur to my recollection, will be added to, or diminished from."

If these autobiographers embellished the story or worried about style, they might compromise the facts in their stories. Any efforts at a skillful telling of the story would be vain and unnecessary given the didactic reason for writing such accounts. They need not even worry about proper grammar and punctuation. The preacher Nancy Towle (1832, p. 5), therefore, began her memoir with this disclaimer: "A brief sketch of the various *changing scenes* of my life, thus, far, I here present you;—not with elegance of style;—to '*hold fast the form of sound words*,' has been my only *aim*" (her emphasis). These religious authors told their stories in what they assumed to be a straightforward, simple, chronological narrative. They could suppose that the commonality of the experience of battling the passions would in itself be interesting to readers.

We could argue, however, that telling an interesting story was still a consideration for them. The preacher Peter Cartwright (1856), who had also managed to acquire some fame as a raconteur, fretted several times in his autobiography over whether his readers would find his life interesting. Even though these religious autobiographers' explicit purpose was to establish that they had gone through the typical stages of a conversion, they also make it apparent that they did not want to bore the reader. Their sentimental descriptions of emotions, such as "trembling hearts," for example, were useful in rousing the readers' feelings. And even though we might expect them to avoid humor and jocularity, some of them, nonetheless, included jokes in their life stories—an inclusion that demonstrated not piety but a sense of humor. Cartwright (1856, p. 41), for instance, related a joke about a lamb butting a dozing congregation member, and the preacher Henry Morgan (1874, p. 139) told a derogatory joke about a black man mistaking a train for the devil. They attempted to integrate the interesting particulars of their lives with a conventional account of a conversion.

Conclusion

For the religious autobiographers, the moral question of the control of the passions was a crucial issue in a story of self. Their characterization of the self gave these authors a conventional way to interpret their own weaknesses of the flesh and to explain all events in their lives no matter how enigmatic. Their interpretations of self, however, were not simple. They recognized that questions of responsibility for one's own actions are not easily resolved.

To compose a story of a conversion, they need only turn to the Bible or books such as *The Pilgrim's Progress* for a model account.[50] The Baptist minister Peter Young (1817, p. 57), for example, assumed his readers would understand when he compared the recognition of his own sinfulness to St. Paul's conversion experience: "With Paul, I should cry out, 'Oh wretched man that I am.'" Furthermore, the religious autobiographers heard others at church tell narratives about their conversions. As the physician Faye Lewis (1971, p. 84) recalled about her childhood, "A session of 'testimonies' was a regular part of the revival meetings . . . during which the more courageous arose and told the assembly of their own personal experiences in sin, and the victories of spirit over flesh."

This model of the self began to be disputed, particularly in the late nineteenth century, as Darwinism and advances in the behavioral and social sciences began to elaborate alternative explanations of human behavior and development. The Darwinian theory of evolution, along with the nineteenth-century geological discoveries of fossils, cast doubt for some on the religious interpretation of the history of humankind—particularly the story of creation and Adam's "fall" in the Garden of Eden. Some autobiographers who lived through this period commented on this change, as did

James Fagan (1912, p. 38): "My experience was only an illustration, on a small scale, of the intellectual excitement that was being aroused at the time, all over the world . . . For one thing, the Book of Genesis and miracles of every description in Biblical history were on trial at the bar of the 'Missing Link.'" Such ideas, however, did not simply supersede religious interpretations. Some Protestant theologians were able to respond to Darwinian controversies by absorbing evolutionary ideas—incorporating, for example, a concept of development in which natural selection, far from disproving religious teaching, could be interpreted as part of God's plan.[51]

Religious autobiographies continue to be published in considerable numbers, although, since the 1930s, they are no longer the largest category of autobiographies. More recent versions of these works usually contain modifications and adjustments in the model of the self in response to contemporary ideas, for example, fewer mentions of original sin, God's direction of human affairs, predestination, or the need for an emotional conversion. The Catholic priest and bishop Fulton Sheen (1980, p. 3), for instance, referred to original sin and the "frailty of human nature" in his autobiography, yet he also included a discussion of social justice and "man in society," and he incorporated psychological concepts such as the libido, the unconscious, and the psychology of conversion.[52] He asserted that we must "take all the findings of our psychological age and use them as a springboard for the presentation of Divine Truths" (p. 74). In a study of twentieth-century conversion narratives, Virginia Brereton (1991, p. 48) found that "the most far-reaching twentieth-century cultural influence has been evangelicalism's growing awareness and appropriation of psychology, of the therapeutic." Brereton added that conversion has come to mean "an occasion of psychological healing, when a divided, unhappy personality could be integrated."

We could argue that a conception of the self stressing the battle between the "passions" and reason well preceded these nineteenth-century religious autobiographers' concerns (for example, Plato's metaphor of the soul as a charioteer with a pair of horses—one vicious and one noble) and has continued to exist in one form or another (e.g., Freud's ideas about the id and ego). But even for an abiding issue such as self-control, the specifics of a person's beliefs will be tied to what the historian Carl Becker ([1932] 1965) called the "climate of opinion"—the culturally shared understandings extant during a person's lifetime.

Chapter Four $\mathcal{M}$ ASTERS OF FATE

Will it, and it is thine. No longer grovel as though the hand of fate were upon thee.
SELF-HELP BOOK FROM 1856

Although it might appear that the concept of the self-made man has been the prototypical American story since the birth of the nation, this idea did not crystallize in the United States until the middle third of the nineteenth century (Weiss 1969).[1] Moreover, it was during this same period that some American autobiographers (both businessmen and others) began to use this story of an individual who achieves success by his own efforts as the basis for telling about their own lives.[2] In so doing, they employed a model of the self distinct from that of the religious autobiographers. They supplanted the idea of a sinful self to be changed only by divine intervention with a notion of a self with considerable promise if it is "developed." Their metaphor for under-

standing the self was not transformation but cultivation—with its connotations of labor, nurture, and growth. From this perspective, the banker
Roeliff Brinkerhoff's declaration (1900, pp. 23–24) in his autobiography
that "the course I actually did take was the very best I could have adopted for
the best development of the mental and physical forces given me" was not
egocentric and self-indulgent, as many religious autobiographers would
have considered it, but instead was praiseworthy.

Historical Background

During the nineteenth century and into the early twentieth century in the
United States, there were differing, although overlapping, interpretations
of what constituted the self-made man (Cawelti 1965). For some persons,
being self-made primarily meant the development of "character." Benjamin Franklin's ([1793] 1923) memoir, although written before "self-made"
became a catchword, no doubt could be taken as a model of such character
building because of his ample advice on self-discipline and hard work.[3] In
addition, many self-help books and school texts in the nineteenth century
preached the virtues of character building. In the McGuffey readers, for example, students found many such maxims: "The industrious boy is happy
and prosperous," A "noble and beautiful character" is "the best of possessions in the world," and so on (Mosier 1965, pp. 103, 107).[4]

In contrast, a second definition of the self-made man placed the emphasis on self-culture: the development of a person's intellectual or spiritual self
through individual effort with the objective of "fulfillment" (Cawelti 1965).
Here the stress was not only on moral traits but also on the development of
intellect. The term *self-culture* first appeared in English in 1838 in an essay by
John Stuart Mill, who had been impressed by German ideas about personal
culture as found in the *bildungsroman* (Bromwich 1989).[5] In the same year,
the Unitarian clergyman William Ellery Channing delivered a set of lectures he entitled "Self-Culture," and the term was soon used by Emerson,
Lowell, and others.[6] Those who adopted this idea had faith in the power of
education to improve human beings, and they believed that an individual
had a moral responsibility to develop his or her own self.

From the late 1820s until the Civil War, the lyceum provided a means for
self-culture (particularly in New England and the Middle Atlantic states)
by presenting lectures and debates in villages and towns (Bode 1956). Later
in the century, the Chautauqua adult education program also offered plays,
concerts, lectures, and eventually correspondence courses and home-
reading programs to those who wished to cultivate themselves. James Fagan

(1912, p. 104), a railroad signalman and writer, recalled the prominence of self-culture in the late 1800s: "Society at the time, from top to bottom, was absorbingly interested in personal culture and development of every description. In the year 1881, self-culture was the supreme topic in the public mind."

Finally, a third version of the concept of the self-made man highlighted the financial success of the businessman.[7] Sherwood Anderson ([1924] 1969, p. 84), who rebelled against such an idea, recalled its advent: "A new kind of hero, tarnished somewhat later, filled the popular eye . . . Everyone was singing a new little song: 'Get on. Make money. Get to the top. A penny saved is a penny earned. Money makes the mare go.'" After the Civil War, self-help manuals and many children's books (such as those of Horatio Alger, Oliver Optic, and Harry Castlemon) helped to promote this mythical story of the self-made businessman. Alger's books, with total sales estimated at seventeen million, detailed the rise of a self-made man from rags to at least a "secure white-collar position," albeit with the help of a kindly benefactor (Weiss 1969; Cawelti 1965, p. 109).

Businessmen's life stories were among the top five categories of American autobiographies from the 1870s through the 1930s.[8] Collections of brief biographies of successful businessmen were also published, such as Freeman Hunt's *Lives of American Merchants* ([1856] 1969) and Charles C. B. Seymour's *Self-Made Men* (1858). In these stories, readers are to assume that financial success was evidence of a man's industry and economy. Sherwood Anderson ([1924] 1969, p. 213) noted the popularity of such stories during the last half of the nineteenth century: "Like all young Americans I had read innumerable tales of men who had begun with nothing and had become great leaders, owners of railroads, governors of states . . . Abraham Lincoln walking miles through a storm after a hard day's work to borrow his first book, Jay Gould the young Wall Street clerk."

Each of these renditions of the idea of the self-made man contained different definitions of success, yet they were similar in attributing achievements to individual effort. For autobiographers, the first two versions—the themes of either character development or self-culture—were particularly adaptable as a basis for their life histories. A story only highlighting fortune building and competitiveness, however, was not as commendable for an autobiography, even for business successes like Andrew Carnegie.

The development of these notions of the self-made man in the nineteenth century was intertwined with other historical events. The themes of character and willpower, for example, relate to the shift in theological doctrine toward Arminianism with its greater faith in human potential. Additionally, the Industrial Revolution in the United States, in theory, widened the opportunities for social mobility. As Ebenezer Thomas (1840, p. 34), publisher of several Cincinnati newspapers, declared in his autobiography, "The aristocracy of wealth and family have been compelled to give way to the aristocracy of mind; all [the] most distinguished men of the present day are self-made."[9] The possibility of financial success through industrious-ness, according to the historian Irvin Wyllie (1954, p. 13), helped provide the "foundations for the powerful nineteenth-century cult of the self-made man." And for those who did not become business successes, the 1862 Homestead Law and the existence of a frontier offered Americans the prospect that they could, in the words of the cliché, "go West, young man," and start from scratch with free land.

The concept of the self-made man also showed an elective affinity with the scientific thought of the time—particularly the ideas of development and evolution.[10] In the latter half of the nineteenth century, the theories of Charles Darwin, Jean-Baptiste de Lamarck, and Herbert Spencer offered a scientific explanation of human development.[11] Darwin's theory of the ori-gin of species advanced and extended ideas about evolution and develop-ment in existence since at least the early nineteenth century.[12] Ideas about evolution, particularly those of Herbert Spencer, were widely circulated in the United States.[13] Richard Hofstadter ([1944] 1955, pp. 4–5), in his dis-cussion of the intellectual uses of Darwin's ideas, maintained that "in some respects the United States during the last three decades of the nineteenth and at the beginning of the twentieth century was *the* Darwinian country."

Andrew Carnegie (1920, p. 206), like many autobiographers, men-tioned how ideas about evolution had personally influenced him: "Spencer and Darwin were . . . high in the zenith, and I had become deeply interested in their work. I began to view the various phases of human life from the standpoint of the evolutionist." Clarence Darrow (1932, p. 250) also proudly noted that his parents "had all of Darwin's [books] as fast as they were published." For autobiographers, Spencer's ideas about the survival of the fittest and the evolution from simple to complex were particularly use-ful to explain not only the development of species but also the individual life course. If evolution toward perfection were happening on a general level, then this might be true also for individuals. On this subject, John Moody ([1933] 1946, p. 178), the successful publisher of a manual of indus-trial securities, explained in his autobiography: "We humans are merely what evolution tells us we are: struggling creatures slowly climbing to a higher plane."

Ideas about evolution led some autobiographers to consider the rela-tionship between their own development and the physical environment.[14] In order to survive, as Spencer contended in the *Principles of Psychology*

(1855), human beings must adjust to the environment. Spencer adapted Lamarck's theory of acquired characteristics, which was widely debated in the latter half of the nineteenth century and into the early twentieth century (Jordanova 1984). Lamarck postulated that an organism responds to environmental pressures by adapting itself through changes in its physical constitution in its own lifetime, and, furthermore, these modifications could then be inherited by offspring (Cravens 1978; Curti 1980; Morss 1990). By adjusting its behavior to changes in the environment (that is, by developing new habits), an animal could biologically change. Lamarck's conclusions were particularly useful in supporting the argument that the human species—both on a general and individual basis—could improve. It was an appealing idea that a man might pass on to his children what he gained by "exercising" his faculties such as reason and will, thereby actively contributing to their development as well. Furthermore, a self-made man could believe his success proved he was among the "fit."

These autobiographers, therefore, raised different questions about the self from those of the religious autobiographers: What is the relationship between the self and the physical environment? Can the self develop or evolve over a lifetime by a person's own efforts? Can we understand such change scientifically? Together, the answers to these questions led to an optimistic view of the self. Andrew Carnegie (1920, p. 339) rhapsodized about the "truth of evolution" and human potentiality: "Man was not created with an instinct for his own degradation, but from the lower he had risen to the higher forms. Nor is there any conceivable end to his march to perfection. His face is turned to the light; he stands in the sun and looks upward."

Theory of the Self

In the model of the self used by the religious autobiographers, human nature was the key element in understanding a person's behavior. But for those who adopted a view of the self as something to be developed, human nature played a less determinative role. Such a self is not unalterably handicapped by human nature for it can be cultivated by a person's own endeavors. And among the components of the self, the idea of will came clearly to the forefront.

Human Nature

These autobiographers questioned the idea that human beings are innately corrupt and cannot win the battle of self-control without divine intervention. Georgiana Kirby (1887, p. 29), a member of the utopian community of Brook Farm during its short existence in the 1840s, told her readers of her disgust with the idea of original sin: "Adam and Eve ate the forbidden apple, and in consequence the whole world was degraded. Every heart was vile, and should be conscious of the burden of sin . . . The whole idea was revolting, monstrous." It was more likely, from this standpoint, that human beings have the capacity for both evil and good—in other words, human nature was malleable.[15] As the spiritualist Andrew Jackson Davis (1857, p. 35) noted in his autobiography, this view constituted a different assessment of human nature: "In briefly analyzing the history of moral philosophy from the early eighteenth century to the mid-nineteenth century, we have seen a tendency to deny the doctrine of man's total depravity and to restore 'natural man' to the original purity of an Adam who possessed capacities for either good or evil." Thus Kirby (1887, p. 135) argued that she had "faith in human nature," and the minstrel Ralph Keeler (1870, p. 274), in his advice to travelers, was charitable in his viewpoint of humanity: "He will find in the human nature with which he comes into contact in every land the sum of the good invariably preponderating over that of the evil."

Nonetheless, these autobiographers still treated the passions as something to be mastered. This was particularly true for those who emphasized the importance of character development. Although human beings have the potential for goodness, the capacity for wrongdoing remains. From this perspective, the solution lies not in God's hands but in the individual's development of "character" and use of willpower. If human nature were plastic, it could be shaped and developed. It is possible to have a "better self" (Kirby 1887, p. 69) or to cultivate one's "better nature" (Morgan 1874, p. 22). Now the fundamental problem was a personal failure to develop will, not the impairment of human nature in general.

These autobiographers could discuss wrongdoing without using theological ideas by explaining such behavior as a matter of bad habits (which could be eliminated since they were not innate). John Moody ([1933] 1946, pp. 79, 49), summarized this viewpoint: "What we used to call sin was at the worst mere error," and evil was the result of "vicious habits." Similarly, Sophia Wyatt (1854, p. 204), a hotel proprietress, discussed "sloth" not as sin but as something that might become "habitual." The explanation for why human beings "know what is good, but do what is bad" shifted from the idea of a corrupt human nature toward the notion that such behavior is a matter of learning.[16] Any vice, therefore, could be overcome by training and the inculcation of good habits. "Habit" was far from being a new idea, of course, and it generally referred to behavior that had become customary and unthinking through frequent repetition. What had changed in the nineteenth century, however, was the placement of this idea of habit (as un-reflective behavior) into a physiological framework that made it possible to offer a more "scientific" explanation of human wrongdoing as "bad habits."[17] In Lamarckism, habit (as the way in which animals accommo-date themselves to the environment) was a key aspect of evolution (Richards 1987; Morss 1990). Human beings, as William James and others argued, could "re-form" themselves by developing new and commendable habits through the repeated exertion of willpower (Curti 1980).[18] Once persons developed good habits, they need not consciously exert will.

From this perspective, the ability to develop *willpower,* a term first ap-pearing in English in 1874, was a capacity that all human beings (males and females) possess. One need not be transformed by God's grace in order to cultivate this power. And because anyone could develop will, these autobi-ographers need not claim to be unique in this respect. Although this may seem at odds with the individualistic premise of the "self-made man," these authors modestly maintained that they were examples of what anyone could do. As the writer of a popular business manual at the turn of the cen-tury sermonized, "What men need most is not talent but purpose, not the power to achieve, but the will to labor through difficulties" (Nichols 1904, p. 33). Natural endowments could even be a detriment—talented persons might foolishly believe they had no need to develop character.

The Components of the Self

Nineteenth-century American religious autobiographers discussed reason, will, and above all, the passions as key considerations when thinking about the self. Similarly, the nineteenth-century autobiographers who adopted the idea of self-development also used the simple tripartite scheme of fac-ulty psychology dominant for much of the nineteenth century in the United States. But for them, the emphasis switched from the passions to the faculty of will.

PASSIONS. In this optimistic model of the self, the passions were a manage-able component of the self. Rather than fatalistically emphasizing the neg-ative in the category of passion and emotion, these autobiographers discussed emotions such as generosity and kindness that represented the good side of human nature. Andrew Jackson Davis (1857, p. 253), for exam-ple, described a person's "instinctive sympathy," and Georgiana Kirby (1887, p. 79) characterized someone as a "man of the finest sensibilities, im-pulsive with generous instincts." The category of passions was divided into positive and negative—with the term *sensibilities* sometimes used to distinguish "refined" and beneficial emotions such as compassion, sympathy, and benevolence. As the philosopher Charles Taylor (1989, p. 22) has observed, "With the decline of the specifically theological definition of the nature of a transformed will, a formulation of the crucial distinction of higher and lower in terms of altruism and selfishness comes to the fore." If the autobiographers described their own emotions, it was likely that they would illustrate their sensibilities.

There were at least two related interpretations of the source of these finer human emotions. One explanation was that individuals foster proper feelings and virtue through "moral culture"—learning to cultivate positive emotions and regulate the passions.[19] A second explanation, following the influential ideas of Lord Shaftesbury and Francis Hutcheson in the eighteenth century, was that human beings have an inborn "moral sense" or "propensity" that tells them intuitively what is right. The idea of a moral sense placed the source of morality "within" an individual—connecting it to the emotions (particularly empathy). If benevolent emotions were the result of an innate moral sense, it was possible to engage in virtuous conduct without being purified by the grace of God. To explain why human beings, nevertheless, engage in wrongdoing, it was necessary to add that evil can be the result of a person's failure to cultivate this innate moral sense. For example, Calvin Fairbank (1890, p. 128), an ardent abolitionist, used these terms to describe another who had not developed such sensibilities: "He entertained no social sympathy, which acted as a restraint upon his brutality."

REASON. Here reason is not a feeble and flawed advisor to the will. Instead, reason, which represents a "higher" stage of development, can be cultivated (particularly by males). Reason was to be celebrated as a faculty that helps "the human animal," as the lawyer J. W. Arbuckle (1942, p. 45) worded it, "to lift himself above the brute." It plays a part in emancipating a person from the sway of the passions, even if the wish to do what was right had as its source the "moral sense." Reason, nevertheless, was still not as significant as the faculty of will. Theodore Roosevelt (1900, p. 725) wrote on this subject in the magazine *Outlook:* "In the great battle of life, no brilliancy of intellect, no perfection of bodily development, will count when weighed in the balance against that assemblage of virtues, active and passive, of moral qualities, which we group together under the name of character."

Mental development did not mean the acquisition of knowledge but rather the attainment of mental *discipline* and self-direction—the ability to employ reason as a tool for problem-solving.[20] These autobiographers overlaid the notion of will on the idea of reason. James Fagan (1912, p. 165), for example, wrote of his realization that "it would be necessary for me to treat my mind as I would my business or my body; that is to say, I was called upon to direct its energies and superintend its activities." A few pages later, he confidently asserted that "the brain and the mind are my servants, my *Will* is their master" (p. 168). Similarly, John Moody ([1933] 1946, p. 53) described how he learned "to guide and control [his] mind, to concentrate and reason logically."

Such mental discipline could be acquired by "exercising" the faculty of reason. Georgiana Kirby (1887, p. 13), who associated with persons such as Ralph Waldo Emerson during her residency at Brook Farm, lamented that her "reasoning faculty" had not been "properly exercised in a good school." And nearly half a century later, Lincoln Steffens (1931, p. 164) employed this idea that "evidently the brain is like any other muscle." Using a biological metaphor, some autobiographers asserted that ideas were "food" for the brain. Andrew Carnegie (1920, p. 339), for instance, explained how he was fascinated by the idea that "man has absorbed such mental foods as were favorable to him, retaining what was salutary, rejecting what was deleterious." A primary way to obtain such "food" was through self-education—by reading or taking part in Lyceum or Chautauqua activities.[21]

Such mental development was not dependent on original endowment. These autobiographers modestly depicted mental maturation as something anyone could accomplish—even those slow of comprehension. I found few autobiographers boasting that they had great native intellectual abilities. Instead, some of them appeared eager to proclaim that they did not originally equal others. Georgiana Kirby (1887, p. 33) divulged she "was anything but precocious, being very slow of comprehension, as well as unready with language," and the banker Roeliff Brinkerhoff (1900, p. 19) remarked, without any apparent sheepishness, that he "was not as bright as some others, and made no claim to meteoric gifts in any direction."[22] Such autobiographers could hope that readers would admire their humility and give them credit for the effort and willpower that must, therefore, account for their successes.

A concomitant belief was that persons who relied too much on their original talents would fail to develop the all-important faculty of will. As Irvin Wyllie (1954, p. 36) noted in his study of the self-made man, the term *genius* often was negatively linked with the adjectives of "lazy, vain, impatient, and undisciplined." In addition, "overexercising" the faculty of reason could enervate other faculties such as the emotions.[23] Extensive reading and study, therefore, might be at the expense of physical or mental health and could cause a person to become sickly and pale. Adopting such a theory, James Fagan (1912, p. 23) noted that his continuous study "resulted in a mental condition that was altogether too morbid and introspective." And H. L. Mencken ([1940] 1955, p. 175) quipped that, as a result of his childhood enthusiasm for reading, he "acquired round shoulders, spindly shanks, and a despondent view of humanity."

WILL. Will was undoubtedly the most crucial faculty for these autobiographers. Fagan (1912, p. 106), for example, explained that his theme was how his will "consciously and persistently, has been hewing a personal trail through a forest of difficulties." We can see the centrality of the concept of will not only in these autobiographies, but also in the self-help literature published in the latter half of the nineteenth century and the early decades of the twentieth century.[24] The will apparently carried no significant danger (the peril of being self-willed) as it had for the religious autobiographers; instead it was the means by which one could transform oneself. As John Stuart Mill ([1859] 1991, pp. 68–69) wrote:

> According to [Calvinistic theory], the one great offense of man is self-will . . . But if it be any part of religion to believe that man was made by a good Being, it is more consistent with that faith to believe, that this Being gave all human faculties that they might be cultivated and unfolded, not rooted out and consumed, and that he takes delight in every nearer approach made by his creatures to the ideal conception embodied in them, every increase in any of their capabilities of comprehension, of action, or of enjoyment.

Usually these advocates of self-development did not explicitly define the term *will*, although they generally meant the capacity of individuals to control their own actions. Will was a vaguely understood inner energy source to which any human being has access, and exercising willpower meant acting with resolution and controlling the passions.

These autobiographers, like their religious counterparts, worried about self-control, but they saw the answer to be the exertion of willpower. They discussed self-control not only in biblical terms such as sin and temptations of the flesh, but also as relating to vices and virtues that affected their success in their occupations, for example, laziness or industry, dishonesty or integrity, improvidence or frugality. In looking back over his life, the schoolmaster Elihu Shepard (1869, p. 210) summarized his moral virtues in this manner: "I had generally been temperate, studious, industrious, frugal, enterprising, and successful in all my business where I directed it myself."

Individuals who developed an ongoing resoluteness and firm determination acquired "character." In the nineteenth century, as the historian

Warren Susman (1984, p. 273) has summarized it, "*Character* was a key word in the vocabulary of Englishmen and Americans." Character meant that a person was hard working, self-disciplined, thrifty, and trustworthy. Autobiographers earlier in the nineteenth century had generally used the word *character* to refer to a person's distinctive qualities—good or bad. For example, Mrs. K. White (1809, p. 29) described the Indians who had held her captive in this way: "I could not but observe the following favorable traits in their character." By the latter half of the nineteenth century, however, more of my sample of autobiographers began to use the term *character* to refer to a set of moral virtues to be developed.[25] Autobiographers such as Georgiana Kirby (1887, p. 137) advised readers that "it was *doing* patient, faithful repetition of service . . . that disciplined the will and created character."

The development of character, according to a nineteenth-century manual on pedagogy, involved "the discipline of the will to act habitually in view of those motives which release the soul from bondage to low and selfish desires."[26] "Character was never something you had," Alfred Kazin (1951, p. 15) recollected about his childhood education in the 1920s, "it had to be trained in you, like a technique." Character involved the *habit* of making the right choices so that individuals need not expend will every time they made decisions. Such choices could then be "unthinking" and automatic. The popular inspirational writer Harry Emerson Fosdick (1923, p. 24) explained in a book he wrote on character that "freedom is the positive substitution of inward self-control for external restraints." In this vein, Kirby (1887, p. 225) argued in her autobiography that persons must develop a "fixed character" from early self-discipline or they will "remain perpetually in the disciplinary state."[27]

One of the prescribed places to develop character was the workplace. Here a person could cultivate and exhibit work "habits" such as perseverance, industry, and honesty. Work was a prime way of disciplining the self and avoiding those idle hands that "do the devil's work." Roeliff Brinkerhoff (1900, p. 235) thus extolled the benefits of his vocation: "Bankers are stimulated by the requirements of their occupation to habits of integrity, industry and a moral life."

Instead of being virtuous by claiming a resignation to God's will, these autobiographers became praiseworthy by taking their development—both mental and moral—into their own hands. They were enthusiastic about human potential—neither resigned to a weak human nature nor troubled about the influence of the social environment on the self as later autobiographers were. Life for them could be summed up in the cheerful adage, "Where there's a will, there's a way."

Changes in the Self

Although these autobiographers believed they could improve themselves, they did not assert that such a change could happen easily. Any improvement must be the result of a long-term cultivation of self. How they traced the story of such a development was dependent upon which version of the self-made ideology they adopted. In general, they told stories of either mental or moral development—in line with Aristotle's (1962, p. 33) observation that there are two kinds of virtue: intellectual and moral.

Those who believed in self-culture could use their autobiographies to detail mental development over a lifetime. "I built up the physical first, the intellectual afterwards," declared the clergyman Lyman Beecher (1865, p. 38) in a statement typical of those who believed in self-development. If they wished to tell a tale of self-culture, it was easy to adapt the conventional story of a religious conversion. A rendering of the story could include a germinal period during which the autobiographer was "slumbering." Then there may have been a pivotal moment of illumination—perhaps an "awakening"—that stirred the mental capacity that implicitly was already there. This awakening did not involve shedding one's former self as it did in a religious conversion but rather was the triggering of a process of development. The result was not an immediate maturation, for effort and hard work were necessary. As the spiritualist Andrew Jackson Davis (1857, p. 44) explained, "During infancy, the inmost spirit of man is slumbering in the cerebral substance." Davis then switched to the metaphor of growth: "As with germs in the soil, so it is with the gradual growth and upspringing expansion of the mental energies" (p. 44).

A common catalyst for such an awakening was an insight kindled by the reading of a particular book. Not any book, however, could qualify—pulp fiction and dime novels did not play such a role. For H. L. Mencken ([1940] 1955, p. 163), reading *Huckleberry Finn* was "the most stupendous event" in his life. For the novelist and critic Ludwig Lewisohn (1922, pp. 103–4), John Fiske's *Cosmic Philosophy* fostered "an awakening intellect." Although writers are probably more inclined than others to claim the significance of books in their lives, they were not the only ones to do so. The businessman John Moody ([1933] 1946, pp. 217–18), for example, reported that a book by G. K. Chesterton was "the first breath of fresh air that I had mentally breathed for many, many years."

Some of these autobiographers described critical moments in their lives as "turning points," an expression apparently first used in English in 1851 by John Ruskin to refer to a pivotal point in a person's life. Among my autobiographers, the first to use *turning point* was the physician J. Marion Sims in the 1860s. Later, Edward Bok (1920, p. 109), a Dutch immigrant who eventually became editor of *The Ladies' Home Journal*, assumed that such an idea was commonplace when he made reference to "the turning-point which comes in the life of every young man." With the "turning point," the literary scholar Stephen Shapiro (1968, p. 439) has commented, "Life's long arcs become the sharp edges of literature." Structuring an autobiography around such a dramatic change helps make it an interesting story. Henry James (1987, p. 438) recognized this with his response to a friend's suggestion that his life story contained a "turning point": "Let me say at once that I welcomed the suggestion—for the kindly grace of it, the element of antique charm and bedimmed romance that it placed, straight away, at the disposal of my memory; by which I mean that I wondered whether I mightn't find, on ingenious reflection, that my youth *had* in fact enjoyed that amount of drama. I couldn't, I felt, be sure; but the question itself, and its accompaniments, appealed to me."[28]

The aim of self-culture was mental discipline and the formation of a philosophy that could serve as a tool to manage the problems of life.[29] "Where there had been chaos there was now order. My mind was at rest. I had a philosophy at last," rejoiced Andrew Carnegie (1920, p. 206) in the story of both his successful career in business and the development of his mind. James Fagan (1912, p. 41) also described his evolution into an individual "with a certain point of view in regard to life and living." This objective was similar to the goal sought in the typical *bildungsroman* in which a young man developed "a point of view in practical matters and above all a 'Weltanschauung'" (Bruford 1975, pp. 29–30).

Autobiographers who wished to emphasize their moral development also made use of the concept of a turning point. They might describe, for example, a sudden recognition of the value of willpower—a moment of illumination comparable to the insight triggering a process of self-culture. Fagan (1912, p. 16), for example, claimed it to be a crucial discovery that "the consciousness of will-power should actually add to the strength of my muscles." Another turning point in moral development involved the acquisition of "decision of character"—a milestone that some persons in the nineteenth century expected to be part of adolescence (Kett 1977). Andrew Jackson Davis (1857, p. 296) used just such a phrase to describe a change in himself during adolescence: "Decision of character I had recently acquired." Although the recognition of the importance of willpower may have been a sudden insight, the full development of character was a gradual process requiring the inculcation of good habits and the elimination of bad ones. Thus Linda Richards ([1911] 1915, p. 76), the first trained nurse in the United States, reminded her readers, "The habits of a lifetime were not to be overcome in a few weeks or months." If the acquisition of character was based merely upon a sudden insight, it would be too effortless.

A good beginning for the formation of character, in keeping with the Horatio Alger myth, was being born into a poor family. None of these autobiographers, however, alleged it was good to remain in poverty throughout one's life for the sake of character building. "To begin, then, I was born . . . and, as the saying is, 'of poor but honest parents, of good kith and kin,'" proudly wrote Andrew Carnegie (1920, p. 2). A person born into poverty must work at an early age and become self-sufficient. In contrast, if one were born into a wealthy family, as Agnes Meyer (1953, p. 28), a publisher of *The Washington Post,* cautioned, "Dependence upon material possessions inevitably results in the destruction of human character." Rachel Watson (1871, p. 18) phrased it more vividly in her story of domestic life in the wilderness: "Strong characters . . . are not made on beds of down and fattened on sweets and dainties." Such a belief in the value of a spartan childhood was common enough to be mocked by autobiographers as well. Ralph Keeler (1870, p. 16) ridiculed the convention that an autobiographer "almost invariably comes of 'poor but honest parents.'" And Lincoln Steffens (1931, p. 63) jokingly bemoaned his misfortune of having well-to-do parents: "I grieved . . . My father and mother did not die when I was young . . . I didn't have a chance; I could not go out and suffer, strive, and become a success." Having begun life in a poor family made the autobiographer's success more dramatic and more admirable.

From this perspective, working at an early age was valuable for cultivating the habits of industry, honesty, and thrift.[30] In an 1883 survey of five hundred successful men, three-quarters of them chose to credit their achievements to the inculcation of work habits during childhood (Wyllie 1954, p. 43). We can find this attribution made by the editor of Ichabod Washburn's (1878, p. 19) brief autobiography, when he concluded that Washburn's financial successes in the hoopskirt wire business "had their foundation in the spirit, traits and habits of the youth." And the humbler the job, the better it was for developing character. John Moody ([1933] 1946, pp. 33–34), who began his career as a "stamplicker" for a Wall Street firm, recalled his youthful conviction that this was true: "I . . . promptly assumed the role of the ambitious American youth who is bent on becoming a self-made business citizen. I would look for an errand-boy job and stride to affluence and success in the true Horatio Alger manner." This story of initial employment in a lowly job, however, did not apply in a story of the development of character in a woman. Georgiana Kirby (1887, p. 225) described instead a process of self-discipline: "To be consciously on one's guard against temptation; to undergo a daily inspection of one's motives and behavior; to bring every separate thought and act before the judgment-seat of conscience, is an experience every youth should pass through . . . The large majority who so need it never pass through this valuable discipline, and hence have no fixed character."

Such autobiographers also believed that a rural childhood was ideal for developing character.[31] Life in the country meant physical hardships to which persons must adapt. Following evolutionary theory, such an argument connected the physical environment (e.g., terrain or climate) to self-development.[32] As Andrew Carnegie (1920, p. 6) wrote, "Where one is born is very important, for different surroundings and traditions appeal to and stimulate different latent tendencies in the child." The lawyer J. W. Arbuckle (1942, pp. 90–91) also made reference to the effect of the physical environment: "I realize that I have inherited a stern strength, and for this I thank a long line of Scotch-Irish fathers and mothers toughened by tramping, with bare shanks, across the bogs and through the Highland snows." In contrast, Sherwood Anderson ([1924] 1969, p. 353) mocked adventure stories and westerns in which a "rather mean, second-rate chap" went into the forest, "took up land," and a "great change comes over him."

Finally, those autobiographers who told of their lives as successful businessmen (usually along with a moral account of self-development) traced noteworthy career steps—the first job, the first paycheck, the first savings, the first investment, and so on. The lumber dealer Daniel Abrey (1903, p. 21), for example, proudly informed his readers that he had three thousand dollars in the bank after only three years of marriage. And the editor Edward Bok (1920, p. 325), whose Pulitzer-prize autobiography sounded as if it came straight from Horatio Alger, included a chronology in which he listed his first job (washing windows) and his first pay (fifty cents per week). Such a detailing of financial milestones made evident the clear-sighted, step-by-step determination of these autobiographers to be a success (at least in retrospect).

I did not find any of them, however, arguing for a cutthroat philosophy of "dog-eat-dog" as the basis of their own successes or declaring that wealth was a paramount goal. Improving oneself was admirable; coveting riches was not. John D. Rockefeller (1913, p. 20), for instance, attempted to fend off any critics when he wrote, "I know of nothing more despicable and pathetic than a man who devotes all the waking hours of the day to making money for money's sake." And Roeliff Brinkerhoff (1900, p. 235) declared, "I have never had an ambition to be rich." We can contrast this with a later autobiographer, Lee Iacocca (1984, p. 9), who candidly recalled his materialistic goal: "I was after the bucks."[33] Yet Iacocca, too, framed this admission as a youthful aspiration.

Like the religious autobiographers, these authors did not highlight their early years. Childhood, as Clarence Darrow (1932, p. 81) noted, was to be "the special time for forming habits necessary in determining conduct," and, for businessmen, it was the time to begin the modest job that would lead to a successful career. Few pages were required to describe the commencement of character development or self-culture. These autobiographers did not find it necessary to talk about the sins of childhood, although some of them did gleefully recall a few pranks. They did not treat such mischief, however, with remorse, but more indulgently as childish exuberance or "animal spirits." John Moody ([1933] 1946, p. 22) happily recalled, "And I was a bad boy; perhaps the town's star scamp." Shenanigans could be interpreted as evidence of that inner energy source that eventually could be developed into willpower. "What resources do the young possess," asked Georgiana Kirby (1887, p. 70), "except animal spirits?" And James Fagan (1912, p. 6) advised his readers that "the individualism and self-assertion contained in this state of gypsy-like lawlessness must be noticed in passing." Play, according to a theory circulating in the late nineteenth century, served as a rehearsal for adult activities—giving those who were successful at playing games a competitive advantage in their future activities (Flugel 1933). We can find this theory reiterated by autobiographers such as Lincoln Steffens (1931), who commented that trading games are preparation for a business career.

The Role of Society and Significant Others

Some of these autobiographers assumed, from a Lamarckian perspective, that the environment affects individual self-development. But here, environment generally meant the physical environment—the availability of sustenance, the harshness of the climate, and so forth—those factors, in other words, to which a person (and a species) must adapt in order to survive. Environmental conditions (particularly adverse ones) could trigger a process of self-development because persons must adjust to these conditions. In such an understanding, however, there was little consideration of the influence of the social environment. The idea of sociocultural determination developing in the late nineteenth century (see Chap. 6) did not easily harmonize with the story of a self-willed moral or mental development. Society, instead, remained the setting or the stage for a person's self-development.[34]

The social institution of formal education also was granted little influence. These autobiographers, like the religious autobiographers, placed no great value on schooling. We might expect autobiographers who focused on mental development to extol the benefits of education, but for them to accord a significant amount of influence to the process of formal education would be to acknowledge that this part of their development had not been self-willed. It was preferable to be an autodidact. The early McGuffey readers advised children that "education, moral and intellectual, of every individual, must be, chiefly, his own work" (Mosier 1965, p. 100). A person might learn a significant amount from a self-initiated reading program, and such reading was a virtuous and profitable use of leisure time. Consequently, tributes to the merits of reading, such as Andrew Carnegie's (1920, p. 47), were not uncommon: "The treasures of the world which books contain were opened to me at the right moment." In addition, the argument that people could educate themselves through books was a democratic one—implying that one didn't need fancy schooling to develop one's mind (Rubin 1992).

In the matter of moral development, schoolteachers and parents may have firmly believed that character could be imparted through the discipline of school and by textbook maxims and exemplary tales. But when it came to writing their personal stories, these autobiographers related character development not to school but to work. Among those who wrote of their business careers, some of them even displayed a scorn for formal education. This disdain accords with Irvin Wyllie's (1954) observation, in his book on self-made men, that business opinion was skeptical about higher learning until the 1890s. These autobiographers did not yet view education as a vehicle for social mobility. John Moody ([1933] 1946, p. 33) recalled that when, as a youth, he did express a desire to go to college, he was "emphatically reminded that self-made men, who had never seen the inside of a college, were really the backbone of America." Henry Adams ([1906] 1918, p. 348), in his famous autobiography about his own education, commented on this general attitude toward formal education: "Education counted for nothing . . . An administrator, organizer, manager, with medieval qualities of energy and will, but no education beyond his special branch, would probably be worth at least ten times as much." More was to be gained, as the lumberman Daniel Abrey (1903, pp. 9–10) said, "by observation, intercourse, and personal acquaintance than from any theoretical knowledge obtained from books, or instruction received from others."

We might guess that other persons also do not figure prominently in a life story that has, as its theme, self-sufficiency and a process of self-development. But some of these autobiographers did allow that others were important in their lives, especially in terms of their part in the autobiographer's mental or moral development—as mentors, as catalysts who triggered the process of self-culture, or as inspirational examples. An older and, hence, more mature friend or a teacher who took a personal interest in the autobiographer may have played the role of guide for mental development. Lyman Beecher (1865, p. 43) gave credit to Timothy Dwight, president of Yale and professor of theology, who "had the greatest agency in developing my mind." And Georgiana Kirby (1887, p. 58) named as influential in her life a woman able to "discuss any subject."

For the development of character, another person could serve as a role model. The autobiographers telling a tale of moral development found that a personal hero could help steel their resolve to develop character.[35] "It is a tower of strength," declared Andrew Carnegie (1920, p. 18), "for a boy to have a hero." Reading biographies of famous men could help a person find such heroes. John Stuart Blackie (n.d., p. 104) wrote in his book *On Self-Culture: Intellectual, Physical, and Moral* that "[t]here is no surer method of becoming good, and it may be great also, than an early familiarity with the lives of great and good men."

These autobiographers, like the religious autobiographers, put their mothers on the proverbial pedestal. "Her pure and beautiful life," Daniel Abrey (1903, p. 10) told his readers, "is guiding mine." Likewise, Andrew Carnegie (1920, p. 33), reminiscing about his mother, declared that "anything low, mean, deceitful, shifty, coarse, underhand, or gossipy was foreign to that heroic soul." Hard work, too, was added to the list of their mothers' virtues. "My mother," claimed the preacher Henry Morgan (1874, p. 21), "was the embodiment of industry," and the schoolmaster Elihu Shepard (1869, p. 10) described his mother as "a small, healthy, active, and industrious woman." Mothers were exemplars of goodness (although not of self-culture). They did not, however, mold character in their children since the process of moral development required personal effort to exercise the faculty of will. After all, as John D. Rockefeller (1913, p. 152) pronounced in his autobiography, "The only thing which is of lasting benefit to a man is that which he does for himself."

Although some of these autobiographers did discuss, on a general level, the importance of the family in building character, they did not recall their own childhoods with such an emphasis.[36] This, too, would take away from their claims of being self-made. Furthermore, it was difficult to specify what concrete parental actions build character. Carnegie (1920, p. 23), for instance, only made the general remark that his mother "was always looking to home influences as the best means of keeping her two boys in the right path." And Agnes Meyer (1953, p. 10), the first woman reporter for the New York *Morning Sun* before her marriage to financier Eugene Meyer, was able to come up with only one concrete detail: "The real torment of our lives, considered vital to the formation of a sturdy character, was the cold bath into which we plunged every morning." When speaking of raising their own children, such autobiographers offered hazy tenets such as encouraging self-reliance and not "spoiling" the child.

In contrast to the portraits of their mothers, these autobiographers' descriptions of their fathers were less consistent. It was not as clear what role they thought the father should play in a child's development. One possible answer in a story of self-culture might be that of intellectual mentor. This was a role, after all, that mothers apparently did not assume. But none of my autobiographers described their fathers as having time to do anything more than offer encouragement or serve as a model of mental development.[37] Lyman Beecher's (1865, p. 19) father, who was a blacksmith, was "one of the best-read men in New England," and Elihu Shepard's (1869, p. 9) father was "a fine scholar." Overall, these autobiographers made little reference to their fathers' personal merits as a family member, but instead referred to their industry and integrity in the workplace.

Spouses and children, too, did not warrant any extensive discussion. Although the sociologist Wendy Griswold (1981, p. 751) found in her study of American novels published from 1876–1910 that "adult heterosexual love [was] the key to the plot" for many of them, such love got scant attention in these autobiographies of self-development. Instead they focused on actions and achievements that related to self-development instead of their personal relationships. If male autobiographers mentioned their wives at all, it generally was to characterize them in terms of their moral virtues. Elihu Shepard (1869, p. 196) boasted that "industry, frugality and economy were striking traits in the character of Mrs. Shepard." And Andrew Carnegie (1920, p. 218), who did not marry until his fifties, spoke admiringly of his young wife: "The Peace-Maker has never had a quarrel in all her life, not even with a schoolmate, and there does not live a soul upon the earth who has met her who has the slightest cause to complain of neglect . . . She is incapable of acting or speaking rudely; all is in perfect good taste. She is always thinking how she can do good to those around her." As for the autobiographers' children, they could not figure prominently in such a story for they had not played the roles of mentors, models of character or self-development, or heroes.

Finally, in significant contrast to the religious autobiographers, these chroniclers of self-development did not routinely use the idea of Divine Providence to explain events in their lives. As Martin Marty (1972, p. 93) succinctly commented, "Providence had turned into progress." Life's meaning was to be found in the evolution to perfection, and there appeared to be comprehensible laws of nature. Personal failure was not attributable to the mysterious workings of Providence; it more likely meant a lack of effort or character. Each individual assumed greater accountability for failures and successes. An 1895 self-help book by Orison Marden illustrated this assignment of responsibility to the self with its title: *Architects of Fate.*

Telling the Story

"This is a story of education, not of adventure!" exclaimed Henry Adams ([1906] 1918, p. 314) in his autobiography. "It is meant to help young men . . . but it is not meant to amuse them." Like the religious conversion narratives, autobiographies of self-development were ostensibly for didactic purposes—to serve as a model of self-culture or exemplary development of character. They portrayed life as a matter of working hard for the sake of self-development. As Sherwood Anderson ([1924] 1969, p. 352) noted, "There was a notion that ran through all storytelling in America [in the late nineteenth century], that stories must be built about a plot and that absurd Anglo-Saxon notion that they must point to a moral, uplift the people, make better citizens, etc." These autobiographers made it clear that they were writing of their achievements because others had urged them to do so. Their stories were to have greater significance than just the account of one person's experiences, and they did not appear troubled if their individual stories followed a conventional story of self-development. Furthermore, since the stress was on the instructive value of such narratives, they need not worry much about literary style. They used plain, unadorned titles such as *The Autobiography of . . .* , or *Reminiscences,* and they often stuck to a simple chronological narration.

Although they surely were proud of their accomplishments, they, too, tried to be modest in their accounts—letting the (carefully chosen) evidence speak for itself. If they were to brag, it was best to boast only of working hard or "trying their best," since such effort represented a moral virtue that anyone could cultivate. None of my autobiographers used the term *self-made* for themselves. They reserved this term for others or for a general discussion of the philosophy of character building. By lauding others for being self-made, they left it to the reader to recognize that similar praises were also due to them. Furthermore, although it has been customary for some commentators to equate American autobiography with a stress on uniqueness and individuality, we can find that even these "self-made" men courteously offered the democratic argument that they were not unique. It appeared that they agreed, in principle, with the philosophy espoused by Edward Bellamy ([1888] 1967, p. 152) in his well-known novel *Looking Backward:* "All men who do their best, do the same." The process of self-development was an individual one, but all theoretically had the potential to go through it. The resultant self, one's "best self," could be achieved by anyone. But, of course, not everyone did.

For those telling a story of mental development, they could make their self-culture apparent by discussing their mature philosophies of life, citing quotations from literature, and mentioning respected authors or books. Andrew Carnegie (1920), for example, quoted Burns, Pope, Arnold, and Carlyle, and he referred to many writers, philosophers, scientists, composers, and poets. For those autobiographers detailing the development of character, they could demonstrate their own possession of it by avoiding boastfulness, abstaining from disrespectful or ungrateful remarks, and refraining from a story of a ruthless pursuit of success and money.

Since a theme of their stories was development over a lifetime, these autobiographers used metaphors to describe their lives that connoted action, advancement, and growth. Carnegie (1920, p. 39), for instance, described the beginning of his career as having a "foot upon the ladder" that he "was bound to climb," and he referred to the "race of life" (p. 42). From such a viewpoint, in contrast to biblical teachings, the race, after all, was to the swift. But these "modest" autobiographers would be quick to add that "swift" did not mean natural abilities but only the application of effort.

Private thoughts and feelings were generally not the focus of these autobiographies; conduct and actions were more important. When these autobiographers looked at themselves introspectively, however, they generally assumed it was not difficult to understand their own actions, motives, and thoughts. They apparently did not share the concern over self-deception that was the province of the religious autobiographers, nor did they feel compelled to comment on the vagaries of memory as would later autobiographers. Problems of memory, instead, would suggest a failure to have properly cultivated this faculty.

Conclusion

The historian Richard Weiss (1969, p. 12) has argued that basic questions in the twentieth century about humankind have been these: "Is man free or is man determined by forces beyond his control? Is man responsible or merely a helpless and therefore blameless object in the hands of a capricious fate?" Based on autobiographies, however, we can see that similar questions were raised in the nineteenth century when individuals pondered what it meant to be human. The religious autobiographers worried about the strength of the passions, and they puzzled over the question of moral responsibility.

Likewise, the autobiographers in the nineteenth and early twentieth centuries who placed an emphasis on moral development wished to govern the passions. But for them, the temptations of the flesh could be managed in a matter-of-fact way without divine assistance. Human beings could free themselves from the determinism of the body through decisive effort. "Freedom is a matter of character and willpower," James Fagan (1912, p. 267) asserted, borrowing a quotation from Charles Eliot, former president of Harvard University. These autobiographers appeared confident the human species was moving toward perfection. And for the individual, as a self-help author proclaimed, "The scale or range of self-improvement is illimitable" (Fowler 1852, p. 23).

As we can see, these self-made autobiographers selectively used prevailing ideas to think about selfhood. Rather than relying primarily on the Bible for an understanding of human nature, they also used ideas adapted from the scientific writings of the day—reading moral implications into this literature. They appropriated the idea of evolutionary development, yet most of them rejected what the historian Hamilton Cravens (1978, p. 35) has called the "cold, messy, and perhaps haphazard process" that Darwin articulated.[38] George Bernard Shaw ([1921] 1947, p. 255) once wrote that "what damns Darwinian Natural Selection as a creed is that it takes hope out of evolution, and substitutes a paralyzing fatalism which is utterly discouraging." But this is not how these autobiographers interpreted Darwin's ideas. They did not declare that life was a jungle, and they did not emphasize the lack of design or the role of chance in the evolution of species. They preferred a Lamarckian viewpoint, and they persevered in seeing meaning in the universe in the evolution of human life. Darwin once wrote in his notebooks that "man in his arrogance thinks himself a great work worthy the interposition of a deity. [M]ore humble & I believe truer to consider him created from animals" (Moore 1979, p. 317). Such a view, however, was not appealing to these autobiographers.

By the 1920s, however, Sherwood Anderson ([1924] 1969, pp. 324–25) was not alone in debunking the idea of the self-made man: "Suppose some fellow were to come along who was really on to the entire emptiness of the whole success theory of life." The novelist and critic Ludwig Lewisohn (1922, pp. 158–59) also contemptuously proclaimed, "The current connotations of the word [success] are enough to make a voluntary outcast of any self-respecting soul." Others began to attack the basic Horatio Alger myth and to complain, as did William James (1920, p. 260), about the "worship of the bitch-goddess SUCCESS" and the "squalid cash interpretation put on the word success" in the United States.

Students of this period have attributed the decline of the myth of the self-made man to several factors. One was a general disillusionment with the methods of the "self-made" entrepreneurs—methods that muckrakers in the early twentieth century demonstrated were not based on the virtues of character (Wyllie 1954). As Lincoln Steffens (1931, p. 79) concluded, "The hero business was, like everything else apparently, not what it was cracked up to be." Furthermore, as more persons took corporate jobs in the twentieth century, the myth of the self-made man who goes from rags to riches in his own business was less applicable.[39] World War I also disabused many of the notion that human beings were irreversibly on a "march toward perfection." Agnes Meyer (1953, p. 62) recalled the disillusionment: "The pessimism of the postwar era as to human nature . . . led to a revival of the doctrine of original sin." And Louise Whitfield Carnegie noted in the introduction to her husband's autobiography that he was unable to complete his life story once World War I began because of his dejection over what he perceived as a retrogression in human history (1920, p. v). Finally, psychological ideas about unconscious motivation as well as sociological ideas about the influence of the social environment on the self helped cast doubt on the belief that people need only character and effort to be architects of their lives.

I am not claiming, however, that self-improvement and character building are no longer topics in autobiographies. As Americans, we remain familiar with the story of the self-made man. Lee Iacocca (1984, p. 357), for example, gave this advice in his best-selling autobiography: "People say to me: 'You're a roaring success. How did you do it?' I go back to what my parents taught me. Apply yourself. Get all the education you can, but then, by God, *do* something! Don't just stand there, make something happen. It isn't easy, but if you keep your nose to the grindstone and work at it, it's amazing how in a free society you can become as great as you want to be." Iacocca and his ghostwriter, however, merged this philosophy with twentieth-century psychological and sociological ideas that I discuss in the following chapters. And Iacocca, like many other contemporary autobiographers, is not as sanguine about the possibilities of self-development. For contemporary autobiographers, W. E. Henley's poem published in 1888, which encapsulated the model of self-development, is no longer quite so appropriate: "I am the master of my fate: / I am the captain of my soul."

Chapter Five THE *U*NCERTAIN SELF

All the new social and psychological theories had this in common: they suggested the need for profound revision in the concept of the self. By the end of the nineteenth century, the self seemed neither independent, nor unified, nor fully conscious, but rather interdependent, discontinuous, divided, and subject to the play of unconscious or inherited impulses.   T. J. JACKSON LEARS

"We are importing the plague," remarked Sigmund Freud to Carl Jung when they visited the United States in 1909.[1] Since then, numerous commentators have agreed—perhaps not with Freud's choice of metaphor—but with the view that his ideas, as well as the field of psychology in general, have had a considerable impact on thought in the United States and throughout the Western world.[2] By the late 1930s, the psychologist C. E. Spearman (1937, pp. 3–4) could comment that "never before, it would seem, have all sorts and conditions of men betaken themselves with such ardor to 'psychology' . . . There has come upon us a corresponding deluge of psychological books, journals, pamphlets, and what not."[3]

With the goal of understanding human behavior scientifically, psychologists pursued questions that hitherto had been the domain of novelists, philosophers, theologians, and poets. The theories and vocabulary developed by psychologists, in turn, have added to the stock of ideas available to make sense of what it means to be human.[4] Such a science offered the prospect that human behavior could be systematically studied and explained. Thus Clarence Darrow (1932, p. 332), who as a lawyer had practical reasons for trying to understand human behavior, offered this enthusiastic assessment in his autobiography: "Sane ideas of human conduct are not much over fifty years old, and the last thirty years have done more for the understanding of man than any five hundred that preceded them. We now know something about the causes of human behavior."

It is not surprising, therefore, that American autobiographers have been among those interested in what the science of psychology had to offer.[5] The literary scholar Thomas Cooley (1976, pp. 18–19) has even maintained that "among the altered conditions that contributed to new ways of thinking and writing about the self in America after the Civil War, perhaps none was more formative than the rise of modern psychology."[6] In my sample of autobiographers, I found that more of them in the late nineteenth century began to consider the irrational and the unconscious in themselves as relevant to questions about the intentionality of human action. They began to look at the "battle within" in different terms—discussing the troubling "passions" in the more neutral terms of instincts and drives. And they no longer assumed that introspection was a simple task.

Historical Background

The founding date of psychology as a science is often said to be 1879—the year Wilhelm Wundt founded his laboratory in Leipzig for experimental psychology (Misiak and Sexton 1966). The word *psychology,* however, was first used in the late seventeenth century, and writers such as Samuel Taylor Coleridge and John Stuart Mill helped popularize it in the first half of the nineteenth century. Psychology texts, such as J. F. Herbart's *Text Book of Psychology,* began being published as early as 1816 in Germany. And by 1886, psychology was well enough established to earn its own heading in the Encyclopaedia Britannica—no longer subsumed under the rubric of metaphysics (Flugel 1933).

The publication of Herbert Spencer's *Principles of Psychology* in 1855 introduced the word *psychology* to many readers in England and the United States.[7] During the 1870s and 1880s, college courses in the subject became the norm, and by the 1890s, the first departments of psychology were established in the United States (Evans 1984). In addition, popular magazines, books, and self-help manuals spread psychological theories and concepts such that it is likely that many literate persons in the United States were aware of psychology by the late nineteenth century.[8] In my sample of autobiographers, the spiritualist Andrew Jackson Davis (1857) was the earliest to use the word *psychology*. But it was not until the early twentieth century that it became more routine for these autobiographers to incorporate and adapt psychological ideas.

Beginning in the late nineteenth century, motivation had become a central topic for psychologists.[9] John Atkinson (1964, pp. 8–9), in detailing the history of the psychological study of motivation, explained how such an interest developed out of Darwin's ideas about the evolutionary process: "If men and animals are not qualitatively different, but instead represent different points on a continuum of increasing complexity . . . then the instinctive, irrational, and automatic tendencies formally attributed to animals also should play a vital role in human behavior." Psychologists became interested in the causes of human behavior that were not conscious and rational, and they examined biological aspects of human behavior that might help explain motivation and that could be studied empirically such as instincts, hereditary influences, emotions, reflexes, impulses, and drives. They asked how much of the behavior of human beings can be attributed to the fact that they are animals with inherited traits and instincts, and they considered how human beings are similar to and different from other animals.

Overall, this interest in motivation meant that faculty psychology, with its basic tripartite division into emotion, reason, and will, began to fall from favor in the late nineteenth century and, along with it, the stress on will as an essential explanatory variable in human action (Hilgard 1987).[10] Many psychologists, instead of discussing goal seeking by human beings as a matter of will, viewed it with a more deterministic emphasis on goal seeking as a matter of drives or motivation—assuming that will itself could be reduced to impulses or feelings. As one 1950s psychology textbook put it, "Psychologists have come to regard the varieties of behavior attributed to 'will power' as expressions of the relative strength of motive."[11] The concept of motivation includes both conscious and unconscious motives and therefore is not limited to voluntary activity as is the concept of will.[12] Will was important in the psychological theory of William James, but experimental psychologists and behaviorists effectively banished it as subjective and difficult to observe (Hilgard 1987).[13]

Furthermore, the idea of will did not fit neatly into the debate that had developed in the late nineteenth century over the effects of the environment versus heredity on human behavior.[14] Darwin's cousin, Francis Galton, introduced the alliterative phrase "nature and nurture" in 1874, and he, along with others, argued that nature was more important than nurture (Hale 1971; Fancher 1979). The German biologist August Weismann, whose work became known in English-speaking countries in the 1880s, also began to undercut the Lamarckian theory of acquired characteristics by arguing that such traits were transmitted independently of the environment and any personal efforts at exercising the faculties (Curti 1980).[15] Additionally, in 1900, the scientific community rediscovered Gregor Mendel's work in genetics, which gave support to those who were arguing for the importance of heredity in the constitution of individual traits.

Psychologists approached the topic of motivation in several ways. One is the interest in the influence of heredity on human behavior that can be found, for example, in the developmental psychology that emerged at the end of the nineteenth century (Morss 1990). This type of psychology, based on evolutionary ideas, included studies of infancy, childhood, and adolescence as "stages" in the lives of all human beings. Early developmental psychologists, similar to Darwin in his "A Biographical Sketch of an Infant," hoped they might single out the inherited aspects of human nature from what human beings acquire as part of experience (Hale 1971; Riley 1983).[16] This scientific attention to childhood spread beyond psychology, and in the late nineteenth century educators and women's clubs established child study groups, following the guidance of Hall, to study the development and proper rearing of children (Ross 1972).

An interest in heredity also included the topic of instinct. As the historian John Burnham (1988, p. 32) has pointed out, psychologists believed that part of inheritance was "structural—one's constitution—but another part was supposed to be dynamic—the instincts." An instinct, by William James's ([1890] 1950, 2:383) definition, was "the faculty of acting in such a way as to produce certain ends, without foresight of the ends, and without previous education in the performance." Instincts, according to Darwin in *Descent of Man* ([1871] 1981), were instruments of survival and adaptation. Although the idea of instinct had been used for centuries to explain behavior that appeared to be natural and did not involve conscious design, psychologists who followed evolutionary theory tried to develop this vague explanation of human motivation into a scientific one.[17] Instinct theory was in vogue in the United States from roughly the 1890s until it began to be discredited in the 1920s (Cravens 1978). At that point, some psychologists substituted the concepts of "drive," "impulse," or "goal-directed behavior" to explain what biologically impels human action.[18]

The topic of motivation was also prominently reflected in the work of Freud, who, like other psychologists, looked to the importance of instincts. Freud's writings also raised provocative questions about the irrational and the unconscious in human motivation. As Max Weber commented in 1918, "The spheres of the irrational, the only spheres that intellectualism has not yet touched, are now raised into consciousness and put under its lens."[19] The psychologist J. C. Flugel (1933, p. 286) expressed it eloquently when he accounted for the early appeal of Freudian ideas:

> With Freud, psychology first began to bear some semblance to a science to which men could look for real help in unravelling the puzzles presented by their own and others' behavior. Here were no mere general laws of mind, too abstract and remote to be of any use in dealing with practical problems . . . Here, at last, was some real light on the motives underlying our loves and hates, our interests, our longings, our work and play, our difficulties, failures, maladjustments and general unreasonableness.

Freud's conception of the unconscious challenged the commonsense idea that we can explain behavior in terms of will and conscious reason. Freud ([1920] 1938, p. 252) advanced the disquieting ideas that "each one of us . . . is not even master in his own house" and that each "must remain content with the veriest scraps of information about what is going on unconsciously in his own mind."[20] As the sociologist Anthony Giddens (1979, p. 38) observed, Freud, along with Marx and Nietzsche, was a "radical critic of the claims of the Cartesian *cogito*," since he "can be seen as questioning, in a profound way, the reliability of consciousness as 'transparent to itself.'"

Emotion, too, can be subsumed under the category of motivation, and the scientific eye turned upon it as well in the late nineteenth century.[21] Emotion can be conceived as a determinant of action that falls outside the realm of voluntary behavior. Furthermore, psychologists could study and measure emotion as a state of arousal and a physiological reaction. From the standpoint of faculty psychology, it had been easy to conceive of emotion, reason, and will separately. But now psychologists examined the connections between thought and emotion (Atkinson 1964).[22] How do emotions affect thought processes? And, conversely, what part does thought play in emotion? As Herbert Spencer ([1855] 1899, p. 133) wrote, "That passion perverts judgment, is an observation sufficiently trite; but the more general observation of which it should form part, that emotion of every kind and degree disturbs the intellectual balance, is not trite, and even where recognized, is not duly taken into account." Furthermore, those researchers who were developing a physiological conception of the human brain (e.g., studying reflex action and the nervous system) helped to undermine dualism by examining the physiological relationship between mind and body, reason and emotion (Hilgard 1987).

Although one of the objectives in studying heredity and instinct was to determine what all human beings share by nature and how this affects their behavior, these questions also related to an interest in individual differences—particularly the complexity of the individual's makeup. Individual differences first became a subject in general psychology textbooks in the United States during the first decade of the twentieth century (Davis and Gould 1929). This was a topic that Wilhelm Wundt declared to be typically American— *"ganz amerikanisch"* (Flugel 1933, p. 208).[23] We can connect this attention to individual differences to evolutionary theory—particularly the notion of the survival of the fittest. That is, what individual variations (such as intelligence) relate to successful adaptation to the environment?

A concern with unique endowment and individual differences led to a consideration of "personality"—a term increasingly used in the late nineteenth century (Hilgard 1987).[24] Here the term *personality* referred to the set of behavioral and emotional characteristics of a person (such as intelligence) that "determine his unique adjustments to his environment" (Allport 1937, p. 48). Previously, in common parlance, *personality* meant existence as a person.[25] Although William James used the term in relation to cases of split or multiple personalities, the idea also came to be associated with individual differences (Hilgard 1987). By 1937, Gordon Allport (1937, p. 3) could begin a textbook on personality with the declaration that "individuality is the supreme characteristic of human nature."

Such a definition of personality, in contrast to the idea of character, is not as laden with moral connotations and could be perceived as more scientific.[26] As Allport (1937, p. 52) summed it up, "Personality is character devaluated." The notion of will is not crucial to the concept of personality as it was for character. Furthermore, *personality* emphasizes individuality, while the concept of character does not. Some psychologists even began to treat character as nothing more than a personality trait (Davis and Gould 1929). The historian Warren Susman (1984, p. 279) has observed that we can see these changing interests by looking at the topics chosen by the popular self-help writer Orison Marden: from *Character: The Grandest Thing in the World* in 1899 to *Masterful Personality* in 1921.[27]

Common to all these psychological topics was the assumption that human behavior could be understood in scientific terms.[28] But, at the same time, a scientific approach in itself was not sufficient to engage autobiographers. Psychological theories and concepts must be useful in illuminating and interpreting their own choices and actions in life. These autobiographers, therefore, did not so readily employ behaviorism to explain their own lives, despite its dominant position in psychology from the 1920s until the 1950s, because it offered no arguments for self-control and individual responsibility. Behaviorism might be useful when thinking about changing other persons' behavior, but, when it came to contemplating one's own actions, it could be regarded as an attack on freedom and dignity since it dismisses people's intentions and beliefs.[29]

Theory of the Self

We can find American autobiographers developing an interest in motivation in a parallel fashion to psychologists. Any part of psychology that might elucidate why persons choose one course of action over another (for reasons of instinct, drive, unconscious motivation, etc.) was of potential interest to autobiographers. Therefore, despite significant differences in conceptual and methodological orientation between psychoanalysts and the experimental psychologists in the first half of the twentieth century, their shared attention to the subject of motivation attracted the attention of autobiographers. Their work might explain actions that are "unthinking" and offer ways of controlling such behavior. Furthermore, the possibility that there are unconscious determinants of behavior is important to consider because it raises the key issue of responsibility for one's own actions.

Human Nature

The late nineteenth- and early twentieth-century autobiographers who used psychological concepts were less likely than either the religious or the self-development autobiographers to use the term *human nature* to explain their own actions. They did not dismiss this fundamental topic, however, but they translated it into the more "scientific" language of heredity, instincts, and drives. As Wayne Shumaker (1954, p. 90) noted in his study of English autobiography, "Hereditary and environmental influences now assumed the centrality which had formerly been accorded to actions and observations; and the materials as well as the methods and purpose of autobiography changed radically." These autobiographers, like their predecessors, were curious about what they shared with all human beings. Science, perhaps, offered a means by which they could better understand the biological aspects of their own (and others') behavior.

One particularly interesting topic for autobiographers was heredity. By 1912, an author of a self-help book on character was able to assert confidently that "the idea of heredity has been lodged beyond displacing in the mind even of the average man" (MacCunn 1912, p. 1). Autobiographers could demonstrate that they were conversant with the scientific debates of the day about evolution by discussing heredity. Georgiana Kirby (1887, p. 154), who knew many intellectuals through her association with Brook Farm, referred to "the subject of the inherited tendencies which prevails at the present time among thoughtful Americans." The banker Roeliff Brinkerhoff (1900, p. 269) declared that "the governing forces of every human life are to a very large extent the forces of heredity." And Andrew Carnegie (1920, pp. 5–6) asserted that "the doctrine of inherited tendencies is proved every day and hour."

But heredity was not just a topic for idle curiosity. It was relevant for the important question of what is voluntary in a person's behavior. It would seem that heredity, since it relates to traits that are not a matter of choice, would have too deterministic a connotation for these autobiographers concerned about taking responsibility for their own lives, but they were able to make creative use of such an idea. For one thing, heredity was useful for explaining other persons' behavior—particularly that which previously had been called sin. George Walling (1887, p. 332), chief of police in New York from 1874 to 1885, discussed not sin but the "hereditary viciousness" of some criminals. Transgressions could now be explained as characteristic of human beings in earlier stages of evolution or as a "lapse into animality."[30] Walling declared that a considerable amount of crime "springs from the instincts of nature, and . . . will be committed by human beings, whether savage or civilized" (p. 596).

For the autobiographers themselves, heredity was something to be modified, made use of, or overcome. In contrast to Divine Providence, heredity was a constraint they could understand and manage. As the historian Bernard Wishy (1968, p. 132) observed in his study of American notions of child nurture, people sometimes used the notion of hereditary tendencies to explain behavior in others (e.g., "the slum child"), but when it came to the behavior of children in the "nice home," they discounted its role. These autobiographers agreed in principle with the assertion in an early twentieth-century child study manual that "in a sense a child chooses his heredity, for while he may not choose any other than his own, he may choose to neglect or improve any part of his own. He may select his noblest competence and let his ignoble ones lie dormant, thus turning capacity into character."[31] The railroad signalman James Fagan (1912, p. 27), following this line of reasoning, approvingly repeated his cousin's advice that heredity and environment "have no terrors to the man with a purpose in life, and a will." Similarly, Roeliff Brinkerhoff (1900, p. 429) observed that "with the brute, environment, heredity, and instinct . . . are every thing, and with a man they amount to much, but after all a man, in the main, is what he believes." In these two quotations, we can see how these autobiographers resourcefully combined the concept of heredity with ideas about self-development and will that I discussed in Chapter 4.

These autobiographers also selectively used the idea of heredity to explain a few of their individual traits—generally to illustrate how they were different from others. If they made allowance for the role of inheritance in their own makeup, they were more likely to do so in terms of admirable traits. Fagan (1912, p. 68), for instance, commented on "the roving, adventurous spirit" that he inherited. It was also useful, for the sake of modesty, to claim a praiseworthy trait to be inherited, thereby attributing it to fortune. Andrew Carnegie (1920, p. 3) used such a tactic: "I think my optimistic nature, my ability to shed trouble and to laugh through life, making 'all my ducks swans,' as friends say I do, must have been inherited from this delightful old masquerading grandfather whose name I am proud to bear." But even so, these autobiographers were careful about what merits they would claim as inherited. I did not find, for example, any autobiographers boasting that they had inherited extraordinary intelligence. Moreover, for those with a reputation that needed to be rectified, they could claim that shortcomings were the result of inherited traits. The minister R. G. Williams (1896, p. 9), for instance, blamed his ancestors for his former wickedness and drunkenness: "They were very ungodly men, and I inherited the same disposition and a similar nature."

Instinct is another topic that autobiographers found to be interesting as a possible cause of human behavior. Attributing much significance to instinct, however, can result in a deterministic view of human beings as slaves to these internal forces. It surely must have been unsettling for people to begin to notice "lines of force," as Henry Adams ([1906] 1918, p. 426) observed in his autobiography, "where [they] had always seen lines of will." Some autobiographers kept the discussion of instinct on a general level, as did Clarence Darrow (1932, p. 86) when he pronounced that "every instinct that is found in any man is in all men." But when it came to their own makeup, they focused more on the question of why they were not enslaved by any instincts that were potentially deleterious. They might admit, however, to being influenced by positive or morally neutral ones such as the "romantic instinct" (Keeler 1870, p. 23) or "climbing instincts" (Brinkerhoff 1900, p. 10).

Those autobiographers who continued to believe in self-development and Lamarckian evolution made a connection between instinct and habit. Before the work of Weismann, as John Burnham (1988, p. 56) pointed out, "Instincts were seen to have their origins in the habits developed by one's ancestors." William James, in an influential 1887 article, had defined instincts as "habits to which there is an innate tendency."[32] A debate continued into the early twentieth century on how to distinguish instincts from habits (Flugel 1933). If instincts are actually habits, then they can be managed. Thus James ([1890] 1950, 2:390) also maintained that "no matter how well endowed an animal may originally be in the way of instincts, his resultant actions will be much modified if the instincts combine with experience." The popular self-help writer Harry Emerson Fosdick (1923, p. 144) reflected this idea when he argued that instincts could be shaped for new uses:

> For our primitive instincts are neither to be surrendered to nor to be stamped on and cast out. They are about the most valuable part of our native equipment. They are our original motive force, and our business with them is not to crush them but to expand their uses, to organize them around new purposes and direct them to new aims.

Some autobiographers also invoked instincts as a natural part of self—in particular, the sexual "instinct," which had become a serious topic in the writings of Freud, Havelock Ellis, and others.[33] Among the autobiographers in my sample, I found that those who published after 1920 were more likely to discuss their own sexuality forthrightly—contributing to a trend that has continued to the present day. Such discussions, of course, are not without precedent. In his *Confessions,* Rousseau ([1781] 1953), for example, revealed his sensual pleasure as a child when spanked by Mademoiselle Lambercier, his childhood encounter with a pederast, and his adolescent penchant for "haunt[ing] dark alleys and lonely spots where I could expose myself to women from afar off in the condition in which I should have liked to be in their company" (p. 90). But for the religious autobiographers and the self-development autobiographers, such discussions of sexual behavior did not fit into their stories of exemplary lives. Autobiographers interested in motivation, however, helped further a sexual vocabulary of motives.[34] Rather than regarding sexuality as something to be regulated scrupulously, some of these twentieth-century autobiographers adopted the idea that the sexual instinct is natural and, hence, good. At the same time, however, as the historian Nathan Hale (1971, p. 421) discussed in his study of the American reaction to Freudian thought, they "toned down the unruly nature of the sexual instincts."

For some autobiographers, this trend meant an abstract discussion of sexuality—perhaps mentioning Freudian ideas or at least noting that the topic was in vogue. The financial publisher John Moody ([1933] 1946, p. 205), for instance, spoke disapprovingly of "sex-mania" and "the popularity of the books and plays which now pandered to the cravings of a Freudian-minded age, which thought it had to learn the art of 'self-expression.'" And the popular novelist Gertrude Atherton (1932, p. 436) mentioned how earlier generations did not anticipate that "the day was not far off when homosexualism and kindred subjects would be topics of casual conversation at tea tables, cocktail parties, invade the movies, and be flaunted by those in search of high prestige."

On a personal level, these autobiographers selectively used the topic of sexuality. Most of the autobiographers in my sample from the first half of the twentieth century did not see an extended analysis of their sexual behavior as necessary for self-understanding, nor did they wish to suggest that sex was a compelling drive in their lives. Those who did contemplate their own sexuality usually limited their discussions to milestone events to which readers can relate: their first knowledge of sex, the first stirrings of sexual feelings during adolescence, or perhaps their first sexual experience. Lincoln Steffens (1931, p. 13), for example, described how an older boy explained sex to him when he was a child: "He began there in that dark, tight, hidden little hut to tell me and show me sex. It was perverse, impotent, exciting, dirty." Steffens went on to relate how he was perplexed, as a boy, by his first feelings of sexual arousal brought about by riding a horse.

Steffens was also willing to consider the idea of preadolescent sexual feelings when he commented that "parents seem to have no recollection and no knowledge of how early the sex-life of a child begins" (p. 13). Other autobiographers, however, vehemently denied any sexual feelings before adolescence and proclaimed their own childhood innocence. "It has become the habit of our Freudian era," commented the writer Ellen Glasgow ([1954] 1980, p. 54), "to represent the infant mind as oppressed by a heavy burden of sex . . . For myself, I cannot recall that I speculated about sex, or singled out this instinct as a special province of wonder." Vladimir Nabokov ([1951] 1966, p. 150) also debunked the notion of childhood sexuality as he recalled his preadolescent self: "We lay on the grass and discussed women. Our innocence seems to me now almost monstrous, in the light of various 'sexual confessions' (to be found in Havelock Ellis and elsewhere), with tiny tots mating like mad. The slums of sex were unknown to us." Likewise, H. L. Mencken ([1940] 1955, p. 135), reminiscing about his youthful days in the late 1800s, insisted that "the humor of the young bourgeoisie males of Baltimore, in those days, was predominantly skatological [sic], and there was no sign of the revolting sexual obsession that Freudians talk of."

These autobiographers interested in motivation also diverted more of their attention from traits shared with their fellow human beings to the topic of individual differences—what constituted their own unique personalities.[35] The publisher, reporter, and social reformer Agnes Meyer (1953, p. 348), for example, referred to the fusion of "inherited and acquired characteristics" that make up the "dynamic, functioning unity which alone is worthy of being called personality." Other autobiographers made proclamations like that of the lawyer J. W. Arbuckle (1942, p. 34): "I become conscious that I am myself and not a mere unit, an identity and not a mere entity." And Gertrude Atherton (1932, p. 22) declared: "It was my ambition to be as 'different' as possible."[36] These are comments that the religious autobiographers would not have made.

It appears that the literary scholar Wayne Shumaker (1954, p. 29) is correct in his observation that autobiography, once based on the deductive notion that the truth about human existence is "already known in its essentials," has come to be based on the inductive idea that an understanding of human life and human nature can only be developed by the "slow accumulation of particulars."[37] These autobiographers, in contrast to the religious and the self-development autobiographers, now saw value in contemplating their unique life experiences for the purpose of understanding themselves rather than demonstrating fundamental truths about human life.[38] The sociologist Georg Simmel ([1917] 1950, p. 78) had commented on such a trend in the nineteenth century: "Now, the individual . . . also wished to distinguish himself *from other individuals.* The important point no longer was the fact that he was a free individual as such, but that he was this specific, irreplaceable, given individual" (his emphasis).[39] Such autobiographers felt freer to move away from a didactic presentation of self as role model. Those who paid more attention to individual differences were not, of course, the first to notice that human beings are not identical.[40] Nevertheless, as the philosopher Charles Taylor (1988, p. 316) has argued, "No one ever doubted that there were individual differences, that one person differed from another. What is new in the modern era is that these have a specific kind of moral relevance . . . Nowhere before the modern era was the notion entertained that what was essential to us might be found in our particular being."

Components of the Self

Faculty psychology had fallen out of vogue in the late nineteenth century, but these autobiographers still had reason to discuss such "faculties," since thinking, choosing, and feeling are fundamental aspects of human behavior. They began, however, to use other terms for these faculties as well, such as consciousness, motivation, and emotion. As Theodore Sarbin (1986a, p. 85) has observed, even psychologists have continued "to talk and work as if the three-way split of the faculties had continuing validity." In this chapter, for ease of discussion, I will continue to use this simple classification in order to compare the changed interpretations of the self. We could, however, apply other divisions of the self such as Freud's division of the psyche into conscious and unconscious. And we could combine emotion and will into the category of motivation.

REASON. Psychological theories about the interrelationship of cognition and emotion offered potential grounds for pessimism about human rationality. If we agree that emotions influence thought, we are led to question the possibility of objectivity as well as the value of introspection as a means of investigating human consciousness. Scientific analysis of the workings of the mind, therefore, gave additional ammunition to those who wished to attack reason. The religious autobiographers had discounted the ability to reason as one of the weak faculties of imperfect human beings, but now there was another line of attack. As the writer Ellen Glasgow ([1954] 1980, p. 268) recalled about the 1920s, "The intellect, with its record of long service and of rigid systems, was condemned even by its former disciples." Thus we can find Lincoln Steffens (1931, p. 692) writing in his autobiography: "That reason was no approach to the minds of other men I had learned. After a few attempts with logic on myself, I had seen to my surprise that it was no use reasoning with myself. The way to influence others was to appeal to their emotions or change their environment or both. I would try that on myself." Likewise, Clarence Darrow (1932, pp. 210–11) expounded on the topic of reason: "Reason has very little to do with human action. Reason is simply a method of comparing and appraising; it is always used to justify what the emotions demand. How far the reason of man can be used to inhibit emotions may be a subject of debate, but it can go but a little way. The structure of man determines his course under certain circumstances."

In particular, Freud's contention that a considerable part of what goes on in the human mind is unconscious raises serious doubts about the human ability to introspect reliably. Such a possibility, then, is disconcerting for autobiographers who wish to "know thyself." The religious autobiographers, too, had been anxious about the possibility of self-deception, but they did not explain it in these terms. Twentieth-century autobiographers such as Lincoln Steffens believed that Freudian analysis could lead to greater self-knowledge of one's own motivation.[41] He, along with others, was intrigued by Freud's ideas about the emotional influence of parents on a child, the importance of libido, and the workings of the unconscious mind.[42]

Within a decade of Freud's visit to the United States, some autobiographers had begun to consider his ideas.[43] Lincoln Steffens (1931, p. 655), well-placed in intellectual circles, recalled that he learned of Freudian theory in the second decade of the twentieth century: "It was there and thus that some of us first heard of psychoanalysis and the new psychology of Freud and Jung, which in several discussions, one led by Walter Lippmann, introduced us to the idea that the minds of men were distorted by unconscious suppressions, often quite irresponsible and incapable of reasoning or learning." By 1915, the topic of psychoanalysis reached magazines, and by the 1920s the popularization of Freudian thought was under way in the United States even though many persons had not read his writings (Hale 1971). Freud (1925, p. 95) himself commented that psychoanalysis had become "extremely popular among the lay public" in America, although he lamented that it had been "watered down." Autobiographers, to varying extents, adopted and modified his ideas and those of his followers that dealt with aspects of human behavior that they wished to discuss, for example, neuroses, repression, libido, catharsis, inferiority complexes, and sublimation. For instance, John Moody ([1933] 1946, p. 221) wrote, "In our day we have invented a new term called the inferiority complex. It is an expressive term and covers a multitude of sins; most of us are afflicted with it in one form or another."

Freud gave autobiographers further reason to analyze their own thoughts, feelings, and motives extensively. Using his ideas, they might be able, for example, to understand why, on occasion, they had acted irrationally and not in their own best interests. If they considered such ideas, they could no longer confidently write, as did Edward Gibbon ([1796] 1984, p. 39) in his famous memoir that "I must be conscious that no one is so well qualified as myself to describe the series of my thoughts and actions." Instead, it was possible that people often do not understand their own motivation, and that a good deal of human behavior is not the result of conscious reasoning but instead the product of drives, instincts, and repressed impulses and feelings. Furthermore, some portions of the unconscious may resist entry into consciousness—a theory that makes a metaphor of "depth" appropriate when referring to the mind.

Some late nineteenth- and twentieth-century autobiographers speculated about the unconscious and showed their familiarity with the topic. Georgiana Kirby (1887, pp. 134–35) made note of a trend in the late nineteenth century toward using the words *consciousness* and *unconsciousness* in everyday conversation. Henry Adams ([1906] 1918, p. 433) lamented that he "failed to fathom the depths of the new psychology, which proved to him that . . . his power of thought was atrophied, if, indeed, it ever existed." And the novelist Gertrude Atherton (1932, p. 259) observed that "the human mind has an infinite capacity for self-delusion." Later in her autobiography, she exclaimed, "So scant a knowledge have we of our depths!" (p. 529).

Autobiographers could use the idea of unconscious motivation to analyze others' behavior. "But he often did not know," wrote Lincoln Steffens (1931, p. 513) about Theodore Roosevelt, "why he did what he did, gave reasons instead of his actual motives for conduct." James Fagan (1912, pp. 214–15) declared to his readers, "In forming opinions of people one's mental camera is usually on the watch for characteristics that jut out, unconsciously or otherwise, in language or behavior." And in a more contemporary autobiography, the businessman Lee Iacocca (1984, p. 104) commented about another: "I don't want to play psychiatrist here, but I had a theory about where his fears came from."

Although these autobiographers viewed the human mind as complex and with unplumbed depths, they seemed far from enamored by the implication that such depths in their own minds were resistant to being raised to consciousness. The sociologist Philip Rieff (1959, pp. 36–37) commented on an analogous opposition to this Freudian idea among some psychologists:

> That this depth, this immense fund of unacknowledged contents, exists so far out of the reach of consciousness that it must be lodged, metaphorically, in another part of the psyche, is just the extremity upon which Freud insisted . . . I would hazard a guess that the cause of widespread hostility to the idea of the unconscious among non-Freudian psychologists . . . is . . . its critical implications, and, moreover, Freud's resigned modesty about just how much any man can do to alter the fates working themselves out of the unconscious.

Some autobiographers from the early twentieth century more readily adopted the idea of the *subconscious* to refer to mental activities below the threshold of awareness that can be brought to consciousness.[44] Henry Adams ([1906] 1918, p. 433), for example, asserted that "the only absolute truth was the sub-conscious chaos below, which every one could feel when he sought it." Likewise, Lincoln Steffens (1931, p. 313) wrote, "I had not realized till that moment the subconscious fear in which I was working, the depth of my dread."

It is more reassuring to believe that reason, somewhat paradoxically, could be used to understand and manage subconscious or unconscious motivation. For those who were interested in the unconscious, it was likely that they hoped by recognizing its existence they could understand and eventually manage this aspect of human behavior. As the historian Nathan Hale (1971, p. 346) observed, "Most of the Americans developed psychoanalysis into an ethical system. Its first commandment was to face 'reality,' to know one's own inner desires the better to control and sublimate them." Introspection was important for such control. Eldridge Cleaver (1968, p. 15) stated this expressly in his bestseller *Soul on Ice,* written while he was in Folsom Prison: "I had to seek out the truth and unravel the snarled web of my motivations. I had to find out who I am and what I want to be, what type of man I should be, and what I could do to become the best of which I was capable." The possibility of gaining an understanding of these inner depths was more congenial to these autobiographers than the idea that they could not be masters in their own houses.

WILL. As psychologists turned aside from the concept of will, so, too, did these twentieth-century autobiographers to a considerable extent. They stopped trumpeting the virtues of character, and more of them began to talk about "motives."[45] In particular, the idea of unconscious motivation, as Nathan Hale (1971, p. 249) observed, threatened to destroy "the older faith that 'character' rested squarely on fully conscious moral choice." Many people today still use the ideas of will and character, but these concepts no longer hold pride of place for autobiographers as they once did for those who told a story of self-culture or self-development.

Once autobiographers paid closer attention to instincts, impulses, and drives, they began to consider that the direction of their lives may not simply be the result of exertions of will. John Moody ([1933] 1946, p. ix), for example, approvingly cited the statement that "the life of a man is a diary in which he means to write one thing and writes another." Fewer of these autobiographers used metaphors for life connoting control (the pilot at the helm of a ship)—returning instead to the long-standing metaphors of a quest or a journey. Although they were no longer enamored with the concepts of will and character, nevertheless they did not replace them with a strictly deterministic viewpoint of human behavior. Some still found the idea of will useful as a way of explaining how people can overcome inherited "tendencies" or instincts. There were also those who chose to denounce these new theories of human behavior. Moody ([1933] 1946, p. 206), who preferred ideas about self-development, ridiculed the belief that "we were slaves of our libidos or our ductless glands, and could not change our destiny even if we wanted to." Likewise, Ellen Glasgow ([1954] 1980, p. 227) dismissed both the "patter of Freudian theory" and the idea of "molding both causes and effects into a fixed psychological pattern."

EMOTION. These autobiographers approached the subject of emotions in a different manner than their earlier counterparts. Instead of focusing on passions as compulsions to be mastered or describing emotions that displayed to the readers their "sensibilities," they tried to interpret the role that the full range of emotions played in their lives.[46] Clarence Darrow (1932, p. 32) thus appeared proud that he could say, "I had a strongly emotional nature which has caused me boundless joy and infinite pain." Autobiographers now found it worthwhile to discuss internal emotional conflicts, repressed emotions, and emotional discord with others. They did not restrict themselves to "elevated sentiments"; they considered irrational impulses and emotions.

Some of these autobiographers subscribed to the romantic notion that they should not restrain emotions and impulses (at least some of them), but instead they should express and explore their feelings. A common interpretation of Freudian thought was that a person would be happier if he or she were less repressed. From this perspective, impulses and passions are a source of creativity, and they offer insight into one's true self because they are spontaneous and not calculated. Ellen Glasgow ([1954] 1980, p. 267) recalled such ideas from the 1920s:

> It was not long before the rebellion broke away . . . from reason, broke into a desultory guerrilla uprising of the primitive, and into a final tremendous assault upon the intellect . . . The war had been the great liberator of instinct, and . . . the new prophets of Freudian psychology were crying aloud to the multitude . . . Sensation was so effortless, so unbridled, so direct in motive, and so democratic in method . . . Sensation was a lavish gift at birth.

Ludwig Lewisohn (1922, p. 155) also reflected this viewpoint when he described his decision to "let my reasoning be guided by a strong and hitherto unsuspected impulse which stirred somewhere in the depths of consciousness."

In contrast, reason, by interceding between stimulus and response, destroys spontaneity and undermines the motivating power of the passions. As Charles Taylor (1989, p. 116) has observed, "The notion has been developed that rational hegemony, rational control, may stifle, desiccate, repress us; that rational self-mastery may be self-domination or enslavement." Accordingly, the novelist Rebecca Harding Davis (1904, p. 90) disparaged what she described as the typical New Englander, who "has cultivated habits which verge on closeness . . . with the expression of feeling, and even—his enemies think—with feeling itself." The passions, instead, were to be honored. Gustave Flaubert ([1857] 1981, p. 125) had earlier encapsulated this romantic viewpoint in *Madame Bovary* in the words of Rodolphe: "Why preach against the passions? Aren't they the only beautiful thing in this world, the source of heroism, enthusiasm, poetry, music, the arts, everything?" In this spirit, Lewisohn (1922, pp. 136–37) offered advice to his readers:

> The passion of love is the central passion of human life. It should be humanized; it should be made beautiful. It should never be debased by a sense that it is in itself sinful, for that is to make the whole of life sinful and to corrupt our human experience at its very source.

This model of the self, however, does not recommend unfettered "release" of one's emotions, for there remains significant concern about what Agnes Meyer (1953, p. 43) called "the lonely battle for self-control."[47] Alexander Pope's ([1734] 1969, p. 27) much earlier comment about humankind seems appropriate here: "In doubt to deem himself a god, or beast; / In doubt his mind or body to prefer." On the one hand, it might be harmful to restrain impulses and emotions. But, as Max Weber (1949, pp. 124–25) has observed: "We associate the highest measure of an empirical 'feeling of freedom' with those actions which we are conscious of performing rationally—i.e., *in the absence of physical and psychic 'coercion,' emotional 'affects' and 'accidental' disturbances of the clarity of judgment*" (his emphasis). Thus Agnes Meyer (1953, p. 188) concluded in her autobiography that she needed to find a way "through the turmoil of modern life toward a new balance of demonic passion and calculated order, of spontaneity and responsibility, of freedom and self-discipline." In general, these autobiographers took the situation into account when claiming the value of spontaneous impulse. This is in accord with the anthropologist Catherine Lutz's observation about American life that there are some situations (usually in private life) where it is believed that emotionality is good as an expression of engagement and connection. In other circumstances (usually in public life), however, emotionality is often linked to irrationality and a lack of self-control.

Changes in the Self

The story told by these autobiographers was not one of self-transformation or self-development. Their ambition was not to develop the "best self" (in the sense of being self-controlled) that anyone potentially could. Rather, the goal more likely was to gain insight into the essence of one's unique self.

Thus James Fagan (1912, p. 72) proclaimed in his *Autobiography of an Individualist,* "The problem for me . . . was simply to find myself." Likewise Lincoln Steffens (1931, p. 51), in a gently self-mocking style, recalled his youthful decision that "I would 'find' myself, as my kind of people did." A thorough self-examination, therefore, should include a consideration of their own motivations: their instincts, impulses, drives, and unconscious or subconscious thoughts and feelings. What they hoped to discover in such self-scrutiny was not the intrinsically sinful self that the religious autobiographers were looking for, but an understanding of the unique and complex self.

The theme of the autobiography could then be this process of "finding oneself" or gaining a sense of identity.[48] The actor Anthony Quinn (1972), in this general spirit, organized his autobiography around discussions with his analyst. The search for self implied there was something "there" to be discovered, yet by allowing that childhood events can shape the self, they did not simply look for some immutable essence present from birth. A practical way of going about discovering the "truth" about themselves was to look for patterns in their past actions and experiences (Barbour 1992). The act of writing an autobiography could help accomplish such a goal by forcing its writer to introspect and commit to paper a particular portrait of self. Thus the illustrator, editor, and television host Alexander King (1958, p. 364) wrote, "I suppose that all through the writing of these pages there trembled in my heart a sort of submerged hope that the story of my life would finally come to form a meaningful pattern . . . Well, I'm happy to say I've found it, all right, the moral and the meaning, too, even if you can't always see it too plainly." Such autobiographers may be distressed by the results of self-analysis or by the sense of closure once the narrative is completed. Clarence Darrow (1932, p. 440) made such a realization: "This is the first autobiography that I have ever written. Strangely enough, as it draws to a close, it gives me the feeling of an obituary carved on a marble stone."

The concept of a turning point is useful for such a tale, but here this pivotal moment involves neither a transformation of self (and subsequent behavior) as in a conversion nor the initiation of an active process of self-development. The turning point was more likely an epiphany—an illuminating moment of self-understanding that offered a way of making sense of one's life. These autobiographers depict a transformation not in the self but in how they understand the self. Agnes Meyer's (1953, p. 106) epiphany came from a dream: "The voyage home from Europe was a turning point in my life . . . because I had a terrible nightmare that gave me an insight of permanent influence upon my life."[49]

If such autobiographers subscribed to Freudian ideas, then they might not want to overlook the seemingly trivial details of their lives in a meticulous self-examination, since Freud had argued for "the thoroughgoing meaningfulness and determinism of even the apparently most obscure and arbitrary mental phenomena" (Jones 1953, p. 366). Alexander King (1958, pp. 109–10), for this reason, recalled a conversation he had with a girl when he was ten, a memory that he reasoned must contain a clue to his own personality: "For nearly fifty years I have recalled this conversation every few months. It comes unbidden into my mind from the depths of memory, and sometimes I used to feel that its emergence signified a key, a clue, or a parable applicable to some current emergency in my life." Such a focus on minor details, however, runs the risk of boring the readers.

For autobiographers interested in explaining their unique histories, childhood assumed greater significance than it had for their earlier counterparts. The search for self included a careful look at the past, particularly childhood, for clues. By my count, American autobiographies that focused *solely* on the author's childhood increased from twenty-one published in the entire nineteenth century (1 percent of that century's total) to 176 published in the first half of the twentieth century (4 percent of the corresponding total).[50] Furthermore, even among the twentieth-century autobiographers in my sample who wrote about their entire lives, they devoted a significantly greater proportion of pages to their childhood than earlier autobiographers.[51] This interest in childhood was particularly the case for autobiographers who accepted the Freudian idea that childhood events were fundamental in shaping adult behavior. The childhood occurrences that became significant were not simple childhood joys or blissful innocence, but instead conflict-laden or traumatic events, which they assumed to have lasting effects throughout life. George Orwell (1954, p. 29) simply presupposed this view of childhood when he once warned that "whoever writes about his childhood must beware of exaggeration and self-pity." On the other hand, H. L. Mencken (1940, p. 149) sarcastically rejected such a viewpoint: "In those . . . days no one had yet formulated the theory that a few licks across the backside would convert a normal boy into a psychopathic personality, bursting with Freudian complexes and a rage against society."

Some early twentieth-century autobiographers also characterized childhood as a "stage" of life during which the instincts predominated. James Fagan (1912, p. 6) deemed childhood "the wilderness stage," and John Moody ([1933] 1946, p. 22) explained it in this manner: "Regular boys tend to live in caves, to pull little girls around by the hair, to roam in gangs, to view property with a communistic eye, to rejoice in destruction, and to be thrilled by battle, murder and sudden death." And George Francis Train (1902, p. 50), a shipping magnate, offered this explanation for his childhood temptation to steal a knife: "I looked around, with all the inherited cunning of savage and barbarian and predatory ancestors in a thousand forests and for a hundred centuries." All this discussion of youthful vigor and bestial origins, as commentator Anthony Rotundo (1990, p. 230) has pointed out, applied to males only; it would be difficult to find early twentieth-century recollections of savage girlhoods. Viewing childhood as the "wilderness stage" fit in with G. Stanley Hall's recapitulation theory that individual development follows the evolution of the species and that any wrongdoing by children was a normal part of biological maturation (Kett 1977).[52] Such a theory allowed autobiographers to argue that they had outgrown any wrongdoing that naturally accompanied such a stage—leaving no cause for censure.

Hall (1904) was also influential in advancing the notion of adolescence as a "stage" of life.[53] Rousseau and romantic writers had developed the idea of adolescence as a time of *Sturm und Drang,* and Hall tried to give such an idea a scientific basis by construing adolescent turmoil as a natural accompaniment of the abrupt transition from one stage of evolutionary development to another (Morss 1990). Adolescence, according to Hall, represented a "transition from preconscious animality to conscious humanity" (Gould 1977, p. 143). This notion of adolescence as a time of discontent was adopted by some of these autobiographers. Hannah Solomon ([1946] 1974, p. 29) described the "traditional questioning of an adolescent," Agnes Meyer (1953, pp. 30–31) mentioned the "adolescent turmoil of mind and emotions," and John Moody ([1933] 1946, p. 32) asserted that "fourteen or fifteen is the age when the average boy passes out from the placid harbor of parental protection into the storm-tossed sea of adolescence." The editor and writer Albert Jay Nock (1943, p. 291), however, was skeptical of such an idea: "Somehow I had completely missed out on the eruption of *Sturm und Drang* which is supposed, I do not know how correctly, to accompany adolescence." Such descriptions of adolescence contrast with the religious autobiographers' representation of this period of life as significant only as the appropriate time for a religious conversion.

Henry Adams once predicted in a letter that the time was not far off when "psychology, physiology, and history will join in proving man to have as fixed and necessary a development as that of a tree; and almost as unconscious" (Cooley 1976, p. 53). Adams, nevertheless, did not apply this notion of stages to his own life history. The idea of stages involves changes that all human beings share (an emphasis that might appeal to readers), but uniformity of experiences was not the primary focus for those interested in their own constitution. Furthermore, the idea of a fixed set of stages was presumably too deterministic for many of these autobiographers.

Such autobiographers, however, do acknowledge that changes in the self are not simply a matter of steadfastly directing one's own destiny. In the words of Ludwig Lewisohn (1922, pp. 18–19): "The world is wide and its paths are many and the fate of no man is quite his own to shape." More of them began to discuss the role of chance in their lives.[54] The religious auto-biographers had interpreted their lives as full of meaning, and they had scrutinized unexpected events closely to look for the designs of Divine Providence. The self-development autobiographers, too, had found meaning in evolution and the laws of nature. But for those who could discern no apparent meaning in the universe, they could only explain some events as random, uncontrollable, and a matter of chance. Alexander King (1958, p. 2), for example, considered the role of chance: "Once a playful wind blew a scrap of paper up against me, and on it, quite by accident, was charted the new direction of my life for the following five years." It was more acceptable now for these autobiographers to admit that not all the significant events in their lives could be ascribed to careful foresight and planning. Further-more, as the literary scholar John Sturrock (1993, p. 80) has observed, the idea of chance can be useful for achieving dramatic effect in a story by high-lighting the irony that minor events may have major consequences. And fi-nally, autobiographers might use the idea of chance in the manner that Shakespeare described in *King Lear:* "This is the excellent foppery of the world, that when we are sick in fortune—often the surfeit of our own be-havior—we make guilty of our disasters the sun, the moon and the stars: as if we were villains by necessity, fools by heavenly compulsion."

The Role of Society and Significant Others

Autobiographers who thought about human motivation considered "inner forces" within the individual. In this explanatory scheme of human behav-ior that focuses on the internal self, society may not play much of a part. But since some drives or impulses such as aggression may harm others, "society" needs to place controls on these forces. Autobiographers could, therefore, view society as an external constraint on the self. This consideration of the relationship between self and society, however, I am reserving for the fol-lowing chapter.

"Relationships" with significant others did become more important for these autobiographers to discuss than for their earlier counterparts.[55] Some students of autobiography have argued that females, in general, focus more on relationships than males do, but in this type of psychological autobiography both men and women show an appreciation of the importance of interpersonal relationships in shaping the self. A history of interaction with significant others, particularly the emotional nature of such relationships, offered insight into their own selves. Particularly important were relationships with parents during childhood.

The novelist Gertrude Atherton (1932, p. 44) wrote that she had once been jealous of her beautiful, vivacious mother, and she declared, "My mother and I had been antagonistic for years." This would have been an unlikely comment from those autobiographers who depicted their parents as role models. But from a psychological perspective, autobiographers like Anthony Quinn (1972, p. 97) find such things as the tyrannical behavior of a father to be significant. Yogi Berra (Berra and Fitzgerald 1961, p. 36) also recalled, for example, how his authoritarian father often hit him. At the supper table one evening, when the youthful Berra did not eat all his bread, "all of a sudden his hand flew out and cracked me right across the mouth so hard I almost went out of the chair" (p. 47). These events now can be seen as significant in understanding the adult personality. Such a trend toward describing family emotional dynamics and disturbances, along the line of Christina Crawford's best-selling *Mommie Dearest* (1978), has continued to this day such that a number of commentators in the 1990s have observed that "the dysfunctional memoir is the oeuvre of the decade" (Streitfeld 1996, p. 162). The family here is not a haven of unconditional love; it is a caldron of conflicting motives and emotions.

No longer do such autobiographers describe their parents strictly in sentimental terms.[56] Although many autobiographers have continued to describe their mothers in a favorable light, some now have felt it necessary to discuss their mothers' emotional nature and emotional influence. Readers are told not only of the mother's strengths but also of her faults, desires, and weaknesses. There was no longer a guarantee that she would be idealized and her moral uprightness emphasized. Georgiana Kirby (1887, p. 15), for instance, complained that "anxiety on the part of my mother, her consequent irritability, and the inevitable disorder made home a place to escape from, rather than cling to." Ludwig Lewisohn (1922, pp. 17–18) offered this characterization of his mother: "Her strength never lay in nimbleness of mind; neither then nor later did she reflect closely; it lay in the fullness and richness of her emotional nature." And Victor Perera (1986, pp. 17–18), a writer and former editor at the *New Yorker*, in a full chapter on his mother, described her "chronic laziness," "childlike dependence," "sloth," and "irresponsibility," and he included the observation that she "was not very bright."

In the mid-twentieth century, Philip Wylie ([1942] 1955), in his well-known *Generation of Vipers*, introduced the term "momism" and alleged that mothers are "vipers" who attempt to emasculate their male children by encouraging their dependency. In Wylie's words, "[A mother's] policy of protection, from the beginning, was not love of her boy but of herself, and as she found returns coming in from the disoriented young boy in smiles, pats, presents, praise, kisses . . . she moved on to possession" (pp. 208–9). Such a notion, related to the popularization of Freudian ideas, had been developing over the decades as demonstrated by the psychologists Stephanie Shields and Beth Koster's (1989, p. 48) analysis of child-rearing manuals for the years 1915–80, in which they found that "mothers are portrayed as having the tendency to 'overreact' emotionally" and that "their unrestrained passions [are] harmful to both daughters and sons."[57]

Agnes Meyer (1953, p. 107), mother of five children, discussed such a notion on a general level: "I feel sorry for the modern mothers who have not one but a whole swarm of famous psychiatrists to confuse their thinking and spoil their fun by reminding them constantly that love is a dangerous business. What with the women who reject their children and those who bring them up with a thermometer in one hand and a book on psychology in the other, many American children are having a hard time." Yet Meyer added, "Nothing seemed . . . more abhorrent than a mother's boy." Wilmarth Sheldon Lewis (1967, p. 89), a wealthy book collector, approvingly recalled his schoolmaster's advice that "the greatest danger to his future lay—in his mother." Lewis, writing in the third person, reported he began to understand "the genesis of the mother's possessiveness, hatred of her husband and her unconscious wish to emasculate their son" (p. 91). More recently, Victor Perera (1986, p. 20) analyzed his relationship with his mother: "It's true she was intensely possessive of me, but only by fits and starts, so that I was able to elude her smothering attentions for varying intervals."

From this perspective, male autobiographers who acknowledged strong ties to their mothers might be accused of having an Oedipal relationship or being the dependent victim of a "smothering" love. In the 1870s, Henry Morgan (1874, p. 22) could boast of his relationship with his mother with no trace of embarrassment or self-consciousness: "I was the idol of her heart, the center of her affections . . . Where I played was her Eden . . . I wanted no other companion, she wanted no other society." By the 1920s, however, Ludwig Lewisohn (1922, pp. 18–19), decried his mother's devoted love of him: "Utterly she transferred the center of her being to another. It was wrong! Wrong to herself." Thus, as the poet Stephen Spender (1951, p. 196) once suggested in his own autobiography, "There is in modern love an awareness of the psychological motives involved which must be without parallel in past time." Or, as Ernest Hemingway (1964, p. 108) wrote in his memoir, "Families have many ways of being dangerous." Dependence and the fear of losing the love and approval of one's mother (and father) was now of analytical importance (Kagan 1983).

Fathers also do not escape this closer scrutiny. In the nineteenth century, the portrait of the father often stressed his ability as a breadwinner, but as autobiographers became interested in family dynamics they began to discuss their fathers' traits more critically. Lewisohn (1922, p. 14), for instance, analyzed his father's "lack of intellectual restraint, his habit of utopian scheming, [and] the harsh self-assertiveness by which he strove to deaden his own sense of failure and insignificance." The autobiographers' emotional relationships with their fathers were now noteworthy. Victor Perera (1986, p. 9) granted that his father "fed, roofed, clothed, bedded down at night [his family] from an inherited reflex of duty," but what was more significant was that "he had no real love for us." Earlier, Agnes Meyer (1953, pp. 10–11) wrote, "Now that I look back upon my extraordinary Oedipus complex, I am well aware that my father was not the luminous personality I loved as a child nor the somber figure that haunted my adolescence like a nightmare." Such autobiographers, however, still did not accord fathers the same degree of emotional influence as mothers—perhaps because they spent less time with their fathers and because of the fathers' assumed lack of emotional demonstrativeness.

The inadequacy of the father's emotional expressiveness, in fact, has been a subject since the mid-twentieth century for autobiographers in my sample. Ellen Glasgow ([1954] 1980, p. 15) reported that her Calvinistic father "never committed a pleasure," and that he "gave his wife and children everything but the one thing they needed most, and that was love." Worden McDonald (1978, p. 28), notable as the father of the 1960s singer Country Joe McDonald, also found his own father's inexpressiveness worth discussing: "I know now that he loved us too, but he just couldn't talk about it." And the writer Adam Hochschild (1986, p. 27), whose relationship with his father was the subject of his memoir, reported that his father's emotions "showed only through the cracks," and that they were never able to discuss their relationship with each other. In this vein, the lawyer J. W. Arbuckle (1942, p. 94), was remorseful about his inattentiveness to his own children: "When my children came to the formative period of their lives they were in a measure robbed of my companionship and encouragement." The father's efforts at providing for the family might now be interpreted as a misplaced preoccupation with financial success at the expense of the emotional needs of family members.

Some of these autobiographers described problems in their parents' marriage and how this adversely influenced their own lives and outlooks. Gertrude Atherton (1932, p. 24) recounted how her parents quarreled constantly before their divorce and how she "grew up with the idea that the matrimonial condition was a succession of bickerings." The physician Faye Lewis (1971, p. 94), for her part, reported the friction between her parents: "Evidence of strain in our parents, which we children did not understand, became very upsetting at times causing us to wonder fruitlessly what mother was crying about; why father was so cross." These autobiographers also were more likely to discuss their own marital relationships and love affairs in greater detail. An important variable, however, was whether the relationship was intact; autobiographers understandably find it imprudent to broadcast the problems of a current marriage. Thus Worden McDonald (1978, p. 110) tempered his forthright remark about his marriage that "Florence and I have had some fierce fights over the years" with the added reflection that "we have also shared a tremendous amount of love and pleasure." In contrast, the novelist Gertrude Atherton (1932, p. 125), since she was widowed, was quite blunt about her dislike for her husband and her difficulty with pretending to mourn at his unexpected death: "I knew the others were watching me like hawks. They were quite aware that I had no love for George, but if I manifested indifference to his untimely end I should be accused of bad taste, and if I looked too solemn I should be condemned as a hypocrite."

In summary, the portraits of personal relationships by these autobiographers were more multidimensional and psychologically detailed than those of many earlier autobiographers. They no longer believed, as did autobiographers such as Andrew Jackson Davis (1857, p. 61), that such matters were private: "The curtain that hung between our house and the world—which folded in obscurity the private afflictions of our family—I will not roll up." Other persons are not described primarily in terms of idealized roles such as those of parents or spouses. They are not confined to the role of heroes, idols, mentors, or exemplars; they are now considered to have a significant emotional (and determinative) impact on the autobiographer.[58]

Telling the Story

"We psycho-analysts were neither the first nor the only ones to propose to mankind that they should look inward," wrote Freud ([1920] 1938, p. 252), "but it appears to be our lot to advocate it most insistently and to support it by empirical evidence which touches every man closely." Such a look inward, which became the fundamental task for some of these autobiographers, meant the authors need no longer tell the story of an exemplary life—except perhaps to illustrate a commendable search for self-knowledge. They need not exemplify a religious conversion or affirm the value of mental or moral self-development. The stress could be on communicating their experiences (Marcus 1994). They could now assert that what made autobiographies interesting and useful were the variations in how persons lived their lives. Thus the New York society leader Ward McAllister (1890, p. v), in answering his own question about what makes a memoir engaging, replied that "the one thing needful is individuality." Much later, Faye Lewis (1971, p. vii) declared she was writing her autobiography because she had led an unusual life.

This stress on individuality, differences, and unique experiences rather than a common human nature or an exemplary life justified a wider range of stories for autobiographers to tell. In the interests of inductive science, the purpose of autobiography, as a "democratic province," was not to show us how life should be lived but to show us how life (presumably) is lived. And a greater variety of autobiographers, who don't all have public accomplishments to tell about, may teach us more realistically, perhaps, about ordinary life. At the same time, however, it is likely that they didn't want to be too atypical. They still assumed that there remained enough of shared common ground or even universal human experiences for readers to find assistance in interpreting their own lives. In the words of the writer Richard Rodriguez (1982, p. 7): "If my story is true, I trust it will resonate with significance for other lives."

In their autobiographies, such authors believed it was commendable to explore their thoughts, feelings, and motives in contrast to focusing on outward actions and events. To introspect adeptly in an autobiography was an admirable goal; they took it for granted that this was a difficult task that not all had the insight to accomplish. Here the focus on self was not to be disparaged as vain, self-absorbed, or effeminate, although it still might be possible to stray too far in these directions.[59] Clarence Darrow (1932, p. 7) was only mildly defensive when he stated the goal of his autobiography: "My ambition is not so much to relate the occurrences as to record the ideas that life has forced me to accept; and, after all, thoughts, impressions and feelings are really life itself." Darrow did not feel compelled to paint a portrait of himself as a man of action only. The religious autobiographers had also focused on inner thoughts and emotions as part of a search for the sinner within, but they did so to humble themselves. In comparison, these psychologically oriented autobiographers justified such a self-examination as a way to fathom the complexity of the self.

How, then, can individuals explore their "inner depths" in an autobiography? How do they articulate their subjectivity in public terms? Or, as the poet Paul Zweig (1968, p. 246) put it, what is "the language of public privacy"? Furthermore, if autobiographers acknowledged the difficulty of exploring the unconscious, how could they hope to understand and articulate their own motives? Was introspection reliable? The physician Faye Lewis (1971, p. 94) recognized such a problem in her autobiography: "The abrasions of the spirit come less readily to the surface of the mind for voluble release, being more painful to recall, and possibly more telltale in their interpretations."

Writing a story of self was no longer a simple matter of recollecting the "facts."[60] More of these autobiographers conceded the subjectivity of their own accounts, and they became more reflexive about the complexity of the autobiographical task, as in Clarence Darrow's (1932, p. 6) comments on this subject: "Autobiography is never entirely true. No one can get the right perspective on himself. Every fact is colored by imagination and dream." H. L. Mencken (1940, p. v), too, displayed such an awareness: "These casual and somewhat chaotic memoirs of days long past are not offered . . . as coldly objective history. They are, on the contrary, excessively subjective, and the record of an event is no doubt often bedizened and adulterated by my response to it. I have made a reasonably honest effort to stick to the cardinal facts . . . but no one is better aware than I am of the fallibility of human recollection." Likewise, Thomas Hart Benton (1937, pp. 77–78), known as a muralist of Americana, made it clear that he knew his accounts were subjective: "My own brother, to whom I showed my accounts of the Missouri of my childhood, dubbed me a fabricator of the worst sort. He maintained that my father sat in the smokehouse rather than in the privy for his figuring, and he insisted that our cow, Bleu, was not given to the contrariness I claimed for her."

Such autobiographers may question memory—not because they see it as a faculty that may be weak through lack of exercise, but because the interrelationship of mind and emotion may cause memories to be altered or repressed.[61] Hannah Solomon ([1946] 1974, p. 3), a founder of the National Council of Jewish Women, mused in her autobiography, "Is memory to be trusted, or has time, in passing, so obliterated the poignancy of experiences which distressed us or enhanced our joy that we are unable to record them in true proportion?" Memory, from this perspective, cannot be so confidently trusted as it had been by the businessman George Francis Train (1902, p. 2): "From the time I was three years old up to this present moment—a long stretch of seventy years, the Prophet's limit of human life—I can remember almost every event in my life with the greatest distinctness. This book of mine will be a pretty fair test of my memory." Instead, memories may be colored and given significance by later events in a person's life. As Clarence Hawkes ([1915] 1946, p. 9) wrote in the story of his blindness, "The dividing line between memory and imagination is so vague and mysterious that it is often almost impossible to tell where memory leaves off and imagination begins."

Once autobiographers arrived at the point of doubting this usual source of information about the self, they began to offer disclaimers such as James Fagan's (1912, p. 7), "If my recollection of my adventures is even partially reliable . . . "; or Andrew Goldstein's (1973, p. 1), "The Dates, Names and Facts Are True within the Impression But the Impression is Subject to Memory and Bias." Some autobiographers also respond to this problem of the fallibility of memory by asserting that what was significant, after all, was not what occurred but what they recalled. Henry Adams ([1906] 1918, p. 43) put this clearly: "This was the journey he remembered. The actual journey may have been quite different, but the actual journey has no interest for education. The memory was all that mattered."[62] Fanciful recollections can be justified as the voice of the unconscious or as representative of a "deeper" truth.

To make it clear to readers that they are well aware of the problems of memory, some autobiographers include descriptions of how they had caught themselves using inaccurate recollections. Mark Twain (1924, 1:95–96) poked fun at himself several times in his autobiographical writings on this subject: "For many years I believed that I remembered helping my grandfather drink his whisky toddy when I was six weeks old, but I do not tell about that any more, now; I am grown old and my memory is not as active as it used to be. When I was younger I could remember anything, whether it had happened or not; but my faculties are decaying now, and soon I shall be so I cannot remember any but the things that never happened." Twain also observed that when human beings repeat a story many times over the years, the result is "one part fact, straight fact, fact pure and undiluted, golden fact, and twenty-fours parts embroidery" (p. 313). In a similar manner, Lincoln Steffens (1931, p. 7) interjected this caveat into his recollections of childhood: "I can call up only a few incidents, which I think I still can see, but which I may have constructed, in part at least, out of the family's stories of that time." On the other hand, H. L. Mencken ([1940] 1955, p. 4), always the iconoclast, professed in his autobiography that he "took no stock in the theories of psychologists who teach that events experienced so early in life are never really recalled, but only reconstructed from family gossip." Yet, in his preface, Mencken conceded that "as Huck Finn said of 'Tom Sawyer,' there are no doubt some stretchers in this book, but mainly it is fact" (pp. vi–vii).

These autobiographers also had good reason to engage in frankness—confessing what they may have preferred to keep private. As the critic Kenneth Burke (1939, p. 391) once observed, Freud "perfected a method for being frank."[63] Similar to Rousseau's famous efforts in his *Confessions,* these autobiographers believed that if they truly wished to know themselves, they should face the contemptible aspects of their lives as well as the effects of drives or instincts on their behavior. Malcolm X (1965, p. 151) spoke to this when he explained in his autobiography:

> I want to say before I go on that I have never previously told anyone my sordid past in detail. I haven't done it now to sound as though I might be proud of how bad, how evil, I was.
>
> But people are always speculating—why I am as I am? To understand that of any person, his whole life, from birth, must be reviewed. All of our experiences fuse into our personality. Everything that ever happened to us is an ingredient.

Such autobiographers addressed aspects of their lives that many nineteenth-century autobiographers, bent on portraying model lives, did not mention, and they could feel virtuous for being so truthful.[64] Such an expectation of candor, of course, might also make the autobiography more fascinating for readers, and those who do not have a life of public achievements may decide to delve into their "private" lives to find interesting material.

One subject eminently suited for frank discussion is sexuality. As I discussed earlier, some early twentieth-century autobiographers approached the topic of sexuality on an abstract level, or they referred primarily to milestone events in the sexual lives of all human beings. In later decades, however, autobiographers become more explicit. The actor Anthony Quinn (1972), for example, tells his readers about his first erection, his masturbation, his libidinous feelings for his sister, and his sexual initiation. Likewise, the writer Victor Perera (1986, pp. 10, 21), while recalling his boyhood in Guatemala, gave his readers a graphic description of his father's "impressive phallus," and he recounted his discovery of his parents in "jointed animality." Although there are some contemporary autobiographers who continue to eschew unreserved details of their personal sexual behavior, we can now easily find life stories whose authors appear to relish such particulars.

Other topics qualifying as frankness are failures, weaknesses, insecurities, conflicts, guilt, and anxieties. Agnes Meyer (1953, p. 58) was forthright about her youthful egotism (now that she considered herself more mature): "For several years . . . I was in love chiefly with myself, an ecstasy that cost me and others much pain before life cured me of this intoxication." Lincoln Steffens (1931, p. 523), too, confided to his readers how he faced his cowardice and his "yellow streak." An article in the 1980s for would-be autobiographers, in fact, advised that "the most awesome of confessions are not so much about actions as about forbidden feelings and passions: greed, lust, wrath, guilt, blasphemy, betrayal or unspeakable desires" (Moberg 1983, p. 33).

Nevertheless, such frankness was still selective. As Philip Roth (1988, p. 164) has recognized, the autobiographical role of "fact-facer" can be a "pose." And there remain limits on how much honesty the audience may find acceptable if they are confronted with what Arthur Koestler ([1952] 1969, p. 38), in a discussion of the pitfalls of autobiography, has called "the embarrassing nakedness of the exhibitionist." In such cases, readers may begin to question the autobiographers' motives for publishing their life stories.[65] The writer Paul Monette (1992, p. 144), after giving a detailed description of a homosexual encounter, asked his readers, *"Is this more than you want to know?"* (his emphasis). Monette understood that such frankness could sabotage his relationship with his readers and might be seen as gratuitous, yet he also recognized that readers with similar stories might admire his impudence. He noted a friend's advice: *"Rub their faces in it, Paulie"* (p. 144).

Autobiographers aware of Freudian theory realized that readers, too, may be using such ideas to interpret the autobiography—looking for omissions, distortions, inconsistencies, rationalizations, or, in a word, self-deception.[66] Such unintentional self-revelation, Mark Twain (1924, 1:235–36) declared, is impossible to avoid in an autobiography:

> And he *will* tell the truth in spite of himself, for his facts and his fictions will work loyally together for the protection of the reader; each fact and each fiction will be a dab of paint, each will fall in its right place, and together they will paint his portrait; not the portrait *he* thinks they are painting, but his real portrait, the inside of him, the soul of him, his character. Without intending to lie, he will lie all the time; not bluntly, consciously, not dully unconsciously, but half-consciously—consciousness in twilight; a soft and gentle and merciful twilight which makes his general form comely, with his virtuous prominences and projections discernible and his ungracious ones in shadow.

The critic Wendy Lesser (1988, p. 27) has called this "the specter that haunts all autobiography—the problem of unintentional self-revelation." I would add that this is a problem particularly for post-Freudian autobiographers.[67]

Some autobiographers have tried to deal with this problem of having readers looking for rationalizations and distortions by bringing up the subject themselves. Alexander King (1958) anticipated such interpretations by prefacing his autobiography with the following announcement: "All the characters in this book are real people, with the possible exception of THE AUTHOR." Similarly, Sherwood Anderson ([1924] 1969, p. 114) followed a discussion of his father with this admission to the reader: "And if you have read Freud you will find it of additional interest that, in my fanciful birth, I have retained the very form and substance of my earthly mother while getting an entirely new father, whom I set up—making anything but a hero of him—only to sling mud at him. I am giving myself away to the initiated, that is certain."

Autobiographers may carefully craft their stories to forestall particular interpretations by the readers. In the nineteenth century, the minstrel Ralph Keeler (1870, pp. 157–58) described an event that many contemporary autobiographers might explain differently in anticipation of readers' interpretations: "I became acquainted with a chubby, handsome boy . . . who excited my admiration in an extraordinary manner . . . I burned with a desire to wrestle with that boy." As another example, Andrew Carnegie's (1920, p. 6) unblushing comments about his mother may lead contemporary readers to a Freudian interpretation: "I feel her to be sacred to myself and not for others to know. None could ever really know her—I alone did that. After my father's early death she was all my own." In contrast, Anthony Quinn (1972, p. 112) recounts for his readers a comment that he made to his psychoanalyst: "I've read Freud. I know all about that shit. No, I never had a mother complex. I never found my mother sexually attractive."

Finally, these autobiographers from the twentieth century may choose to make it apparent to their readers that they realize that imagination has contributed to their self-portraits (Spacks 1976; Eakin 1985). For some of them, fact and fiction is not a self-evident dichotomy, and "telling the truth" in an autobiography has become a more complicated moral obligation. Mary McCarthy (1957, p. 97) abjured any claims of strict truth: "This account is highly fictionalized." And Thomas Hart Benton (1937, p. 7) offered this disclaimer: "I withdraw all claims to an absolute objectivity from my accounts, I waive such claims cheerfully and admit all the implications. I recognize the distorting offices of the self." Such autobiographers may recognize that "real life," as the literary critic Northrop Frye (1970, p. 240) argued, "does not start or stop: it never ties up loose ends; it never manifests meaning or purpose except by blind accident; it is never comic or tragic, ironic or romantic, or anything else that has a shape." Any pattern discerned, therefore, may be the product of the autobiographer's imagination, and the "truth" would be an incoherent and shapeless tale. Lest anyone charge that fictional embellishments or fictional characters violate the norm of truthfulness, such autobiographers can justify them as the result of their imagination or unconscious—products that in themselves may provide more illumination about the author than any recitation of facts. Such fiction, then, is neither intentionally deceitful nor frivolous.

Just as Wayne Shumaker (1954) discovered in his study of English autobiographies, I found that these autobiographers used more of the techniques of novelists such as flashbacks (well suited for the examination of childhood), the inclusion of fictional characters, more elaborate dialogue than they could possibly remember, and more poetic titles such as *Hunger of Memory* for chapters and the book.[68] Furthermore, as the quality of the writing itself has become more important, celebrity autobiographers have often employed professional writers as collaborators. This led the columnist William Safire (1987, pp. 25–26) to comment, "We come now to a problem with many modern memoirs. Autobiography ain't 'auto' anymore; the as-told-to technique is taking over, as celebrated figures under deadline spill what they remember into a tape recorder for 'shaping' by authorized biographers who then go to a list of former associates to fill in more anecdotes." More writers, too, have been attracted to the genre as autobiographies have been recognized as art.

In the construction of their stories, these autobiographers do not limit themselves to a strict chronology.[69] Alexander King (1958, p. 102), aware that his autobiography differed from many earlier ones in this regard, asked these rhetorical questions: "What is the meaning of all these vaguely related anecdotes? An autobiography ought to begin somewhere in childhood and proceed in some decent order toward its conclusion in old age, shouldn't it?" In addition, those autobiographers concentrating on an inner self did not need to anchor themselves as much to the outside world—referring less often to historical events or particular places. In the most subjective of these autobiographies, an index naming places, events, and persons would be out of place.

Conclusion

These autobiographers questioned the optimistic philosophy of the self-made man, and they asked what part heredity, instincts, and unconscious motivation played in their lives. Agnes Meyer (1953, p. 118), for instance, proclaimed that she had acceded to such ideas: "I am convinced no human being is master of his fate, and that we are all motivated far more than we care to admit by characteristics inherited from our ancestors which individual experiences of childhood can modify, repress, or enhance, but cannot erase." Such autobiographers, however, did not wholeheartedly adopt a deterministic model to explain their own behavior. They were discriminating in choosing ideas that suited their purposes in telling their life stories. Although naturalistic fiction in the late nineteenth century commonly contained terms such as "pawns of circumstance," "apelike," "brute," "primitive," and "savage" (Cowley 1950, p. 318), I did not find any autobiographers adopting such a vocabulary to describe their own lives. Writers of fiction (and biography) may find it useful to apply such a deterministic vocabulary to their subjects, but these autobiographers were unwilling to accept the idea that their own actions were fundamentally ruled by instincts, impulses and drives.

A few autobiographers also denounced popular psychological ideas such as those of Freud. H. L. Mencken ([1940] 1955, p. 187), for example, scorned the Freudian "ammunition dump of horrors"; and Vladimir Nabokov ([1951] 1966, p. 14) ridiculed the ideas of the "Viennese Quack": "Let me say at once that I reject completely the vulgar, shabby, fundamentally medieval world of Freud, with its crankish quest for sexual symbols . . . and its bitter little embryos spying, from their natural nooks, upon the love life of their parents." John Moody ([1933] 1946, p. 222) objected to psychology's general tendency of "pulling the pins from under such things as the idea of free-will." That some autobiographers felt compelled to make such declarations, however, points to the salience of such ideas.

Still other autobiographers rejected a narcissistic focus on the self—a criticism that relates to ongoing concerns about vanity in autobiographies (Marcus 1994). Arthur Koestler ([1952] 1969, p. 38) recognized this problem: "With an aching, loving, bitter-sweet nostalgia, the author bends over his past like a woman over the cradle of her child; he whispers to it and rocks it in his arms, blind to the fact that the smiles, and howls, and wrigglings of his budding ego lack for his readers that unique fascination which they hold for him." John Moody ([1933] 1946, p. viii) was one of those to make such a complaint: "Though to-day it seems the fashion for egocentric writers to emit their wail of woe because life had led them into chaos, or because they have failed to find its meaning, I certainly would not dream of writing of my subjective self unless I felt that I had found the answer to life's riddle—and had learned it on the way." Such a theme has been echoed by cultural critics in the twentieth century, for example, Alfred Kazin (1959, p. 127), who wrote that "the age of 'psychological man,' of the herd of aloners, has finally proved the truth of Tocqueville's observation that in modern times the average man is absorbed in a very puny object, himself, to the point of satiety."[70]

Finally, the interest of these autobiographers in the irrational, instinctive, and automatic aspects of human behavior was supplemented by another developing idea about human behavior, that is, the influence of the social environment on the self.[71] Koestler ([1952] 1969, p. 38) had also complained that "the introvert's obsession with himself [in autobiography] makes him neglect the historical background against which he moves." But some autobiographers did ask whether society or their historical backgrounds significantly influenced them. To consider the social environment, however, does not require a complete switch of vocabulary— Freudian ideas such as the unconscious, rationalization, sublimation, and repression remain in our everyday discussions of self. And there also remains the notion of an "inner" self that is uncertain and psychologically complex—an idea only strengthened by the viewpoint of society as an "external" constraint upon the self.[72]

Chapter Six THE *B*ELEAGUERED SELF

> *There is a vulgar tendency in social thought to divide the conduct of the individual into a profane and sacred part . . . The profane part is attributed to the obligatory world of social roles . . . ; it is exacted by society. The sacred part has to do with "personal" matters and "personal" relationships—with what an individual is "really" like underneath it all.*—ERVING GOFFMAN

The American sociologist Lester Ward ([1897] 1926, p. viii) once made a highly optimistic prediction about the future of sociology: "Judging from its rapid rise, and all the signs of the times, it bids fair to become the leading science of the twentieth century, as biology has been that of the nineteenth." Although sociology has not achieved the predominance that Ward foretold, it has played a significant role in the development of a new approach to understanding human behavior. Beginning primarily in the last few decades of the nineteenth century, sociologists provided support for an environmental as opposed to a hereditarian explanation of human behavior. They helped articulate the idea that the environment for human beings was not simply the physical surroundings; it also included the crucial influence of society.[1] From this viewpoint, society and social interaction are significant determinants of behavior. As the sociologist Dennis Wrong (1990, p. 26) has written, "The contention that 'social conditions,' or 'social forces,' or the imperatives of the 'social system' or capitalism or whatever, powerfully shape the lives we lead comes as close to anything does to have been the essence of the sociological outlook from its beginnings."

This sociological model of the self overlaps the same time period as the psychological model described in the last chapter—from the late nineteenth century to the present day. Such a model did not supplant the idea that internal forces such as biological instincts, drives, and inherited traits were important in understanding human behavior; it only added additional considerations. Autobiographers now had both "inner" forces and the "outside" force of society to consider. We can see this change reflected in Clarence Darrow's (1932, p. 961) comment that he had developed, over the years, both a hereditarian and environmental view of criminal behavior: "Up to that time I had the conventional view of crime and criminals. In a vague way I believed that a criminal was somewhat different from other men. He was evil and malignant, because he deliberately chose that way of life. I never had reflected that his composition and environment had any share in his conduct." This recognition of the social environment approached the question of determinism from a new angle: Is society, perhaps, an often-unrecognized influence on how we act? Does this give us additional reason to question the idea that human acts are a matter of free will?

As Raymond Williams (1983, p. 291) has detailed, the term *society* was used before the late eighteenth century to refer to companionship or fellowship. By the nineteenth century, however, people saw *society* "clearly enough as an object" and used it in a general sense such that it "was possible, in new ways, to define the relationship of . . . *the individual and society* as a problem" (p. 294). Among the autobiographers in my sample, I found that this question of the relationship between self and society did not assume prominence until the late nineteenth century. The editor Albert Jay Nock (1943, p. 305–6), for example, acknowledged the inception of such a perspective and scornfully rejected it: "When in the later 'nineties I first observed this fetishistic exaggeration of society's claims against the individual I regarded it as transparent nonsense, as I still do." Such a consideration of the effects of society on the self has continued into contemporary autobiographies. Such autobiographers in the early twentieth century, however, did not relish the deterministic implications of the idea of social influences on the self as we can see in the above quotation from Nock. They preferred to see an opposition between self and society, and they declared that they could resist social forces and any pressures for conformity that might threaten their individuality.[2]

Historical Background

The word *sociology*, coined by Auguste Comte, first appeared in print in the English-speaking world in 1843. Most of the founders of American sociology, however, did not take up sociology until later in the nineteenth century.[3] In 1873, Yale University offered the first college course in sociology in the United States (Bernard 1909), and, in 1889, the University of Kansas established the first American department of sociology (Ritzer 1988). By 1895, the editor of the fledgling *American Journal of Sociology*, Albion Small, confidently pronounced that "sociology has a foremost place in the thought of modern men" (p. 1). Courses in sociology had become common at the college level by 1910 and soon were added to the curriculum at many secondary schools (Cravens 1978).

Much of early American sociology involved a continuance of the social reform movement efforts that had developed in the nineteenth century to correct the problems accompanying industrialization and urbanization. On this subject, the autobiographer James Fagan (1912, p. 104) noted, "The supreme topic in the public mind" by the early twentieth century was "social and industrial betterment." Sociologists viewed crime, poverty, and so forth as "social problems," which resulted, in large part, from the social environment, and which could be studied and eventually managed by changing that environment. Another autobiographer from this period, the banker Roeliff Brinkerhoff (1900, p. 237), approvingly defined social science as "the study of all that relates to social improvement . . . in order to secure right action, which can only come through an enlightened public sentiment."

This attention to social problems can be found in many channels, including theologians in the latter half of the nineteenth century, as the religious historian Timothy Smith noted (1957, p. 148):

> The rapid growth of concern with purely social issues such as poverty, workingmen's rights, the liquor traffic, slum housing, and racial bitterness is the chief feature distinguishing American religion after 1865 from that of the first half of the nineteenth century. Such matters in some cases supplanted entirely the ear-

lier pre-occupation with salvation from personal sin and the life hereafter. Seminaries reorganized their programs to stress sociology.

Religious reformers, such as those involved in the social gospel movement in the late nineteenth century, no longer insisted that social problems were the result of individual sin and a lack of personal responsibility, but instead they argued that it was necessary to eliminate the *conditions* fostering sinful behavior (Curtis 1991). They came to believe that concerted human efforts at the improvement of the social environment were possible.

Social problems also did not escape the notice of many autobiographers in the latter half of the nineteenth century and to the present day. The preacher Henry Morgan (1874, p. 350), for example, was righteously indignant about factory workers' hours: "What untold sufferings are experienced by these slaves of an unnatural system of labor, that compels them to work *sixteen hours a day* for scarcely a subsistence!" Even those autobiographers who played no part in any social reform movements often made it clear that they, too, had a social conscience on such issues as crime, poverty, and the problems of industrialization.

Sociological explanations of social problems, however, were not directly useful to autobiographers for the understanding of their own lives. More apropos was a new "philosophy of man," as the psychologist L. S. Hearnshaw (1987, pp. 172–73) has summarized it: "The nature of man at any given place or time was rooted in history, and shaped by the social circumstances . . . and because these circumstances changed, there was no unchanging human nature."[4] In the 1880s, Lester Ward began to discuss "social forces," and in the late 1890s, the sociologist E. A. Ross delineated the idea of social control and observed that it was necessary for society to "modify individual feelings, ideas, and behavior to conform to the social interest" (Small 1916; Ross 1991, p. 230).[5] This consideration of social forces led to discussions of the link between self and society. A key process in human lives, from a sociological perspective, is socialization rather than a self-initiated cultivation of the self. Hence we must do more than fathom the internal determinants of self to understand human behavior; we must also examine the influence of society on the self.

A concern with the relationship between self and society had been developing before the establishment of sociology as an academic discipline. We can find earlier writers contemplating the effects of society, for example, Rousseau's contentions about the negative influence of society on the naturally good self or, in the United States, Ralph Waldo Emerson's ([1841] 1949, p. 34) assertion that "society everywhere is in conspiracy against the manhood of every one of its members . . . The virtue in most request is conformity."[6] Nineteenth-century socialism and Marxism, too, were fundamentally based on the view that human beings are shaped by social and economic conditions. Nevertheless, my autobiographical evidence supports the sociologist Robert Wuthnow's (1976) observation that it has only been in the twentieth century that such a viewpoint has become widely diffused in the United States.

This philosophy stressing the sociocultural influences on human beings played an important role in the heredity-versus-environment debate in the first half of the twentieth century—with the emphasis on cultural rather than biological determinism. In the 1920s, sociologists such as Luther Bernard and Ellsworth Faris challenged the psychological theory of instincts, and they emphasized the importance of nurture in shaping human behavior.[7] Furthermore, anthropological research conducted in different cultures undermined the idea of a human nature unaltered by culture and society as well as the belief that all cultures naturally evolve through a predetermined set of stages. As the historian Carl Degler (1991, p. 71) has explained, the term *culture* began to take on a new meaning for anthropologists near the end of the nineteenth century: "Until the 1890s [Franz] Boas used the term as his fellow anthropologists did: as another word for civilization or 'high culture' . . . By the end of the 1890s, however, Boas was using culture in the plural, as we do today—every society exhibits a culture . . . After 1910 the usage was common among anthropologists and other social scientists."[8] From Boas's perspective, cultures were not to be explained as different stages in some evolutionary progression, but considered in their own right. This idea of culture provided an environmental explanation for differences in human behavior. Students of Boas such as Margaret Mead and Ruth Benedict promulgated this definition of culture, along with the idea of cultural relativism (Juhasz 1983).

Recognition of the importance of the social environment means a consideration of the relationship between self and society—a topic that can be developed in several ways. Society can be thought of as an "external" force—a part of the environment that constrains the actions of human beings. In such a model, a clear distinction is made between the social environment and the self; it is possible to think of self *versus* society. On the other hand, society can be seen as playing a more profound part in the formation of the self. From this viewpoint, in the words of the sociologist Peter Berger (1963, p. 121), "Society not only controls our movements, but shapes our identity, our thought and our emotions." Here, then, it does not make sense to oppose self and society.

For those who have conceived of society as part of the external environment, a popular image has been that of society as a prison constraining the individual. To exist, society must subdue the "unruly nature" of human beings, but such control comes with a price for individuals—that of the restraint of basic biological drives. Thus Freud ([1930] 1961, p. 43) wrote in *Civilization and Its Discontents,* "A good part of the struggles of mankind center round the single task of finding an expedient accommodation . . . between this claim [to individual liberty] of the individual and the cultural claims of the group." Furthermore, society may be regarded as constraining the self by enforcing conformity among its members rather than encouraging individual differences. In the mid-twentieth century, David Riesman and his associates (1950), C. Wright Mills (1951), William H. Whyte, Jr. (1956), and critics of mass society such as Herbert Marcuse, argued, in essence, that individualism was in decline as we moved toward a society of "other-directed" persons and "organization men." With such a notion of the individual's actions constrained by social forces, it is easy to take the next step and argue that the individual's internal thoughts and feelings, nonetheless, can remain free—that there is an inner core able to resist the demands of society.[9] From this perspective, as John Stuart Mill ([1859] 1991, p. 16) had asserted in the mid-nineteenth century, "the appropriate region of human liberty" was "the inward domain of consciousness."[10]

Beginning in the late nineteenth century, however, theorists such as James Mark Baldwin, Charles H. Cooley, and George Herbert Mead took a different tack in their analyses of the relationship between self and society. Mead (1934), in particular, discussed the social formation of the self. His view stemmed from the idea that the self-reflexiveness of human beings differentiates them from other animals.[11] Such self-awareness gives human beings the ability to monitor and direct their own responses—freeing them from being slaves to their instincts and drives. Biological factors such as heredity and instincts, therefore, are less important in the explanation of human behavior than they are for other animals. And crucially, in Mead's argument, human beings do not have such self-awareness at birth. Instead, self-awareness has a social origin; it develops through social interaction as human beings learn to take the perspectives of other persons on themselves.

Such an understanding of the self leads to the conclusion that it is misleading to counterpose self and society. Society is not just an external part of our environment; it affects our thinking—it gets "inside" our heads. We learn to take into account what others are likely to think about our behavior. Along these lines Cooley ([1902] 1956, p. 36) argued, "A separate individual is an abstraction unknown to experience, and so likewise is society when regarded as something apart from individuals." An individual cannot avoid being shaped by society. Again, in Cooley's words: "Can we separate the individual from society? Only in an external sense. If you go off alone into the wilderness you take with you a mind formed in society, and you continue social intercourse in your memory and imagination" (pp. 48–49).

Any discussion of the meshing of self and society, however, was not as appealing to early twentieth-century autobiographers as the idea that society was an external influence that they could personally resist. Such autobiographers need not have read the writings of any sociologists, for versions of these ideas had filtered into popular books and magazines by the early twentieth century. In a 1912 book on the conventional topic of character, for example, the author incorporated the observation that "the influences of Nature and of Society are inextricably interwoven in their action upon the members of a civilized community" (MacCunn 1912, p. 73). And in a 1920s advice manual, we can find the author counseling his readers that "too much importance cannot be laid on an understanding of one's relation to the powerful social forces that constitute the dynamics of environment" (Fielding 1922, p. xiv).

Theory of the Self

A sociocultural model of the self stresses the relationship between human behavior and the social environment rather than using explanations based on human nature, willpower, or internal motivation. The emphasis is not on an essential human nature, but on a pliant human nature molded by social forces and social interaction. From this perspective, a division of the self into an inner, private self and an outer, social self becomes more appropriate than a partitioning of it into the "internal" faculties of reason, will, and emotions.[12] We can see such an interpretation of the self in the autobiographer Agnes Meyer's (1953, pp. 30–31) claim that she had two "soul-sides": "one to face the world with, the other to show on only rare occasions to people whom I loved and trusted."

Human Nature

In an assessment of early American sociology, Albion Small (1916, p. 755) argued that the concept of *social forces* "amounted to the first impressive challenge of the fatalistic implications of Herbert Spencer's rendering of the evolutionary theory." Autobiographers, too, could bypass any "fatalistic implications" of the idea of inherited traits and instincts by advocating the importance of the social environment instead of the biological aspects of human behavior. If the environment played an important part in shaping human behavior, then any capacities or mechanisms shared by all human beings cannot simply be givens; they must be capable of being modified. The nineteenth-century self-development autobiographers had also argued for the plasticity of human nature—explaining human action in terms of malleable habits and the exercise of willpower. But these twentieth-century autobiographers had a new argument about the influence of the social environment to reinforce this notion of human nature as malleable.

On the other hand, the use of sociocultural explanations of human behavior also introduced the disquieting possibility that the social environment was itself a deterministic factor in human behavior. If the self is shaped by society, then persons' actions might not be as voluntary as they presupposed. Hence the malleability of human nature might be interpreted as tractability in response to society rather than a dormant potentiality to be cultivated by self. What persons hitherto had interpreted as human nature, that is, what is typical in human behavior, might instead be described as similarities that result from conformity to the demands of society. Thus James Fagan (1912, pp. 1–2) lamented in his autobiography that "a large and influential section of public opinion at the present day is persistently emphasizing the central significance of the social stream and the comparative helplessness of the human bubbles adrift upon its surface."

The social psychologists Elaine Aron and Arthur Aron (1986, p. 32) have suggested that we can consider the idea that "most of our 'individual acts of free will' are guided almost exclusively by situational and social influences" to be another blow to human vanity beyond the original three once listed by Freud.[13] The social environment, paradoxically, we can view as both a restraint on human action and a source of freedom. Although culture can help free us from responding blindly to our instincts and drives, we also can regard it as a deterministic factor in human behavior. Clarence Darrow (1932, p. 6), therefore, could make this assertion, "I am interested not in the way that I have fashioned the world, but in the way that the world has molded me," while also declaring, "Instinctively I lean toward the integrity of the individual unit, and am impatient with any interference with personal freedom" (p. 55).

In a study of historical ideas about the self, the psychologist Roy Baumeister (1987, p. 170) argued that "early 20th century citizens saw themselves as utterly in the grip of social forces and powers that were indifferent to them personally." This was not the case, however, with these autobiographers. Since this issue of the deterministic influence of society relates to the moral question of responsibility for their own actions, they had good reason not to adopt such a passive philosophy. Vladimir Nabokov ([1951] 1966, p. 223), for example, scorned such social determinism: "There is in every child the essentially human urge to reshape the earth, to act upon a friable environment (unless he is a born Marxist or a corpse and meekly waits for the environment to fashion *him*)." For some of these autobiographers in the early twentieth century, society became the primary adversary to confront instead of the passions, and it was necessary to wage such a battle to retain the "integrity" of the self. Accordingly, James Fagan (1912, p. 1) first praised the beneficial effects of society on a general level: "True, society reacts on the individual, inspires multitudes of individuals to praiseworthy exertion and development, and thus the commonwealth flourishes." But a few pages later, he groused that he had been "drilled and whipped into civilized form" (p. 8). He went on to complain, "Hitherto Society had been confining me in many ways" (p. 71), and he declared that he was "mentally at war with the artificialities and barbarities of civilization" (p. 88).

Fagan, like other of these autobiographers, did not tell a story of how his life illustrated the universally shared problem of weak human nature. Instead, he had a reason to emphasize his own uniqueness—here defined as nonconformity. In a similar manner, the writer Ludwig Lewisohn (1922, p. 259) proudly maintained, "And I, in my own small and dusty way, was the eternal outcast, rebel, the other-thinking one—guilty before the herd . . . breaker of taboos, creator of new values." Clarence Darrow (1932, p. 285) also professed, "I am, and always have been, with the individual battling for the right to express himself in his own life regardless of the mob." Although human nature was no longer the cornerstone of an explanation of human behavior for such autobiographers, some of them still summoned up the idea of an innocent human nature when they attempted to explain what is debased by contact with society. Lewisohn (1922, p. 245), for example, claimed that what is natural in human beings is noble. The idea of human nature was convenient when trying to explain what is "natural" versus what is "artificial" in human beings.

Components of the Self

In earlier autobiographical models of the self, the relationship among the components of reason, emotions, and will was important in understanding human behavior. But autobiographers who considered the social environment shifted their interest to a contrast between the "real" self and the social self. Some of them also considered the idea that the self may be a multifaceted phenomenon—perhaps even two or more selves.

There are many aspects of the experience of self that can lead people to a feeling of multiple selves. For one, self-awareness involves experiencing the self as both perceiving subject and perceived object. For example, Edward

Bok (1920, p. v), editor of *The Ladies' Home Journal* from 1889 to 1919, wrote, "I have again and again found myself watching with intense amusement and interest the Edward Bok of this book at work." Moreover, it must be an old observation that there are disparities between what people do and what they privately think or feel.[14] And finally, religious writers and others have reported incompatible desires that lead to a sense of more than one self—as Goethe reported in his well-known line from *Faust:* "Two souls, alas! reside within my breast." What was different now, however, was the emphasis placed on the social aspects of a feeling of dual (or multiple) selves.

Psychologists in the late nineteenth century had become interested in the notion of distinct multiple personalities within one person, and they also found it intriguing that persons reported a sense of double selves during the experience of hypnosis—with one self participating and another looking on (Ellenberger 1970; Hilgard 1987). Some commentators began to argue that a feeling of dual selves was normal, and by 1922, an author of an advice manual made this claim: "That every individual possesses a well-defined dual nature is now a thoroughly established scientific fact" (Fielding 1922, p. 1). But it was William James, according to J. H. van den Berg (1974) in his historical study of the concept of "dual selves," who first clearly delineated the idea of multiple selves in a social sense. James ([1890] 1950, 1:294) recognized that "a man has as many social selves as there are individuals who recognize him and carry an image of him in their mind." Here then is what the anthropologist Michelle Rosaldo (1984, p. 146) described as a modern Western model of the self: the opposition of an inner, spontaneous, unique self to a persona "shaped by mask, role, rule, or context." We can relate such a division of the self to the multiplicity of roles in a modern industrial society, which makes it clear that individuals are much more than the "mask" that they wear in any single role (Heine 1971). As Clifford Geertz has suggested, "You can just as easily describe our tremendous emphasis on continuity, sincerity, authenticity, the 'true self' sort of thing, as a reversal of the fact that we are all wearing masks all the time."[15]

Autobiographers, too, began to discuss the idea of dual or multiple selves.[16] Henry Adams ([1906] 1918, p. 433), aware of how the idea of multiple personalities might pertain to all, reported his puzzlement:

> He gathered from the books that the psychologists had, in a few cases, distinguished several personalities in the same mind, each conscious and constant, individual and exclusive . . . The new psychology went further, and seemed convinced that it had actually split personality not only into dualism, but also into complex groups . . . Dualism seemed to have become as common as binary stars. Alternating personalities turned up constantly, even among one's friends.

Sherwood Anderson ([1924] 1969, p. 272) also wrote in his autobiography that "one's body was a house in which had lived two, three, perhaps ten or twelve personalities." Despite their awareness of such an idea, however, few of my autobiographers enthusiastically adopted the idea of many selves. The socially based idea of dual selves was more appealing, that is, the contrast between an inner, sacred self and an outer, social self.[17] Thus Edward Bok (1920, p. v) used this distinction to describe himself: "Edward Bok, editor and publicist, whom I have tried to describe in this book . . . has been a personality apart from my private self."

The "inner" self, in some sense, corresponds with George Herbert Mead's (1934) concept of the "I"—the self as "observer" rather than "observed." As Mead wrote, "[T]he 'I' gives the sense of freedom, of initiative" (p. 177). This inner self is associated with emotion, impulse, and instinct; it involves a person's private feelings and thoughts and thus is the "real" or the "true" self. In the words of the autobiographer Agnes Meyer (1953, p. 188), the inner self is a matter of "demonic passion," "spontaneity," and "freedom." Although the social self varies in response to the social situation, the inner self offers a reassuring sense of continuity.[18]

The sociologist Ralph Turner (1976), in his study of what people mean when they use the idea of a "real self," described a shift in the twentieth century from the belief that a person's real self is manifested when striving to live up to community standards toward the belief that the real self is evidenced by emotions and impulses. We can see this change in emphasis illustrated by looking at autobiographies. The religious and the self-development autobiographers had, in effect, assumed a division between an inferior self dominated by drives and a better self that could control the passions. If they had been conversant with the notion of a "real self," they might have responded that such a real self relates to self-control and the moral obligation of fulfilling one's obligations to others. As S. L. Goldberg (1993, p. 81) observed in his discussion of moral thinking in literature, "That favorite object of many nineteenth-century writers, a 'true' self, alias a 'best' self" was "the will to achieve a perfect moral performance by regulating the ordinary, empirical self."[19] This was the contrast that the editor Albert Jay Nock (1943, p. 292) used when he asserted that "being dichotomous, man is always being put off balance by the promptings of the 'lower and apparent self,' and religion functions as a balancing-pole to bring him into equilibrium again and hold him steady under control of 'the higher and real self.'" Achieving such a real self, consequently, would make human beings more similar to one another.

My twentieth-century autobiographers who used the idea of a real self, however, generally contrasted it to a social self, not to an uncontrolled self dominated by drives. Previously the better self was the one in control of the passions; here it is the one that is less attuned to the demands of society.[20] Such a real self does not bring one into conformity with others; it distinguishes one from the others. By conceptualizing a real self as separate from the outer or social self, it is possible to believe that there is some core untouched by society, some essence, to paraphrase Erving Goffman (1961, p. 152), that is "safe from sociology." The writer Victor Perera (1986, p. 35), for example, emphasized he had an "inviolate private self." Thus one could characterize the types of real selves discussed by Ralph Turner (1976)—institutional self and impulsive self—as freedom from the compulsion of internal passions or freedom from the unreasonable demands of society.

Autobiographers base such an understanding of the real self, in part, on the belief that society does not shape emotions, impulses, or private thoughts (although it may induce a person to hide them). Thus the inner self, which relates to emotions and impulses, is an unsocialized self. What this inner, real self consists of, however, is not obvious since it is not the self as known.[21] Autobiographers such as Agnes Meyer (1953, p. 363) refer to "my innermost self" but don't specify what they mean. What is clearest is that it is not the social self. To attempt to comprehend the nature of this real self, nevertheless, has merit and may become one of the goals of the autobiography—perhaps by "getting in touch with one's feelings."[22]

The "outer" self is the social self. It is this self that is changeable according to the expectations of others, that tries to manage impressions, and that responds to societal expectations of proper behavior. It is this self that accounts for conformity, for dissembling, for "inauthentic" and "fake" smiles, for ritual greetings. Because the nature of the social self is responsive to the situation, it can account for the feeling of multiple selves. With such a viewpoint of the self, it is easy to use metaphors that compare our social selves to actors on the stage—speaking of roles, costumes, performances, and stages as did Erving Goffman (1959).

The social self involves, as the writer Rebecca Harding Davis (1904, pp. 140–41) noted, concealing one's "real" self when under scrutiny of the "public eye." By separating out this social self from the real self, persons can, in effect, offer the disclaimer that their actions done in response to social expectations are not to be judged as part of whom they "really" are (Wuthnow 1987). The behavior of the social self may be explained as a necessary part of community life. "Such a self might also be regarded as adaptive, intelligent, and capable of responding appropriately to shifting environmental conditions," the psychologist Barry Schlenker (1986, p. 21) has commented, "but these more generous judgments are rare." Instead moral worth is reserved for the inner, authentic self.

Some of these autobiographers begin to mention the social interactional skills that constitute the social self. One way to do so was by using still another definition of personality. During the early twentieth century, the term *personality* came to mean not just the distinctive set of behavioral and emotional characteristics of a person, but also a person's "social effectiveness."[23] For example, Cooley, Angell, and Carr (1933, p. 117), in their introductory sociology textbook, stated that "the personality of the individual comprises those qualities which are significant in his association with other people." The psychologist Gordon Allport (1937, pp. ix, viii), therefore, was distressed over the sociological definition of personality as a "man's influence upon others, as his status in the group," and he argued that "the interest of psychology is not in the factors *shaping* personality, rather in personality *itself* as a developing structure." Autobiographers such as Gertrude Atherton (1932, p. 460) began to use this definition that relates to the social self, for example, when she characterized another person as having "little personality." Self-help manuals, too, such as Dale Carnegie's best-selling *How to Win Friends and Influence People* offered advice on managing social interaction and developing "personality" as a social skill.[24]

When it came to discussing their own social skills, however, these autobiographers appear ambivalent. Some made it a point to note their lack of such social skills, for example, describing themselves as "shy," as did the physician Faye Lewis (1971, p. 151) when she recalled that she was "a shy, awkward, uncouth country girl, badly in need of tutoring in social graces, attention to personal appearance, carriage, and manners." Similarly, Yogi Berra (Berra and Fitzgerald 1961, p. 97) described himself as "shy about other people until I got to know them real good." They seemed uneasy with discussions of how they had personally engaged in impression management since such actions might be construed as insincere and based on an excessive concern with the opinions of others. Yet to deny that they did so would be hypocritical and insincere in itself.

For such autobiographers, it was easier to make general remarks on the subject of social selves as did Mark Twain (1924, 2:10): "We are discreet sheep; we wait to see how the drove is going, and then go with the drove. We have two opinions: one private, which we are afraid to express; and another one—the one we use—which we force ourselves to wear to please Mrs. Grundy." But he added no personal examples of how he did so. They also might discuss others in these terms rather than applying such an analysis to their own lives, particularly if they have portrayed themselves as defying social pressures. Thus Ludwig Lewisohn (1922, pp. 223–34) explained why he refused social invitations: "For what was the use of going to places if other people only sent their clothes and manners and left their real selves at home." And Sherwood Anderson ([1924] 1969, p. 21) was writing primarily of his father when he discussed role-playing in everyday life: "My father, like myself, could never be singly himself but must always be playing some rôle, everlastingly strutting on the stage of life in some part not his own." Yet Anderson, after all, does confess here to role-playing, and other autobiographers, in the name of frankness, do admit having engaged in some impression management. The illustrator and editor Alexander King (1958, p. 71), for instance, made this admission: "I am not by nature or character a hypocrite, but when an emergency arises I can be as convincing a phony as the occasion may require."

Finally, a few words about reason and will in this model that postulates an inner and an outer self. Emotions are vitally connected to the inner self and can more easily escape the charge of being influenced by society. But reason, in contrast, could be accused of playing a complicitous role in the social self. As Nietzsche ([1873] 1968, p. 43) put it: "The intellect, as a means for the preservation of the individual, unfolds its chief powers in simulation . . . In man this art of simulation reaches its peak: here deception, flattery, lying and cheating, talking behind the back, posing, living in borrowed splendor, being masked, the disguise of convention, acting a role before others and before oneself." But since these autobiographers did not find their own use of impression management to be a good topic to elaborate in their life stories, such an indictment against reason was not necessary. Some of them did recognize, however, that knowledge and the reasoning process may be shaped by the social context (at least for others). Thus Lincoln Steffens (1931, p. 575) asserted, "I had come so definitely to the conclusion that man's ideas were determined by the teachings of his childhood, by his business interests, by his environment, and not by logic." Such a recognition of the social location of ideas serves as another attack on the possibility of objective reason. But here subjectivity is not so much a matter of a person's particular outlook or history; it is rather something that all community members may share because of their location in a particular culture and era.

In this model of the self, the will does not play an important role. From a sociological perspective, success or failure in the world is not solely a matter of the development of character. The idea of will, nonetheless, was not completely jettisoned. Some autobiographers employed *will* (or self-determination) as a broadened concept—referring to something they could use to resist external influences. Will was necessary, as James Fagan (1912, p. 102) said, to "protect myself from Society and social temptations." Furthermore, although such autobiographers may have argued that they valued impulse, they also continued to recall situations in which they had shown self-control. They valued impulse when they thought of external constraints such as the opinions of other persons, but self-control was important when they thought of drives, desires, compulsions, and certain emotions. They did not want society and convention to rule them, but they did not want to be creatures of impulse either.

Changes in the Self

For the early twentieth-century autobiographers, a theme they could now use in their life stories was their rejection of social influences. The story could be self versus society. In the words of the philosopher Amélie Oksenberg Rorty (1976, p. 316), "Integrity comes to be associated with difference." Here integrity does not refer to the self-control that constitutes character, and difference represents a successful battle against slavish conformity.

From this perspective, early childhood can be conceived as an undisciplined phase of life prior to any significant demands by society. The period before age twelve is a period of "unconscious spontaneity," as Agnes Meyer (1953, p. 27) explained. Young children's behavior may be regarded as authentic; they have not yet learned to engage in role-playing. In the words of Clarence Darrow (1932, p. 77), "The babe is born into the world without any thoughts or inhibitions on any subject. He is equipped with a human organism, and probably a few primitive natural instincts." John Moody ([1933] 1946, p. 37) also used this idea to recall his outlook as a child: "You see my young mind was as yet uncorrupted by the complexities, falsities and warpings of adult experience."

Early twentieth-century autobiographers could easily blend such ideas about uninhibited childhood with evolutionary ideas about natural stages of development, such as those of the psychologist G. Stanley Hall who espoused the recapitulation theory that ontogeny follows phylogeny. Here, however, the "wilderness" stage ends when the child confronts the norms of adult society. As Joseph Kett (1977, pp. 228–29) points out, the child study movement around the turn of the century included an explanation of childhood faults as "the outcome of a collision between natural instincts and arbitrary adult standards." James Fagan (1912, p. 9), for example, characterized his youth as a conflict between "the aboriginal activity and yearning of a hunting and fighting disposition, craving for expression" and the "environment of a determined and methodical plan on the part of a schoolmaster, a minister, and home influences, to turn these half-savage propensities into civilized channels." Thus play is not an idle waste of time or a rehearsal for adult activities; it is a "celebration of freedom."[25]

Childhood may be chronicled as a matter of learning to recognize and then resist the pressures for slavish conformity. Some of these autobiographers admit that they initially succumbed to such influences during childhood.[26] "Young people," the actress Ilka Chase (1941, p. 51) commented, "want to look like peas in a pod, and there is no use trying to make them different." Ludwig Lewisohn (1922, p. 82) also confessed about his childhood, "In one respect only did I fail to achieve a complete conformity. It was in the matter of games." Lewisohn granted that, as a child, he did "absorb, unconsciously, of course, a very large set of moral and social conventions that are basic to the life of the average American" (p. 53). Late adolescence, however, can then be characterized as the time when persons begin to rebel against such pressures. Those who followed the ideas of G. Stanley Hall viewed adolescence as the period of life during which persons develop individualistic traits distinguishing them from others. The artist Thomas Hart Benton (1937, p. 24) described his adolescence as "the inability to conform to accepted behavior patterns, so characteristic of the imaginative in a practical society." Adulthood then brings "maturity"—defined here as the ability to make responsible decisions about one's own behavior with less concern about "fitting in."[27] Autobiographers can display such a mature outlook by writing ironically about their juvenile capitulation to social pressures.

Other autobiographers, however, such as Lincoln Steffens (1931, p. 25), vehemently denied ever succumbing to social pressure—even as a child:

> My pony carried me away not only from business but from the herd also and the herding habits of mind. The tendency of the human animal to think what others think, say what the mob says, do what the leaders do or command, and, generally, go with the crowd, is drilled in deep at school, where the playground has its fashions, laws, customs and tyrannies just as Main Street has. I missed that. I never played "follow the leader," never submitted to the ideals and the discipline of the campus, or, for that matter, of the faculty . . . I could not always face, but I could turn my back on, public opinion.

A similar claim was made by the writer Ellen Glasgow ([1954] 1980, p. 42), who had refused to make the requisite formal debut into Richmond, Virginia, society: "I cannot recall the time when the pattern of society, as well as the scheme of things in general, had not seemed to me false and even malignant."

As I discussed in Chapter 5, some twentieth-century autobiographers have written about the process of searching for the self. A sociological perspective means that they can add to their considerations the effects of society on the self. "The more I traversed 'the terrifying path toward myself,'" mused Agnes Meyer (1953, p. 37), "the more I learned how inescapably I am the child of my clerical forebears and of my Protestant upbringing." To find one's "real" self, one must be aware of the pressures for conformity. As the anthropologist Hortense Powdermaker (1966, pp. 19–20) wrote, "It was part of my growing-up process to question the traditional value and norms of the family and to experiment with behavior patterns and ideologies. This is a not uncommon process of finding one's self."

The Role of Society and Significant Others

Society was now more than the setting for the autobiographers' activities. As Alfred Kazin (1964, p. 216) once observed, "Society is no longer a backdrop to anybody's sensitivity. It is ferocious in its claim on our attention, and so complex as at times to seem a bad dream. We have all suffered too much from society, we are now too aware of what it may do to us." One way that autobiographers have shown their concern with the influence of society on their lives has been by their discussions of "conformity." This term, which can mean "to bring into harmony," here carries a negative connotation of obedience to social standards and a fear of standing out. Autobiographers who discuss conformity usually do not applaud its virtues; instead they scorn the mediocrity of the "common herd" (Atherton 1932, p. 206) or the "lethargic, sheeplike mass" (Chase 1941, p. 277). Rebecca Harding Davis (1904, p. 102), for example, lamented that the "essential duty" for an American had become the necessity "to be one of a majority—to sink himself into the mass."

Such autobiographers may repudiate social conventions or caring about what other people will think of them, and they are not likely to excuse their actions by directly claiming to be a victim of the social environment. Ludwig Lewisohn (1922, pp. 185, 194) disdained the "blind terror of nonconformity" and sneered that "whatever feeble sparks of personality might smoulder here and there are smothered by the morals and beliefs of the mass-life." Agnes Meyer (1953, pp. 154, 29) haughtily denounced "the American steam roller of conformity" and "the stigma which is now frequently placed upon the individual who thinks for himself."[28] It may well be that there have always been rebels against convention, but what is of interest here is how these autobiographers describe such a rebellion as self versus society.[29]

Some of these autobiographers also discuss the connection between society and codes of morality—describing such standards as oppressive and arbitrary. For them, conventional moral codes have their origin in social groups or society (not some transcendental source), and they are a matter of social custom and learning. John Moody ([1933] 1946, p. 207) summarized this viewpoint: "Moral laws, we are being taught nowadays, are but convenient conventions, all right perhaps for our forefathers, but unfitted to this modern age." He was unhappy that "morals have become mere conventions, folkways; always to be revamped to suit the passing spirit of the times" (p. 258). Ludwig Lewisohn (1922, p. 230), who epitomized this attitude, asserted that "we shall not have lovelier private morals until we have destroyed public morality—the fang and claw of Puritan capitalism." And Inagaki Sugimoto (1925, p. 229), in her story of life as an American immigrant, observed, "Our man-made laws of convention have had more power in molding the lives of the people and have left a more lasting stamp on their souls than have our gods." What was to be valued, in contrast, was one's personal moral convictions. Otherwise, much of moral behavior may be an attempt to be respectable and to avoid incurring the disapproval of others. A moral code had greater value if a person created it based on what seemed right to him or her rather than having it socially imposed. Thus Lincoln Steffens (1931, p. 133) reported that he was looking for "an ethics that was not merely a rationalization of folkways and passing laws, forms, and customs."

Attacks on conventional morality and norms sometimes included a debunking of religion, for it was likely that those who wondered about the source and purpose of moral codes might also be skeptical of religious teachings. Clarence Darrow (1932, p. 18) reported that his perspective had changed from his schooldays when he read the McGuffey readers: "Their religious and ethical stories seem silly now, but at that time it never occurred to me that those tales were utterly impossible lies which average children should easily have seen through." Some of these autobiographers maligned the Protestant teachings common in their youth, and they used the term *puritanical* as a reference to carrying self-control too far. Rebecca Harding Davis (1904, p. 94) ridiculed the notion that "most pleasant things in life were . . . supposed to be temptations of the devil," and Ludwig Lewisohn (1922, p. 286) criticized "Puritan barbarism."[30]

These autobiographers also had a new complaint about formal education. On a general level, they might agree that formal education was beneficial and necessary. But for themselves, compulsory education, as an agent of socialization, represented the long arm of society.[31] An advice manual from the 1920s summed it up, "In a sense . . . the school is typical of all these various influencing factors, inasmuch as it represents the dominant spirit of *conformity*" (Fielding 1922, pp. 235–36). Thus the editor Albert Jay Nock (1943, p. 96) spoke of "the magnificent possibilities of the school as an instrument of propaganda." He also described schooling as part of the influence of the "State": "It would be a Sisyphean job to offset the processes of intensive conditioning which the State continually applies to its citizens, beginning from the first day of their conscription into its system of compulsory instruction, and ending on the last day of their lives" (pp. 266–67). And Clarence Darrow (1932, p. 25) alleged that "schools were not established to teach and encourage the pupil to think; beyond furnishing a place for keeping the children out of the way, their effort was to cement the minds of pupils according to certain molds." These autobiographers tended to stress the compulsory and stultifying nature of education rather than the liberating effects that some of the religious autobiographers had feared.

When it came to attributing importance to other persons in their lives, autobiographers now had further reason for discussing "relationships." As the editor Alexander King (1958, p. 350) noted when contemplating what should be in his autobiography, "I can only try not to overlook the circumstances, and particularly, the people who really deeply affected my thoughts and emotions." Others become "significant others"—to use the psychiatrist Harry Stack Sullivan's term. Of particular importance was the idea that others play a part in the formation of one's self-concept and self-esteem.[32]

On the one hand, such autobiographers were likely to denigrate the desire for social approval.[33] An early religious autobiographer, Nancy Towle (1832, p. 21), had also rejected such a concern: "I hence determined, that neither the frowns or the flatteries of mortal worms, should ever move me." But she did so from the perspective that fretting about the good opinion of others distracted her from the critical problem of heavenly salvation. More than a century and a half later, when Paul Monette (1992, p. 236) disparaged his former "ravenous need for approval," he did so because he believed that such concerns led him to mask his true feelings and beliefs. He wrote, "I would say anything to be liked, take on any persona if I thought it would ingratiate me" (p. 236).

On the other hand, intimate relationships are to be valued because of the association between the emotional nature of such bonds and one's "real" self. With one's closest companions, one presumably could drop the social masks and disclose one's real self and one's private thoughts and feelings. Thus Andrew Goldstein (1973, p. 86) wrote in a memoir about the 1960s student movement, "I believe in friends . . . My emotions flow in I and Thou. My sphere is the personal, the tactile." In particular, one's family (at least for males) was a "haven" from the bustle of modern life; home exemplified private life and emotional ties (Lasch 1977). As the lawyer J. W. Arbuckle (1942, p. 152) articulated it, "From this quiet haven each morning have I gone forth." In contrast, life in impersonal society was characterized by some of these autobiographers with such phrases as "the present headlong American race" (Davis 1904, p. 53), "our American rush and hurry" (Richards [1911] 1915, pp. 51–52), and the "material hurrying age" (Hawkes [1915] 1946, p. 104).[34] At home, however, one was not lost in the crowd. From this viewpoint, the emotional aspects of family life—the closeness and the warmth—are good, in contrast to the view of family life that I discussed in the previous chapter, which highlights the hazards of such intimacy.

Autobiographers here have another standard by which to evaluate their parents: the extent of their conformity to social convention. Fathers, in particular, might serve as role models for nonconformity. Clarence Darrow (1932, pp. 7–8) spoke admiringly of this quality in his father, a small-town furniture maker and undertaker: "It is easy for me to believe that my father came of rebel stock; at least he was always in rebellion against religious and political creeds of the narrow and smug community in which he dwelt." And Worden McDonald (1978, p. 30) wrote admiringly of his father's simple acts of resistance: "Papa planted the seeds of rebellion in the minds of his boys. He refused to eat corn flakes, calling them shavings. He said automobiles were ruining the country and that banks, railroads and insurance companies were 'stealing us blind.'" In contrast, the mothers' specialty may have remained, not as a model of nonconformity but as the emotional specialist in the family—which from the perspective of family life as a haven, was good. Autobiographers also might view their parents as agents of society, but I did not find any autobiographers putting it quite this way. Some did, however, speak proudly of youthful rebellion against parental values. Wilmarth Sheldon Lewis (1967, p. 91), a wealthy book collector, assumed that such a rebellion was a natural stage when he described the "struggle between the generations, the oldest in the world, of authority against independence."

Telling the Story

James Fagan (1912) chose to entitle his life history *The Autobiography of an Individualist.* He, like other early twentieth-century autobiographers, pointed out that he was aware of the power of society, but he had personally defied its influence. He painted a portrait of himself as independent, able to resist social pressure, and not overly concerned about the opinion of others—a self-portrait that he must have hoped, ironically, that his readers would find admirable. Such a story of self as nonconformist, however, may present a problem for autobiographers. If they make a distinction between social and real selves, they might wish to eschew the impression management central to the social self. But how can autobiographers remove the "mask of ordinary social intercourse?"—to use the words of the humanistic psychologist Carl Rogers (1970, pp. 27–28).

One answer might be to display the highly valued "real" self to the reader, but the nature of this inner self is not easily discernible. For some autobiographers, revealing one's true self is accomplished by frankly discussing "innermost" thoughts and particularly feelings—part of that "information preserve" kept private or reserved for intimate friends. Autobiographers may use frankness, not so much to ferret out the actual motives for their own actions but to distance themselves from the social self—allowing a consistency between their true feelings and thoughts and the expression of them. They might try to avoid concealing anything for the sake of social norms and inhibitions. Such autobiographers, particularly later in the twentieth century, may also choose to strew their accounts with profanities, in part, to thumb their noses at convention and to provide a more "lifelike" rendering.[35] Autobiographers who want to show the authentic self also might try to distance themselves, as the literary critic John Sturrock (1993, p. 223) has suggested, from "the trickeries of 'style,' which we exploit in order to ingratiate ourselves with strangers." They might even view spontaneous, "artless" writing as more authentic—an idea that harks back to the notion held by some French Romantics that a book, for the sake of spontaneity, should be published without revisions (Furst 1970).

Autobiographers also may openly reflect about the problems of impression management that accompany writing and making public their life stories. They may speak candidly (and by implication, sincerely) to the reader about the problems of constructing a story. As Sturrock (1993, p. 24) also noted, "There is a strand of extreme self-consciousness among some contemporary autobiographers that ought in the future to make any naive practice of the genre impossible." They may engage in role distance—making it clear they have some contempt for the role of autobiographer (Goffman 1961). Yes, they may say to critical readers, we are fully aware we are trying to put ourselves in a good light. They may make a few ironical statements about their self-presentation or toy with the conventions of autobiography. Vladimir Nabokov ([1951] 1966, p. 151), for example, mocked his own autobiographical writing techniques: "Around that time, though, a real romantic adventure did come my way. I am now going to do something quite difficult, a kind of double somersault with a Welsh waggle (old acrobats will know what I mean), and I want complete silence, please."

Some Contemporary Variations

When these autobiographers discussed the meaning of their lives, they confronted, on a personal level, what the philosopher Mitchell Aboulafia (1986, pp. xiii–xiv) has called a contemporary challenge: "To reconcile the apparent truths of modern psychology and sociology—which entail, by and large, deterministic assumptions and conclusions—with the experience of individual autonomy and self-determination." As I have discussed, some early twentieth-century autobiographers avoided what the sociologist Dennis Wrong (1961) has called the "oversocialized viewpoint of man." They preferred to characterize the self as "independent critic and adversary of modern civilization," and they held out for the idea of self-determination in their lives (Sayre 1981, p. 29). By conceptualizing society as an outside force in opposition to an inner self, they could believe that it was possible to resist the influence of society. Although they viewed the independent self as beleaguered by society, they reported their own selves to be strongly fortified.

The more insistent claims of self versus society, however, seem to have been modulated in the latter half of the twentieth century.[36] I find fewer contemporary autobiographers making it a point to denigrate conformity or the "masses," and fewer celebrate the real self. They seem to recognize that they cannot quarrel with the idea that society is a formative influence upon the self—that the dichotomy of self *versus* society is too simple, since no one's thoughts, actions, and emotions can be kept free from sociocultural influences. Virginia Woolf's ([1939] 1976, p. 80) comment in the 1930s is no longer quite so appropriate: "The consciousness of other groups impinging upon ourselves; public opinion; what other people say and think . . . has never been analyzed in any of those Lives which I so much enjoy reading, or very superficially."

Furthermore, if contemporary trends in the human sciences and literary theory continue to be related to changes in autobiography, it is likely that more autobiographers may explore the idea that there is no essential "real self" waiting to be discovered, but rather that persons create their own notion of self (as a symbolical object). Instead of seeing the autobiography as a vehicle to "find" themselves, they may argue that they are "constructing" a self and that they have changeable, situational selves or identities (Eakin 1992; Sturrock 1993). The poet Gloria Anzaldúa (1987, p. iii), for example, described her own life in this way: "Living on borders and in margins, keeping intact one's shifting and multiple identity and integrity, is like trying to swim in a new element, an 'alien' element." Such a postmodern viewpoint also contributes to a reflexiveness about the rhetorical nature of the autobiographical task and a willingness to experiment with the structure of the autobiography. Any radical experimentation with autobiographical form, nevertheless, remains unusual. Many readers today apparently continue to prefer autobiographies that aspire to being a subcategory of history.[37] The literary critic Ira Nadel (1987, pp. 131, 133) has argued along these lines that the "narrative and structural conservatism" of the general category of biography account for its increasing popularity among readers, who are uncomfortable with contemporary experimental techniques in novels such as "narrative discontinuity, erratic time-shifts, and complex methods of characterization, [which] present a world divorced from the empirical experiences of the reader."

In recent decades, as commentators have increasingly raised the issues of multiculturalism and identity politics, another contemporary variation for some American autobiographers has been a focus on the perplexing question of identity—how group identities (race, ethnicity, gender, or sexual orientation) contribute to the self an essential quality that is not the result of socialization and is a crucial part of self-definition. This interest in group-based identity is part of a broader change that the sociologist Nathan Glazer (1975, p. 177) and others have observed since the mid-1960s, when it became increasingly popular for Americans to identify themselves as a member of a particular ethnic group rather than simply say, "I am an American."[38] This trend has included later-generation white ethnics, for whom active ethnic identification is symbolic and voluntary, and those nonwhite, for whom identification with ethnicity or race, from the standpoint of wider society, is ascribed and not an option (Gans 1979; Waters 1990). Those who are interested in telling a life story that emphasizes ethnic identity are more likely to be from the latter group, and their contributions have helped raise critical interest in autobiographies as a vehicle for members of marginalized groups now to tell their own stories. A focus on identity means that these autobiographers are likely to reflect on the question of what is innate in the self and what is imposed. Some of them develop an essentialist model of the self, while also acknowledging the influence of society upon that self.

Despite many differences between and within these groups, some members of marginalized groups, when writing their autobiographies, have adopted a similar approach that contains significant divergences from earlier models of the self. For one, identity becomes a key term—in particular, ethnic identity. The concept of identity has come into widespread use since it was promoted in the 1950s by the work of Erik Erikson ([1950] 1963, p. 282), who noted that "we begin to conceptualize matters of identity at the very time in history when they become a problem." Philip Gleason (1992,

p. 140), in recounting the history of the term *identity*, has suggested that the word became popular because it related to developing concerns about the effects on the individual of living in a mass society. That is, what are sources of identity within a mass society? What differentiates human beings from one another in such a society, and, in particular, is ethnicity a significant difference? Erikson (1975, p. 43) argued that the terms *identity* and *identity crisis* "seemed naturally grounded in the experience of emigration, immigration, and Americanization" as new Americans were expected to "merge their ancestral identities in the common one of self-made men."

But what "ethnic identity" means is not an easy question. A topic worth investigating, therefore, is how autobiographers make use of the idea of ethnic, racial, or other group identities. What are their stories about differences and similarities among human beings? Gleason (1992, p. 131) observed that psychologists and sociologists have defined the term *identity* differently—with psychologists emphasizing "something internal that persists through change," and sociologists defining it as an "artifact of interaction between the individual and society." He added that we can find this same difference in explanations of ethnic identity. That is, is ethnicity biologically rooted and an immutable aspect of self, or is ethnicity a socially defined category? To what extent is ethnic identity a matter of choice? Autobiographers who use the terms *ethnic identity* or *ethnicity* must confront, on some level, the question of what they mean. Does such an identity stem from a shared genetic inheritance—some biological component that each group member has and that outsiders do not? Does it imply a Lamarckian notion of the biological inheritance of cultural traits? Is it based only on a shared culture? A common experience of oppression? Is ethnicity primarily a useful label? Or is ethnic identity based on a combination of these things?

It is understandably appealing for autobiographers who wish to emphasize their ethnic identity to argue that such differences are innate—for if ethnicity is a matter of culture only, these differences can disappear through the process of assimilation.[39] As George De Vos (1975, p. 10) has noted in his book on ethnic identity, "Some sense of genetically inherited differences, real or imagined, is part of the ethnic identity of many groups." Thus, for some autobiographers, the term *ethnicity*, common since it was first used in this sense in the 1940s, connotes something inborn and essential.[40] Those who use the notion of ethnic or racial identity appear to prefer the term *identity* over the concept of self, which, as the sociologist Stanford Lyman (1994) has pointed out, often connotes individuality. The term *self* may be associated with individual differences (while also being something that everyone has), but the relational term *identity* can be used to refer to what is common among members of a group and how that group is different from others. Gloria Anzaldúa (1987, p. 18) commented in her autobiographical writings, "The individual exists first as kin—as sister, as father, as *padrino*—and last as self."

The question then arises: What do group members share? What is the basis for ethnic identity? We can see the difficulty of answering these questions in comments such of those of Ruben Navarrette, Jr. (1993, pp. xiv, 110), in *A Darker Shade of Crimson: Odyssey of a Harvard Chicano,* when he writes of ethnicity as "something over which I have no control" and of his culture as "a part of my soul really." Also the writer Richard Rodriguez (1982, pp. 5, 7), alongside his efforts to avoid casting himself as "a typical Hispanic-American life," hinted at a biological inheritance: "I assume I retain certain features of gesture and mood derived from buried lives." In a later article, Rodriguez (1989, pp. 8–9) offered this definition of ethnicity: "Memory, response, attitude, mood, coded into the soul, transmitted through generations." He allowed, however, that the term was perhaps only a "public metaphor . . . for a knowledge that bewilders us." Leaving the term *ethnicity* loosely defined allows people considerable latitude when making use of it (Cohen 1993).

Autobiographers writing about ethnic identity may connect such identity to elements of culture such as religion, food preferences, or customs such as holiday celebrations that distinguish the group from others. Anzaldúa (1987, p. 61) wrote that "there are more subtle ways that we internalize identification, especially in the forms of images and emotions. For me food and certain smells are tied to my identity, to my homeland." In particular, it is easy to associate eating together and sharing distinctive foods with intimacy and kinship. Rodriguez (1982, p. 160) recounts how, as an adult, he searched for "evidence of our 'cultural ties'" as he ate dinner with his parents.

A shared language, different from that of the majority group, also can serve as a basis for ethnic identification. Such a language is a barrier to assimilation, and it represents a clearly perceived difference from the majority. Even group members who cannot speak the language may use it as a symbol of ethnicity constituting a fundamental link between themselves and the group (De Vos 1975). This point was particularly a theme of Rodriguez's (1982) autobiography as he meditated on the connection between language and a sense of intimacy. He described how he associated Spanish, learned at home in early childhood, with family ties. In this vein, Anzaldúa (1987, p. 54) offered this quotation: "Who is to say that robbing a people of its language is less violent than war?"

These autobiographers, therefore, may write of ethnic or racial identity as a bond—connecting culture with the shared experiences, similarities, and natural ties of kinship. As the anthropologist Manning Nash (1989, p. 4) has written, "Ethnic ties have been bundled together with other kinds of deep, core, and primary bonds suffused with affect into a category of 'primordial' ties." Nash added that such an idea is inviting: "Finally, the self has a home, with a past, a present, and a future transcending the fragile biological vessel that is its container." This link between culture and identity implies that the relationship is more than common beliefs and customs. The sociologist Ali Rattansi (1995, p. 258) points out that "appeals to ethnicity and cultural difference, by invoking ideas of shared origin, 'kith and kin,' and 'nation' may in fact smuggle in quasi-biological conceptions." We can see this essentialist link when we ask whether anyone could become a member of such a group by simply adopting their culture.

For those who wish to stress ethnic identity, a shared group history becomes a pertinent topic in their autobiographies, enabling them to understand themselves and their links with the past. Stephen Butterfield (1974, pp. 2–3) and others have observed this to be the case in many African American autobiographies: "The 'self' of black autobiography . . . is not an individual with a private career . . . The self is conceived as a member of an oppressed social group, with ties and responsibilities to the other members." Thus, from the subtitle of newspaper reporter Nathan McCall's (1994) autobiography, *Makes Me Wanna Holler: A Young Black Man in America,* we might assume that we are to take his life as representative of a larger category. Or, as Eldridge Cleaver (1968, p. 15) wrote, "I understood that what had happened to me had also happened to countless other blacks." Although such autobiographers may tell of their individual histories, their stories also are balanced by a story of group identity. What the literary critic Genaro Padilla (1993, p. 6) argues about Chicano autobiography applies more generally—in these stories "individual experience and collective historical identity are inextricably bound."

These autobiographers may include, as part of group history, descriptions of how group members have been marginalized and confronted with prejudice, discrimination, and institutional racism. They may cite historical events such as the *Brown* Supreme Court decision (Gates 1994), the civil rights movement, the Chinese Exclusion Act (Fong-Torres 1994), the murder of Emmett Till in 1955 (Hunter-Gault 1992), or the Allan Bakke case (Navarrette 1993). McCall (1994, p. 198) also protested that "the story of Africans brought here as slaves was summed up in our history books in a few short paragraphs, almost as a footnote." And Navarrette (1993, p. 6) lamented that "much of my generation has no knowledge whatsoever of the forms of educational malpractice inflicted upon Mexican-Americans in just this century." Such autobiographers may supply concrete examples of how kith and kin have suffered from discrimination. Rodriguez (1982, p. 120) told of the frustration of his father's youthful dreams of being an engineer. And McCall (1994, p. 84) observed that "the only job contacts *our* parents had—if they had any contacts at all—were for manual-labor jobs."

The responsibility of telling about group history as a part of their personal histories gives such autobiographers a reason to avoid using their life stories to explore the notion of truth and their ability to tell it, or to develop the idea that the self is something they create (Olney 1985). They may treat autobiography as history rather than art to accentuate that they are presenting the facts and the truth of personal experience. They may even use a few footnotes (uncommon in autobiographies) to mark as facts those events that are a part of group history. Taking a documentary approach is not essential, however, for autobiographers such as Maxine Hong Kingston (1976) and Gloria Anzaldúa (1987) have experimented with the form and content of conventional autobiography—using dreams, poetry, and so forth—to develop innovative ways of portraying the self.

This understanding of ethnic identity as something essential or inherent within a person, however, has been the subject of considerable debate. K. Anthony Appiah (1994, p. 156), for example, has written that "one reasonable ground for suspicion of much contemporary multicultural talk is that it presupposes conceptions of collective identity that are remarkably unsubtle in their understandings of the processes by which identities, both individual and collective, develop." Essentialist notions of identity can be contrasted with the approach of those social scientists who consider ideas such as race and ethnicity to be concepts that have been historically and culturally defined (Omi and Winant 1986), and who regard identities as socially constructed categories rather than biologically rooted ties. They generally argue that the concept of ethnic identity is a politically useful vehicle around which to organize as a part of "identity politics" (Lyman and Douglass 1973). What is important from this perspective is not whether there is some objective basis for linking members of the group, but whether persons perceive themselves as belonging to a group and how this affects their actions.

This instrumentalist view of ethnicity has been the direction for many social scientists following the influential ideas of the anthropologist Fredrik Barth (1969), but this is not so clearly the case for autobiographers, who are more likely to find the notion of essential identities and primordial connections attractive. Those who feel that group identity is a crucial part of their self-definition are not apt to assert that such a group identity is only a symbol to be used tactically, or that identities are socially constructed categories. The emotional association of ethnic identity with kinship and community must make it feel like much more than a strategy.

Yet these autobiographers' ideas on self and identity are complex, for they also acknowledge social influences on the self such as the role that the dominant culture plays in the perception of their group as different. Even those who primarily advocate an essentialist notion of self are also keenly aware of the ways in which ethnic identity is not only a matter of primordial ties and personal identification, but also a social identity that has been ascribed to them by others. They ask not only who are we by nature, but also, what has been imposed on us? Gloria Anzaldúa (1987, p. 16), for example, writes, "Culture forms our beliefs. We perceive the version of reality that it communicates."

Stories emphasizing ethnic identity are likely to include the autobiographers' discovery of the influence of the dominant culture on their lives. As many commentators have observed, members of a marginalized group have particular reason to be conscious of the influence of society upon the self. In W. E .B. Du Bois's ([1903] 1961, pp. 16–17) often-quoted words, "It is a peculiar sensation, this double-consciousness, this sense of always looking at one's self through the eyes of others, of measuring one's soul by the tape of a world that looks on in amused contempt and pity." A turning point, therefore, may be the distressing moment in childhood when these autobiographers realized that the dominant culture makes something of differences in their skin color or their ethnic origins. Ruben Navarrette (1993, p. xiii), for example, offered this recollection: "One day, in kindergarten, I walked home from school and confronted my mother with a fundamental question. I told her that there were some children at school whose skin was white and others whose skin was brown. Mine, I noted, was a confused shade of beige. Turning to my mother, I demanded an explanation. 'What am I?'"

Conformity is a topic for these autobiographers, but they discuss it as pressure on the group for assimilation. "We know what it is to live," wrote Anzaldúa (1987, pp. 63–64), "under the hammer blow of the dominant *norteamericano* culture." McCall (1994, p. 232), too, cynically recollected advice that others had given him about "fitting in": "Some professors said that to make it in white mainstream America we had to assimilate, to study the white man and learn his rules." This is a different approach from that of earlier immigrant (usually European) autobiographers who were eager to tell a story of becoming an American. In contrast, these contemporary autobiographers may interpret the idea of assimilation—particularly the disturbing metaphor of losing all distinctiveness in a melting pot—as deterministic on a personal level because of the changes in behavior necessary to accomplish such an integration. As the philosopher Peter Caws (1994, p. 371) has observed, "It has come to be a familiar claim of some advocates of multiculturalism that a culture of one's own (that is, one not imposed from without) is one of the conditions for the achievement of an authentic identity." In this spirit, Navarrette (1993, p. 85) recalled his days as a student at Harvard University: "Resisting assimilation, I wanted to be noticed, seen as different. I wore my ethnicity as a badge." From this standpoint, they may single out formal education as an institution that serves society by exacting conformity—inducing children, in Rodriguez's (1982, p. 72) words, to become "culturally separated" from their parents.

These autobiographers may mildly reproach their parents and their elders for acceding to negative stereotypes or giving in too easily to pressures to assimilate. McCall (1994, p. 12), for example, commented, "Without knowing what they were doing, a lot of adults in black families passed along notions to their young about white folks' superiority." And he added that his stepfather supposed that "you had to ignore all the shit that white people dished out and learn to swallow pride for survival's sake." Navarrette (1993, p. 51) also tells his readers, "I should say that I have never liked hearing either of my parents refer to themselves as 'dumb,' although they are only parroting what they were told so often by so many for so long." Such a critique of parents is quite different from other contemporary autobiographers who complain of dysfunctional families, and it is undertaken from a compassionate viewpoint—excusing one's elders, as did McCall, for not "knowing what they were doing." These autobiographers, espousing the benefits of kinship, are less likely to emphasize family dynamics as important in shaping the self. The more germane problems are at the societal level. Thus James McBride (1996, p. 264) wrote, "Most black folks considered 'finding myself' a luxury." Furthermore, they may wish to avoid perpetuating or fostering any unfavorable stereotypes of their family life.

Another sociological topic for these autobiographers is their dismay at the role-playing to which they have had to resort as a survival skill. Like other twentieth-century autobiographers, they are making reference to a social self. McCall (1994, p. 85) used the idea of multiple social selves when he explained, "The construction job forced me to develop two personalities that kept me in conflict with myself: Away from work I was the baad-assed nigger who demanded respect; on the job I was a passive Negro who let the white man push him around. The suppression of my pride tore me up inside and messed with my head in a big way." He added that "they seldom knew what I *really* thought and felt about things, and I made sure they got few chances to find out." McCall also discussed how "there were always two conversations floating in my head when I interacted with whites. There was what I *thought* and what I *said.* Practically everything I said was calculated to counter some stereotype whites hold about blacks" (p. 253). Such autobiographers may view role-playing as a betrayal of identity, notwithstanding some pride and even glee at fooling those who deserve it. Eldridge Cleaver (1968, p. 103) criticized any black person who would chose "to pretend to be something other than his true self in order to please the white man and thus receive favors."

These autobiographers do not write in terms of self versus society but of the differences between their group and the dominant culture, even though this opposition is played out for them on an individual level. They may express the fear that pressures to assimilate will suppress their own unique culture and consequently the basis of their identity. Here it is the group identity that is beleaguered, not just the self alone. The group identity is the true identity that must first be recognized and then protected. Malcolm X (1964, p. 163), for example, could refer to black persons as having "absolutely no knowledge of [their] true identity." Such autobiographers may argue for cultural pluralism—preserving group identity—rather than assimilation.[41] Nathan Glazer (1975, p. 177), summarizing the transformation of the civil rights movement in the 1960s and 1970s, described a "striking change" in the rhetoric of African Americans from "'we are like everyone else and want only integration,' to 'we are of course different from anyone else.'"[42] At the same time, they may not perceive their own culture as an imposition since they are connecting it with primordial ties.

One particularly important way in which society influences the self, from this perspective, is its effect on how persons think of themselves. These autobiographers, like many sociologists and psychologists in the twentieth century, have come to stress the importance of *self-concept* and *self-esteem* in human behavior. For the purposes of self-understanding, they deem it necessary to discuss the influence of society (i.e., the dominant culture or the dominant "discourse") and others in their thinking about themselves. Such a viewpoint fits in Butterfield's (1974) observation that twentieth-century black autobiographers have turned from the topic of oppression at the level of the social system to a discussion of oppression at the level of culture. They see a close link between self-esteem and the respect and recognition given to their group (Gleason 1992). This belief that it is "healthy" to have a positive estimation of self is a position we can contrast with the misgivings of the religious autobiographers about self-regard.

Such writers may bitterly describe how the opinions of others have shaped how they have thought and felt about themselves. They may discuss how they initially had internalized negative stereotypes of their own group and had fallen victim to self-hatred. Nathan McCall (1994, p. 199) concluded, "Without realizing it, we'd been taught to hate ourselves and love white people, and it was causing us to self-destruct." McCall wrote about what he called his "fragile" self-esteem, and he made this comment about himself and his friends during his adolescence: "On some level deeper than we realized, we hated the hell out of ourselves" (pp. 33, 48). Ruben Navarrette (1993, p. 13) also related an insensitive comment made to him by his high school principal: "He was most likely completely unaware of the sting in his words and the damage that they had done to the self-image of a young man whose talent and arrogance was supposed to make him immune to such pain." And Lorene Cary (1991, p. 5), who wrote of her experience attending St. Paul's prep school, described her "self-loathing" and reported that "in the aftermath of Black is Beautiful, I began to feel black and blue, big and black, black and ugly. Had they done that to me? Had somebody else? Had I let them?"

A lesson to be learned from the lives of these autobiographers, however, is that such problems of self-esteem can be actively corrected. As Gloria Anzaldúa (1987, p. 87) declared, "I seek new images of identity, new beliefs about ourselves, our humanity and worth no longer in question." They may explain that negative evaluations of them within the dominant culture are arbitrary, have no universal standing, and are a reflection of power relations. Despite contemporary complaints, therefore, that too many people claim to be "victims" (Sykes 1992), these autobiographers do not simply adopt this stance for it is a deterministic attribution with connotations of passivity.[43] As part of the politics of identity, group members choose to counter the effects of the dominant culture's stereotypes—not only as a group but on a personal level as well. Thus Navarrette (1993, p. 21) wrote, "At stake, I realized for the first time, was not only my own pride and self-image but also the dignity and progress of a whole race of people." These autobiographers argue that group members must adopt an affirmative outlook on this essential part of the self. McCall (1994, p. 158) explained, it is "a universal principle: that if you change your self-perception, you can change your behavior." Anzaldúa (1987, p. 87), too, maintained that "awareness of our situation must come before inner changes, which in turn come before changes in society."

The autobiography itself may serve as a declaration of freedom from the perspective of the dominant culture, a celebration of the importance of group identity and its significance in one's personal identity, and a demand for respect for one's group and an acceptance of diversity from the wider society. Although some commentators have interpreted the genre of autobiography, as Paul John Eakin (1992, p. 78) observed, as "a stale exercise in a discredited bourgeois mythology" based on Western masculine notions of individuality and achievement, these authors have not rejected it as a form of cultural hegemony but instead adopted it as a means for telling their own stories. They also may hope to educate readers who have not experienced marginalization. Thus, Gloria Anzaldúa (1987, p. 85) wrote: "We need to say to white society: We need you to accept the fact that Chicanos are different, to acknowledge your rejection and negation of us. We need you to own the fact that you looked upon us as less than human, that you stole our lands, our personhood, our self-respect." These autobiographers may explain to their readers what the experience of prejudice and discrimination feels like: "What it was like to be considered less intelligent, less capable, less, less, less by a system . . . " (Navarrette 1993, p. 21).[44] At the same time, they may resist the expectations of readers who hope to be entertained with stories of "authentic" differences (Trinh 1989).

For now, it appears these autobiographers cannot easily ignore relationships with the dominant culture in telling a story of the self; they may be criticized by members of their own group if they do so. As Stephen Butterfield (1974, p. 286) wrote several decades ago: "A future problem for black autobiography to solve may be how to confront human existence without the shadow of the white man—without relying on him, as *diabolus ex machina,* to condition, by negative example, the meaning of a life well lived." Thus Nathan McCall (1994, p. 336) made this observation:

> I can't get past race because white folks won't let me get past it. They remind me of it everywhere I go. Every time I step in an elevator and a white woman bunches up in the corner like she thinks I wanna rape her, I'm forced to think about it. Every time I walk into stores, the suspicious looks in white shopkeepers' eyes make me think about it. Every time I walk past whites sitting in their cars, I hear the door locks clicking and I think about it.

Such autobiographers, as a consequence, combine personal story with cultural critique.

Some of them, despite their emphasis on ethnic identity, also may balk at the notion of a blanket conformity *within* the group and emphasize differences there as well. As they think of how they are similar to group members, they are likely to think of how they are different as well. Even as they feel drawn toward the benefits of community, they may want to distinguish themselves as individuals. Henry Louis Gates, Jr. (1994, pp. xii–xiii), writes of the feeling of "resentment at being lumped together with thirty million African Americans whom you don't know and most of whom you will never know." And such autobiographers may be uneasy with an uncritical idealization of their own culture. Gloria Anzaldúa (1987, p. 21), for example, wrote, "I abhor some of my culture's ways, how it cripples its women." Furthermore, multiple group memberships and identities such as gender, social class, generation, sexual orientation, and religion may draw persons in conflicting directions. These autobiographers may feel a tension between writing a story of "us" as compared with "me," or a story of ethnic identity as opposed, for example, to the identities of "American" or "woman." Any identity such as "black" or "woman" is an ideal type in the sense that it glosses over significant differences between individuals.

Ethnic identity may be particularly powerful, but it is not a person's only identity. Shelby Steele (1988, pp. 43–44), who has written about the "double bind of middle-class blacks," argues that ethnic consciousness has often required that "differences within the race, no matter how ineradicable, had to be minimized," and thus "class distinctions were one of the first such differences to be sacrificed." Similarly, Richard Rodriguez (1982, p. 5) wrote, "Perhaps because I am marked by indelible color they easily suppose that I am unchanged by social mobility, that I can claim unbroken ties with my past." He rejected the burden of being taken as a spokesperson for an ethnic community solely by virtue of his perceived membership in that group, and he added, "But I write of one life only. My own" (p. 7).

As group members achieve material success in society, as Steele (1988, p. 42) has observed, they may adopt values that could be seen as assimilationist and individualistic—"the work ethic, the importance of education, the value of property ownership, of respectability, of 'getting ahead,' of stable family life, of initiative, of self-reliance." This success then creates another sense of double identity (Butterfield 1974). Ruben Navarrette (1993, pp. 74, xiii), as part of what he called an "elite group of young Chicanos," described himself as being pulled in different directions: wishing "to honor tradition, even if [we] first had to reinvent it," and yet, he also wrote of his "unassuming middle-class existence, a reward for my parents' many years of hard work and sacrifice. I have soft hands and even softer experiences . . . And I only occasionally eat tortillas, these days feeling equally at home in a Chinese restaurant as in a Mexican one." Henry Louis Gates (1994, p. xv) also wrote eloquently about feeling divided:

> I want to be black, to know black, to luxuriate in whatever I might be calling blackness at any particular time—but to do so in order to come out the other side, to experience a humanity that is neither colorless nor reducible to color. Bach *and* James Brown. Sushi *and* fried catfish. Part of me admires those people who can say with a straight face that they have transcended any attachment to a particular community or group . . . but I always want to run around behind them to see what holds them up.

These autobiographers agree, in essence, that the dichotomy of self versus society is too simple. They, too, try to balance any deterministic explanations of human behavior—be it internalization of societal expectations, the influence of societal definitions, or biological connections—with ideas of self-determination as well. At least in the case of the effects of society on the self, it remains easier to ascertain such effects in others. More than a century ago, John Stuart Mill ([1873] 1969, pp. 101–2) observed in his autobiography: "What a relief it would be if I could disbelieve the doctrine of the formation of character by circumstances . . . it would be a blessing if the doctrine of necessity could be believed by all [with respect to] the character of others, and disbelieved in regard to their own." The idea of a core executive self that is independent, stable, and self-determining has its abiding attractions for many American autobiographers.

Chapter Seven ONCLUSION:

THE AUTOBIOGRAPHY AS MORAL PERFORMANCE

> *For this is the instructive part of such moral communications, that a man*
> *may learn how it has gone with others, and what he also has to expect from life . . .*
> *If such knowledge is of little use for avoiding evils, it is very serviceable so far as it*
> *qualifies us to understand our condition, and bear or even to overcome it.*
> GOETHE

The genre of autobiography provides us with a valuable written record of how people have thought about the self. By comparing autobiographies over time, we can behold the diversity in this bountiful feast of self-narratives, yet we also can see clearly how these stories of unique lives necessarily link to a larger cultural discourse about the self. We discern the individual voices of the autobiographers, but we also discover culture speaking through the self. These self-narratives, however, have even more to offer when we also recognize them as rhetorical accomplishments. Autobiographers use vocabularies of the self, not only to make sense of their lives but also to present a praiseworthy self to their audiences. They are negotiating their place in relation to cultural norms and values. We can see them do so, for example, when they try to avoid obvious boasting, when they declare they are telling the truth, and when they worry about wasting their readers' time with an uninteresting story. Autobiographies, therefore, give us an opportunity to examine the complex interplay of the micro level of social situation (as autobiographers strategically relate themselves to norms and values) with the macro level of the historical and cultural vocabularies of the self.

This larger cultural discourse furnishes not only ideas about the nature of selfhood but also evaluative standards for model selves and model lives. Autobiographers show us which evaluative standards they are attempting to meet as they offer the stories of their lives publicly. They are aware that others will evaluate their actions, and the potential for feeling pride, shame, or embarrassment as a result gives them good reason to try to guide the readers' judgments of their lives. From this perspective, we can understand Philip Roth's (1988, p. 172) claim that autobiography is "probably the most manipulative of all literary forms," or the literary critic John Sturrock's (1993, p. 19) more kindly worded assessment that autobiography is "the most sociable of literary acts."

Autobiographers offer a public explanation of how they have led their lives. To tell their life stories, they must speak of their beliefs, actions, intentions, choices, and goals. Because they pursued such goals and actions in a social context where others may be harmed or helped, their actions and intentions become moral topics. They demonstrate the truth of Charles Taylor's (1988, p. 298) observation that "selfhood and the good, or in another way selfhood and morality, turn out to be inextricably intertwined themes." Autobiographers need not moralize explicitly or develop a coherent moral philosophy. But when they discuss choices made, emotions felt, and goals pursued, they know that these discussions relate to shared ideals of what is honest, brave, just, kind, and responsible in one's relationships with others.

They are engaging in morality talk that helps to articulate, sustain, or challenge these standards. They are accounting in their autobiographies for their choices and actions—not just in terms of personal goals achieved or personal problems solved but also in response to prevailing moral values. Moreover, they are trying to do so with a narrative whose construction also reflects favorably on them. Because they position themselves in terms of public evaluative standards of what is good and admirable, we can think of autobiographies as moral performances. If they have differed from such standards, they will usually offer an explanation and try to negotiate, in effect, why they ought not to be judged harshly. As Jerome Bruner (1990, p. 121) concluded, "The Self as narrator not only recounts but justifies." [1]

By examining vocabularies of the self over time and in relation to culture, we can see the range of issues that persons have found vital for understanding the self. We can perceive what their concerns are and what they value; what questions they ask and what answers they give. Vocabularies of the self vary, as I have detailed, yet there are also general existential issues that autobiographers must confront, regardless of culture or historical location, simply because life is lived in the company of others. Topics such as self-control, responsibility for one's own actions, and the relative importance of will, reason, and emotion in decision making have moral significance because one's behavior has consequences for others. These issues, likewise, are important in other human institutions, such as the law, political constitutions, education, and religion. Autobiographers describe the working out of such issues in concrete lives.

A key moral issue for these American autobiographers, both explicitly and implicitly, has been how much responsibility they can take for their behavior and for the course of their lives. How freely did they choose their actions in life? For what can they be held accountable? As Hannah Solomon ([1946] 1974, p. 3), a founder of the National Council of Jewish Women, asked as she began her autobiography: "Do we start our pilgrimage conditioned by patterns already ingrained? How far do fate and chance mold our behavior and our lives?" To have some concept of moral responsibility, persons must be able, to some extent, to choose between alternative courses of action and then act on those choices. These autobiographers aim at a conception of human beings that accords them dignity and grants them considerable autonomy in directing their own behavior. Yet they have no simple notion of what freedom means in terms of human conduct, and they may not wish to take responsibility for all their actions. So it becomes important for them to contemplate general questions about human autonomy using contemporary as well as time-honored ideas about what can fetter a person's responsibility for his or her own behavior.

Within the general issue of responsibility for one's actions, there are several auxiliary questions. One is to ask what detracts from persons' responsibility for their behavior. What is done voluntarily and what is out of a person's control? When can persons excuse or justify their behavior? These questions allow a distinction between what persons do and what they intended to do. To assess what is moral in persons' actions, it is necessary to consider what might cause them to act in ways other than they intended. As the sociologist Robert Wuthnow (1987, p. 77) observed, "Moral codes that survive for any length of time are likely to include some way of limiting responsibility." Such limiting factors include what we loosely call "internal" and "external" determinants of human behavior. To what extent, it may be asked, are all persons' actions governed by internal biological factors such as emotions, passions, desires, drives, heredity, or "human nature"? Can emotions, for example, overwhelm a person's reason, as in a "crime of passion"? If autobiographers believe that internal elements such as drives are deterministic, then a key issue becomes that of self-control. In addition, one may ask to what extent are persons' behavior determined by external factors such as God, the devil, Divine Providence, fate, chance, or the social environment?

The nineteenth-century religious autobiographers pondered the effect of both external and internal determinants on their behavior. The most powerful extramundane determinant was that of God's plan for them, and some of them also wrote of Satan holding an insidious and formidable sway over their lives. They might have fatalistically maintained that they had no control over such forces, thereby trying to absolve themselves of responsibility, but, as Max Weber ([1904] 1958) has shown, their thought was not this simple. For them, the problem of what is voluntary in a person's behavior as opposed to what is compelled was an indispensable issue when explaining their life stories. For what, if anything, could they take credit in their histories? We can see the answers given to this question change among Protestant autobiographers as religious doctrine placed greater weight on the role of human effort and works in achieving salvation.

Internal determinants also were an essential part of the religious autobiographers' explanation of human behavior. They described the self-interested "passions" that drive human beings, and they depicted a struggle between personal desires and the need to curb such "appetites" in order to live a morally responsible life with others. Some commentators, such as Charles Taylor (1988, p. 303), have argued that "self-control is a basic theme of our whole moral tradition," and we can see how important regulation of the passions was for these autobiographers. But if we call it self-control in this case, we would be overlooking the complexity of this issue for them. Although self-control can result in an admirable restraint of self-indulgent behavior, the concept also implies what was for many of them a misplaced pride in human ability. It was commendable to curb "animal appetites," but the dilemma was how to accomplish this if, indeed, human beings are inherently weak creatures in need of God's assistance. Furthermore, how could they reconcile the idea of self-control with the belief that Divine Providence governed their lives? They described the self, therefore, as if it were a morality play with a battle between good and evil, but a deus ex machina was necessary to accomplish the miraculous transformation of self.

These nineteenth-century religious autobiographers had to display their humility by admitting their sins and by avoiding the hubris of claiming self-mastery through unaided willpower. Since humility can be feigned or a matter of self-deception, they insisted that emotion be an essential part of a religious conversion—if sorrow for one's sins came "from the heart," it more likely was genuine. They portrayed emotion (including the passions) as a powerful motivator—impelling a person to do good as well as evil. In addition, these religious autobiographers tried to avoid any conceit at being one of God's chosen. Rather than emphasizing their singularity, they stressed a common human nature—a theme that did not exonerate them of the burden of sin but which did, at least, democratize the problem.

In contrast, the nineteenth-century autobiographers who told a story of self-development appeared confident that whatever internal forces impelled them could be managed by the mustering of willpower. They also did not see any external determinants of significant concern, and they did not believe it laudable to resign themselves passively to God's will for the direction of their lives. They seemed eager in their stories to claim autonomy and responsibility for themselves. Yet, at the same time, they were far from describing such a mastery of self as effortless or as the result of unique talents. They still accorded significant strength to the passions, but they claimed that self-indulgent desires could be governed by exercising the faculty of will. Such self-control and self-development could be achieved, as they explained it, by anyone.

What was admirable in persons, from this perspective, were not their unique accomplishments but how such accomplishments confirmed that they had "worked hard," and these autobiographers hoped that their accounts demonstrated that they deserved praise for this virtue. They argued that once the exertion of willpower required for self-control was habitual, a person had character. A habit, which can be demeaned as automatic and unthinking behavior, had moral worth, therefore, if it was established through determined effort and brought beneficial results. For these autobiographers, the best self was a master of fate responsible for his (and her) own behavior and development, and a worthy story described the cultivation of such a self.

In the late nineteenth century, the focus of psychologists and others on motivation and the instincts, drives, and other "automatic" tendencies that may be inborn in human beings raised further doubts about the intentionality of human behavior. How important are such "tendencies" in compelling human behavior? Is it possible that human beings are motivated by drives or instincts to a greater extent than they had recognized? If this were so, a model of the self featuring self-control, will, and character would be unrealistic. Thus autobiographers since the late nineteenth century have delved deeper into the question of human motivation by considering the influence of heredity, instincts, drives, or the "unconscious" upon how they have lived their lives. For them, the nature of the self was less certain than it had been for the religious or the self-development autobiographers, and writing an autobiography appeared to be a more difficult task. The sustained consideration of self that such a writing task required, however, might accomplish the worthy goal of coming to a more thorough understanding of the motives, both rational and irrational, for their actions and choices.

These autobiographers, too, confronted the issue of self-control. They asserted, however, that it was possible for human beings to engage in too much self-control—that repression of instincts, impulses, or emotions could be unhealthy. From this viewpoint, it is beneficial to consider one's own sexuality, not as something to be kept carefully under control but as a natural instinct whose motivating force must be acknowledged. These autobiographers, nevertheless, usually made it apparent that they continued to be troubled by questions of what is voluntary action, and they did not argue unequivocally for the value of impulse. Although they may have extolled the virtues of the "natural," they did not assume that instincts, drives, and emotions need no constraints. Self-control remained a basis for respect, but they argued that it, too, must be in moderation. David Nyberg (1993, p. 149) has described this dilemma well: "As we have learned from Freud's rich psychological images, life is a constant navigation between the Scylla of free expression and the Charybdis of inhibition . . . Deep down we know very well that unmanaged human feeling is a general disadvantage in getting what we want, that it is a serious threat to order, to confident expectation, to trust, all of which we need in our friendships as well as our other relationships. On the other hand, overmanaged feeling can lead to debilitating neurosis." These autobiographers had good rhetorical reasons to make it clear that they realized that emotions must be managed in order to live with others.

Since they believed that emotions play an integral role in the motivation of human beings, they also found it important to consider the cause of many of their emotions—their relationships with others. Of particular relevance was the history of their dependent relationship with parents during their "formative" years. Here the question arises whether experiences during childhood can shape the adult personality and reduce the responsibility of adults for how they act—in contemporary lingo, giving them "emotional baggage." Because the emotional dynamics of relationships became an important topic, these autobiographers now saw it as necessary to paint detailed portraits of the significant persons in their lives.

Some late nineteenth- and early twentieth-century autobiographers also began to consider another "external" determinant of human behavior—the effect of society upon the self. Such a recognition of the influence of the sociocultural environment did not replace the psychological focus on internal determinants of behavior; it simply added another factor to the consideration of what might affect human autonomy. How are individual wants, motives, beliefs, and values shaped by culture? Does this reduce human beings' responsibility for their actions? Autobiographers could now consider whether they had failed to recognize the effect of society on their lives, or at least the extent to which they tried to conform to the standards set by society. If they adopted the perspective that society was an important influence on the self, then the question became not only what must be controlled in oneself for the sake of others, but also at what point do the expectations and standards of other persons or society in general detract from one's own autonomy and responsibility? How much does caring about the good opinions of others influence what a person does? Of course, such autobiographers could now excuse their behavior by proclaiming that they were victims of society or social institutions, but such an argument shifting the blame away from self risked the censure of readers who might see such an excuse as a sign of passivity.

Such autobiographers emphasized that they were different from other persons because they refused any easy conformity. Remaining true to one's "authentic" self became a moral objective and meant resisting the excessive demands for conformity imposed by society through the socialization process and community norms and values. In contrast, actions taken only to comply with the conventions of society or excessive concern with "what people will think" could be viewed as immature or spineless. One ought, by this view, to have a self-generated set of standards for personal behavior rather than mindlessly adhering to conventional moral codes. Furthermore, on the subject of self-control, these autobiographers were more likely than their earlier counterparts to argue that we should recognize that it is society, after all, that requires such self-control (and conformity of behavior). Some of them used the term *puritanical* for excessive self-control—emphasizing the social origin of rigid expectations for human behavior.

These autobiographers also found it useful to argue on occasion that certain social behavior on their part, such as role-playing or impression management, existed as part of a social self required by society. Such a social self, however, could be partitioned off from the inner, "real" self where a person's moral worth was to be found. Emotions and impulses (supposedly uninfluenced by society) were indicators of this real self. Such a connection between emotion and the real self gave these autobiographers reason to stress the value of intimate relationships in their lives. The warmth and affection of home life and close friendships, from this perspective, is a useful contrast to cold and impersonal society.

In more recent decades, proclamations by autobiographers about the virtues of one's real self have diminished. More autobiographers seem willing to acknowledge the importance of society in shaping the self. They are likely, for example, to accept the idea that self-esteem is important for a person's mental health and that others (as well as societal values) are crucial in influencing how we think of ourselves. We can find this significance given to the social sources of self-esteem, for example, among contemporary autobiographers who reflect on the sources of ethnic identity for themselves. Such autobiographers, however, are not ready to drop the self-versus-society theme completely, and they may continue to see as admirable the efforts to resist demands for conformity made by society—specified here as pressures for assimilation. Autobiographers who stress their ethnic identities may argue that ethnicity is an innate source of difference that prevents such assimilation while also providing the basis for a sense of community and strong ties to their own group.

All these autobiographers are constrained by cultural vocabularies of the self, yet they are not, to use the expression of the sociologist Harold Garfinkel (1967, p. 68), "cultural dopes." They are not simply passive reflectors of such vocabularies; they select, interpret, and adapt shared cultural ideas to interpret their lives and to engage in artful self-presentation. Their life stories do not give us a strict history of the prevailing ideas at a particular time; instead, they offer a history of how persons have made use of these ideas as they tell the stories of their lives. We do not find, for example, nineteenth-century autobiographers readily adopting the Darwinian idea of evolution as a haphazard process, although they were able to ferret out a moral significance in evolutionary theory that Darwin had not intended. Similarly, most contemporary autobiographers do not appear ready to abandon, as some postmodernists would have it, the notion of a unified executive self along with its connotations of choice and moral responsibility.

By studying vocabularies of the self, we are then prepared to return to individual autobiographers and see the historically constructed nature of their self-narratives as well as the ways in which each of them is unique. The Scottish immigrant, James Fagan (1912), for example, primarily employed a sociologically based model of the self, but to resist its deterministic implications he wove in older ideas about self-development. Because his stated theme was life as an individualist, he emphasized his "dissatisfaction with Society" (p. 91), and he argued that his cultivation of willpower allowed him not only to overcome heredity and instinct but also to spurn the influence of society. And in his narrative, he showed he was up-to-date by discussing "finding" himself (p. 72), bringing his "subconscious knowledge" to the surface (p. 142), and "awakening to a consciousness of his own personality" (p. 16).

Examining the changes in vocabularies of the self over time can aid those of us who study the self to be reflexive about our own taken-for-granted assumptions about the self. We can see more clearly, for example, how concerns about the effects of society on the self are our contemporary issues. As the political philosopher Quentin Skinner (1969, p. 53) has remarked, "It is a commonplace . . . that our own society places unrecognized constraints upon our imaginations. It deserves, then, to become a commonplace that the historical study of the ideas of other societies should be undertaken as the indispensable and the irreplaceable means of placing limits on those constraints." I would add that the historical study of the ideas of *our* culture can aid us, as well, to recognize our own constraints, presuppositions, and evaluations—not only as scholars but also in our personal attempts to make sense of self.

Appendix A METHOD

Early in my reading about autobiographies, I ran across this comment by the literary critic Francis Hart (1970, pp. 492–93) about characterizations of the self: "The selective 'I' plays one or more of a number of structural roles: The 'I' that has been hidden or misconstrued; the 'I' that has been lost, or gained, regained or sought after in vain; the 'I' that has been cultivated, imposed, preserved, developed." Although I had already realized that there was much of sociological interest in these subjective records of people's lives, Hart's observation helped kindle my interest specifically in the concepts of self we can find in autobiographies, and I undertook this study of self-interpretation in American autobiographies.

Because ideas about the self may change slowly, I selected autobiographies from a long time span: 1800 to the present. The choice of 1800 as a starting date is arbitrary, although it is conveniently close to the year when the term *autobiography* was coined.[1]

I followed the literary critic Paul Delany's (1969, p. 1) definition of autobiography: "Literary works (1) *primarily* written to give a coherent account of the author's life, or of an extensive period or series of events in his life, and (2) composed after a period of reflection and forming a unified narrative."[2] Such a definition includes memoirs (which generally focus on external events) as well as more introspective autobiographies, and it does not raise the issue of the extent to which such an account must be "truthful."[3] I excluded diaries and journals since they do not require persons to summarize their lives from an overarching perspective.[4] Likewise, I did not include oral histories in my analysis since they usually are the result of interviews conducted by persons who guided the perspective developed in such histories. In autobiographies, in contrast, we can see what persons themselves choose to talk about and how they put together the narrative.

Sampling

Two annotated bibliographies list 11,385 American autobiographies from roughly 1800 to 1980 (Kaplan 1961; Briscoe 1982). From these bibliographies, I chose what can be called a judgment sample, which, as explained in a typical social research text (Baker 1994, p. 163), is a nonprobability sample that "considers the most common characteristics of the type it is desired to sample, tries to figure out where such individuals can be found, and then tries to study them." A random sample of autobiographies, where each member of the sampling population has an equal chance of being selected, would be difficult to obtain since as many as one-fourth of American autobiographies, as Kaplan (1961, p. v) noted, are "quite scarce and not easy to find," that is, perhaps only one copy exists in a state historical society or small-town library. Furthermore, most libraries limit themselves to a small number of autobiographies that they deem to be of significant public interest. I was fortunate, however, to have access to the large collection of autobiographies at the New York Public Library, supplemented by trips to the Library of Congress.

Because I was looking for historical variations in ideas about the self over a broad period of time, I chose autobiographies published during each decade—deciding on a minimum of five from each decade from 1800 to the present day for a total sample of 110 autobiographies.[5] Since the bibliographies do not categorize by decade, finding appropriate autobiographies by decade was a matter of an intensive search of the bibliographies. To select autobiographies within each decade, I used what I learned from coding the entire bibliographic listing of autobiographies by gender, decade of publication, and the autobiographer's occupation or primary experience (summarized in Appendix B). If a type of autobiography (such as war memoirs) was predominant during an era, I wanted to include that type—but not only that type. I tried to have a diverse sampling of occupations, and I included members of minority groups. Later in my study, I decided to expand the topic of contemporary multicultural autobiographies—increasing the number of these to ten from the 1980s and 1990s.

I used the date of first publication to categorize autobiographies by decade because I usually could not determine the exact year or years when they were written. This criterion, however, is not without its problems since some are not published until years after they were written. In making my initial choices, I did not include any autobiographies published more than a decade after the author's death. I did, however, eventually include three autobiographies in the decade written rather than published (Benjamin Rush in the decade of 1800–1809, J. Marion Sims in the 1860s, and Clarence Hawkes in the 1910s) since it was made clear in these cases when the autobiography was written.

I chose not to select autobiographies based on when the author was born. One could use the date of birth to select autobiographers for an investigation, for example, of Karl Mannheim's (1952) concept of *generations*. I was assuming, however, that an autobiography is an act of the present (based on a person's current ideas and interests) and that ideas established in one's youth do not remain impervious to changes in the climate of opinion. I did not believe it would be as productive to study autobiographers born in a particular generation regardless of when they wrote their life stories. Some write in early adulthood; others near the end of their lives. The date of publication, therefore, was the most useful way of ordering autobiographers' ideas about the self chronologically.

I also preferred autobiographies written without the assistance of a ghostwriter (Lee Iacocca, Yogi Berra, and Malcolm X are exceptions), since ghostwriters, although they draw from the same vocabularies of the self, may not have the same concerns of self-presentation. They may place a greater emphasis on choosing events that will engage the reader. For example, the historian John Blassingame (1979, p. 372) estimated that abolitionists actually wrote more than half of the slave narratives, and they chose to "focus on the escape from, rather than the routine of, slavery, and [they] are diatribes on unbelievably fiendish masters who terrorized the perfectly angelic slave."

I did not want only famous autobiographers in my sample, but I did not want to avoid them either. I was curious whether they served as models for later autobiographers and whether they picked up or developed new understandings of the self sooner than others. The literary critic Frank Kermode (1967, p. 17) observed that for fiction, "Broadly speaking, it is the popular story that sticks most closely to established conventions; novels the clerisy calls 'major' tend to vary them, and to vary them more and more as time goes by." Is this also the case for autobiographies? Furthermore, I wondered if such autobiographers might have a different understanding of such things as will or fate because of their own successes in life. Thus I included such autobiographers as Mark Twain and Henry Adams in the sample.

I also did not want to overlook female "voices" in my study. Since I found that women constituted about one-fifth of those American autobiographers that I coded, I included at least one female from each decade to equal roughly the proportion of female autobiographers. An influential issue in autobiographical criticism in recent decades has centered on differences between female and male autobiographical writing.[6] One of the earliest books on this subject was a collection of essays edited by Estelle Jelinek in 1980. Some feminist critics contend that women's autobiographies are different from those of men: they are generally more "episodic and anecdotal, nonchronological and disjunctive" with an emphasis on "personal matters," as Jelinek (1986, p. xiii) has summarized it. It is argued that women focus more on family and relationships in their autobiographies than do men, that women place less emphasis on the individualistic "I," and that women are more likely to discuss feelings. But there is not complete agreement about what the gender differences in autobiographies are, and whether they are innate or socially constructed. The feminist scholar Domna Stanton (1984, p. 14), for example, has argued that it is difficult "to separate a manifestation of female difference from a strategic conformity to cultural norms." And Jelinek (1986, p. xiii) conceded that there were "a fair number of exceptions" to the gender differences among autobiographers that she was postulating. The literary historian Linda Peterson (1993, p. 81), in turn, has taken issue with the argument that there is a separate tradition of female autobiography, and she has found in spiritual autobiographies that women, like men, downplayed domestic and romantic themes.

My focus in this study was historical differences in vocabularies of the self used by autobiographers. Although there are certainly gender differences among autobiographers such as career descriptions and presentation of self (e.g., what virtues the autobiographer suggests that she or he possesses), there are also significant similarities. Female autobiographers, using a narrative tradition dominated by men and influenced by similar cultural ideas about the self, do adopt many of the same conventions. We also can see this illustrated in a cross-cultural comparison of autobiographies gathered from Japanese women and American women in Hawaii by the anthropologist Takie Sugiyama Lebra (1984). Lebra was struck by the extent to which the American women presented themselves as autonomous decision makers and the principal characters in their stories, while the Japanese women told stories of accommodations, obligations, responsibilities, and a self immersed in a social world of relationships. Her findings point to the importance of considering autobiographical narratives in terms of their historical and cultural differences as well as gender differences, and suggest that we cannot simply generalize a unified, essential female "voice" that is to be found in any autobiography written by a woman.

To understand adequately how women's stories may differ from the life stories narrated by men, we must also explore the conventions of autobiography and the similarities in how women and men have interpreted and explained their lives. For example, to compare the relative emphasis given to relationships by male and female autobiographers, we should take into account historical changes in discussions of "relationships." Otherwise, ostensible gender differences may be the result of having chosen a male autobiographer and a female autobiographer from different eras. Thus, in this book, I examined models of the self used by both men and women in different historical periods. An in-depth empirical comparison of a large sample of male and female autobiographers (taking into account historical and cultural variations) remains to be done.

Feminist critics also have focused on the way in which the dominance of male voices within the autobiographical tradition illustrates a marginalization of female experiences. It is possible to argue, as did the Personal Narratives Group (1989, p. 8) that "women's personal narratives, whatever form they take, can be thought of as part of a dialogue of domination." We can make a similar case about other groups whose life stories have traditionally been excluded from the autobiographical canon. I have not explored the political question, however, of how autobiography serves as ideology or a legitimation of the status quo. My goal was to explore changes in the content of ideas about the self rather than the uses to which such ideas are put in terms of broader power relations. What voices and values are legitimated in autobiography and how the genre of autobiographies may serve as rhetoric for political or economic interests in society (e.g., through the promulgation of "bourgeois individualism") are other topics to be considered. Work in this direction is established—especially among feminist scholars of autobiography and those studying multicultural autobiography. This work, along with studies of working-class autobiography (e.g., Vincent 1981; Gagnier 1991), emphasizes differences, but we ought to look at similarities as well.

Data

Reading and analyzing autobiographies—making "raids on the articulate"—was an enjoyable project.[7] For each autobiography, I looked at how the author had assembled it, and I recorded all comments (or lack thereof) by the author about these topics:

Ancestry
Autobiographical writing
Changes in the self
Childhood
Children
Death
Education
Emotion
Environment
Fate or chance
Father
Gender
Historical events or personages
Human nature
Influential others
Inherited traits
Instincts
Intellectual trends
Jokes
Justification for writing the
    autobiography

Memory
Mother
Occupation and parents'
    occupations
Psychological terms or ideas
Rationality
Reader, direct statements to the
Relationships
Religion
Self-deprecating comments
Self-descriptions
Selfhood
Sexuality
Sociological terms or ideas
Spouse
Truth in autobiographies
Turning points
Will or character

I preferred the collection of quotations rather than a quantitative content analysis that counted frequently used words in autobiographies, since the latter method can overlook shades of meaning, themes, omissions, emphases, contradictions, irony, and rationalizations. Furthermore, words like *character* vary in meaning over time, so leaving words in context helps us recognize these changes. Doing so also reveals how some phrases and words still in use have changed from their original meaning, for example, "in full possession of my faculties," "countenance," and "sensibilities."

My initial list of topics was not as extensive. After reading a few autobiographies, I realized there were additional topics that I could productively study, so I reread these autobiographies with an expanded list. For example, I did not initially expect autobiographers to concern themselves with subjects such as instincts. When choosing quotations to include in my files, I let my delineation of the topics remain loose so that I would not overlook material that might later seem pertinent. I stored these quotations in computer files by topic and by author (to keep in mind a sense of the author's theme and whole story). Within the topic files, I arranged the quotations chronologically. I also recorded the autobiographer's life span, the age of the autobiographer at the time of writing (if this could be determined), how the autobiographer began and ended the story, whether the autobiographer adhered to a chronology, the number of pages devoted to childhood, the autobiographer's theme (if apparent), and whether the autobiographer used an index, photographs, or drawings. Finally, after looking for patterns in these quotations arranged chronologically, I turned to secondary sources to see if historical events and intellectual trends related to my findings. I also read book reviews from some decades to discover the standards that critics were using to evaluate the autobiographies, and I used the *Oxford English Dictionary* to look for changes in the meaning of words.

Literary theorists who have developed "reader-response" theory would argue that any meaning gleaned from these autobiographies is, to a considerable extent, supplied by the reader.[8] The meaning of the text, consequently, cannot be determined specifically since readers will interpret it differently. One also cannot, as in an interview, ask further questions to clarify the message. Nonetheless, as Wallace Martin (1986, p. 161) has written, it is "wrong to conclude that interpretation must therefore be 'in' the reader, regardless of the words on the page. In order to read them, we must know the language." The author must use conventions and shared understandings to communicate, and an analysis of such conventions is as productive as a compilation of the readers' responses. Readers' interpretations, too, are not simply idiosyncratic; they also use shared cultural knowledge to interpret the text. How readers from different eras or different cultures may interpret the meaning of a text is yet another subject for researchers to examine.[9]

I used the annotated bibliographies compiled by Louis Kaplan (1961) and Mary Louise Briscoe (1982) to code American autobiographies from 1800 to 1980 by gender, decade when published, and the autobiographer's occupation or primary experience (e.g., the adventure of climbing a mountain). Such coding enabled me to sample autobiographies more knowledgeably, and it gave me a sense of the variety of self-histories that have been published. I have summarized this coding in table 1. My coding, however, provides only a rough guide to American autobiographies. Although the bibliographies list a total of 11,385 autobiographies, their inventory is not exhaustive, and there is also some repetition in coverage between the two bibliographies, even though Kaplan's intent was to cover the years from the late 1700s to 1945 and Briscoe from 1945 to 1980.

TABLE I. American Autobiographies, by Occupation or Primary Experience and by Decade

	1800–1809		1810–1819		1820–1829		1830–1839		1840–1849		1850–1859		1860–1869		1870–1879		1880–1889	
	N	%	N	%	N	%	N	%	N	%	N	%	N	%	N	%	N	%
Clergy/Religious	14	51.9	13	34.2	14	27.5	31	40.3	53	40.2	73	36.9	72	30.5	71	33.6	108	31.0
Criminal/Deviant	5	18.5	7	18.4	13	25.5	14	18.2	17	12.9	11	5.6	10	4.2	12	5.7	16	4.6
Military	3	11.1	6	15.8	6	11.8	6	7.8	13	9.8	15	7.6	50	21.2	19	9.0	41	11.8
Doctor/Nurse	2	7.4	2	5.3	2	3.9	—	—	—	—	5	2.5	9	3.8	6	2.8	8	2.3
Educator	1	3.7	—	—	—	—	3	3.9	2	1.5	3	1.5	8	3.4	5	2.4	14	4.0
Lawyer/Judge	1	3.7	—	—	—	—	—	—	2	1.5	3	1.5	1	0.4	4	1.9	7	2.0
Domestic life	1	3.7	3	7.9	—	—	—	—	2	1.5	2	1.0	1	0.4	7	3.3	2	0.6
Business	—	—	1	2.6	2	3.9	2	2.6	1	0.8	10	5.1	8	3.4	10	4.7	26	7.5
Frontier life	—	—	1	2.6	3	5.9	5	6.5	5	3.8	22	11.1	14	5.9	12	5.7	23	6.6
Merchant Marine	—	—	1	2.6	4	7.8	4	5.2	9	6.8	5	2.5	4	1.7	5	2.4	7	2.0
Artist	—	—	1	2.6	—	—	—	—	1	0.8	2	1.0	2	0.8	—	—	1	0.3
Entertainer	—	—	1	2.6	—	—	1	1.3	3	2.3	4	2.0	3	1.3	3	1.4	12	3.4
Slave	—	—	1	2.6	1	2.0	2	2.6	12	9.1	9	4.5	7	3.0	3	1.4	2	0.6
Politician	—	—	—	—	1	2.0	1	1.3	1	0.8	7	3.5	4	1.7	10	4.7	8	2.3
Farmer	—	—	—	—	2	3.9	2	2.6	2	1.5	2	1.0	5	2.1	4	1.9	16	4.6
Immigrant	—	—	—	—	1	2.0	1	1.3	—	—	1	0.5	1	0.4	—	—	2	0.6
Socialite	—	—	—	—	1	2.0	—	—	—	—	1	0.5	—	—	—	—	1	0.3
American Indian	—	—	—	—	—	—	1	1.3	1	0.8	—	—	—	—	—	—	—	—

	1890–1899		1900–1909		1910–1919		1920–1929		1930–1939		1940–1949		1950–1959		1960–1969		1970–1979		Total	
	N	%	N	%	N	%	N	%	N	%	N	%	N	%	N	%	N	%	N	%
Clergy/Religious	141	31.5	129	22.7	151	21.7	134	16.7	122	11.3	114	10.9	81	12.1	40	6.3	108	9.2	1469	17.4
Criminal/Deviant	13	2.9	25	4.4	20	2.9	2C	2.5	25	2.3	17	1.6	10	1.5	5	0.8	37	3.1	277	3.3
Military	57	12.7	75	13.2	111	16.0	62	8.0	48	4.5	53	5.1	16	2.4	31	4.9	39	3.3	653	7.7
Doctor/Nurse	12	2.7	15	2.6	26	3.7	28	3.5	56	5.2	73	7.0	49	7.3	24	3.8	44	3.7	361	4.3
Educator	11	2.5	24	4.2	37	5.3	34	4.2	61	5.7	58	5.6	38	5.7	27	4.3	47	4.0	373	4.4
Lawyer/Judge	4	0.9	11	1.9	17	2.4	17	2.1	25	2.3	21	2.0	20	3.0	23	3.6	30	2.6	186	2.2
Domestic life	3	0.7	3	0.5	4	0.6	4	0.5	2	0.2	4	0.4	3	0.4	5	0.8	13	1.1	59	0.7
Business	22	4.9	36	6.3	44	6.3	69	8.6	82	7.6	56	5.4	23	3.4	27	4.3	45	3.8	464	5.5
Frontier life	33	7.4	45	7.9	46	6.6	65	8.1	70	6.5	48	4.6	10	1.5	8	1.3	15	1.3	425	5.0
Merchant Marine	13	2.9	10	1.8	7	1.0	14	1.7	20	1.9	10	1.0	3	0.4	1	0.2	5	0.4	122	1.4
Artist	4	0.9	3	0.5	5	0.7	11	1.4	21	1.9	21	2.0	14	2.1	20	3.2	35	3.0	141	1.7
Entertainer	14	3.1	6	1.1	26	3.7	43	5.4	56	5.2	58	5.6	79	11.8	89	14.0	152	12.9	550	6.5
Slave	4	0.9	2	0.4		—	2	0.2	1	0.1		—		—		—		—	46	0.5
Politician	17	3.8	41	7.2	41	5.9	42	5.2	50	4.6	41	3.9	32	4.8	43	6.8	74	6.3	413	4.9
Farmer	17	3.8	20	3.5	27	3.9	32	4.0	43	4.0	67	6.4	13	1.9	10	1.6	25	2.1	287	3.4
Immigrant	5	1.1	7	1.2	12	1.7	13	1.6	33	3.1	48	4.6	16	2.4	6	0.9	24	2.0	170	2.0
Socialite	4	0.9	1	0.2	6	0.9	4	0.5	16	1.5	9	0.9	5	0.7	3	0.5	1	0.1	52	0.6
American Indian	2	0.4	4	0.7	6	0.9	3	0.4	6	0.6	3	0.3	2	0.3	10	1.6	14	1.2	52	0.6

TABLE I. (Contd.)

	1800–1809		1810–1819		1820–1829		1830–1839		1840–1849		1850–1859		1860–1869		1870–1879		1880–1889	
	N	%	N	%	N	%	N	%	N	%	N	%	N	%	N	%	N	%
Psychic	—	—	—	—	—	—	1	1.3	—	—	1	0.5	3	1.3	3	1.4	6	1.7
Social reformer	—	—	—	—	—	—	1	1.3	1	0.8	5	2.5	5	2.1	8	3.8	13	3.7
Adventurer	—	—	—	—	—	—	1	1.3	1	0.8	—	—	—	—	—	—	1	0.3
Police	—	—	—	—	—	—	—	—	1	0.8	—	—	2	0.8	2	0.9	4	1.1
Ill/Disabled	—	—	—	—	—	—	—	—	2	1.5	8	4.0	2	0.8	9	4.3	1	0.3
Childhood memoir	—	—	—	—	—	—	—	—	1	0.8	1	0.5	4	1.7	5	2.4	4	1.1
Scientist	—	—	—	—	—	—	—	—	—	—	1	0.5	2	0.8	2	0.9	1	0.3
Social worker	—	—	—	—	—	—	—	—	—	—	1	0.5	1	0.4	—	—	—	—
Blue-collar/Clerical	—	—	—	—	—	—	—	—	—	—	2	1.0	2	0.8	2	0.9	2	0.6
Writer	—	—	—	—	1	2.0	—	—	2	1.5	4	2.0	11	4.7	5	2.4	13	3.7
Other professional	—	—	—	—	—	—	—	—	—	—	—	—	1	0.4	—	—	1	0.3
Racial/Ethnic	—	—	—	—	—	—	1	1.3	—	—	—	—	—	—	1	0.5	—	—
Sports figure	—	—	—	—	—	—	—	—	—	—	—	—	—	—	—	—	2	0.6
Hobbyist	—	—	—	—	—	—	—	—	—	—	—	—	—	—	—	—	—	—
Aviator	—	—	1	2.6	—	—	—	—	—	—	—	—	—	—	—	—	—	—
Miscellaneous	—	—	—	—	—	—	—	—	—	—	—	—	4	1.7	3	1.4	6	1.7
Total	27	100	38	100	51	100	77	100	132	100	198	100	236	100	211	100	348	100

Note: Percentages may not add to 100% due to rounding.

	1890–1899		1900–1909		1910–1919		1920–1929		1930–1939		1940–1949		1950–1959		1960–1969		1970–1979		Total	
	N	%	N	%	N	%	N	%	N	%	N	%	N	%	N	%	N	%	N	%
Psychic	4	0.9	3	0.5	3	0.4	3	0.4	1	0.1	2	0.2	7	1.0	2	0.3	7	0.6	46	0.5
Social reformer	17	3.8	12	2.1	8	1.2	23	2.9	31	2.9	21	2.0	12	1.8	24	3.8	49	4.2	230	2.7
Adventurer	1	0.2	2	0.4	4	0.6	5	0.6	11	1.0	4	0.4	3	0.4	1	0.2	3	0.3	37	0.4
Police	1	0.2	5	0.9	—	—	3	0.4	12	1.1	6	0.6	4	0.6	12	1.9	24	2.0	76	0.9
Ill/Disabled	2	0.4	10	1.8	6	0.9	7	0.9	12	1.1	23	2.2	13	1.9	4	0.6	34	2.9	133	1.6
Childhood memoir	6	1.3	14	2.5	20	2.9	37	4.6	47	4.4	58	5.6	31	4.6	15	2.4	27	2.3	270	3.2
Scientist	2	0.4	4	0.7	1	0.1	4	0.5	13	1.2	16	1.5	14	2.1	7	1.1	16	1.4	83	1.0
Social worker	3	0.7	3	0.5	6	0.9	7	0.9	9	0.8	6	0.6	6	0.9	6	0.9	9	0.8	57	0.7
Blue-collar/Clerical	11	2.5	9	1.6	10	1.4	9	1.1	20	1.9	14	1.3	3	0.4	3	0.5	8	0.7	95	1.1
Writer	17	3.8	32	5.6	33	4.7	65	8.1	121	11.2	122	11.7	84	12.6	81	12.8	100	8.5	691	8.2
Other professional	3	0.7	3	0.5	2	0.3	8	1.0	15	1.4	11	1.1	4	0.6	6	0.9	9	0.8	63	0.7
Racial/Ethnic	—	—	1	0.2	1	0.1	1	0.1	—	—	9	0.9	5	0.7	16	2.5	23	2.0	58	0.7
Sports figure	2	0.4	3	0.5	4	0.6	10	1.2	15	1.4	20	1.9	35	5.2	52	8.2	92	7.8	235	2.8
Hobbyist	1	0.2	5	0.9	3	0.4	6	0.7	8	0.7	4	0.4	5	0.7	5	0.8	4	0.3	41	0.5
Aviator	—	—	—	—	2	0.3	5	0.6	7	0.6	5	0.5	9	1.3	3	0.5	9	0.8	40	0.5
Miscellaneous	2	0.4	6	1.1	6	0.9	10	1.2	19	1.8	21	2.0	19	2.8	25	3.9	53	4.5	175	2.1
Total	448	100	569	100	695	100	802	100	1078	100	1043	100	668	100	634	100	1175	100	8430	100

Note: Percentages may not add to 100% due to rounding.

Overall, there are many problems with coding autobiographies based on one-sentence descriptions in annotated bibliographies. First, the universe of autobiographies is circumscribed by the bibliographer's definition of an autobiography. This problem is underscored by the differences between Kaplan's and Briscoe's definitions. Briscoe, unlike Kaplan, included diaries, journals, oral histories, and collections of letters. Kaplan also omitted "episodic accounts" such as escapes or trips, which meant that he did not include many slave narratives. Both Kaplan and Briscoe chose to include memoirs written by foreigners who spent only a few years visiting the United States.

For my purposes, I excluded diaries, journals, oral histories, collections of letters, memoirs written by foreign visitors, and autobiographies published before 1800. Also, if an author wrote more than one autobiography, I coded only the earliest one published. For these reasons (and because several hundred autobiographies had no date of publication and could not be coded by decade), my tabulation of 8,430 autobiographies does not equal Kaplan and Briscoe's combined total.

A more difficult problem was coding by occupation or primary experience, since many autobiographers have engaged in several occupations or, perhaps, were writing about their careers and their avocations, for example, the autobiography of a businessman who also was an avid book collector. Since I did not want overlap in my coding, I chose the occupation or experience emphasized in the title of the autobiography. If the title gave no clue to the self-perceived importance of occupation or experience, I made my decision based on the annotation. If several occupations were listed, I used the occupation named first. To do a more accurate coding would require reading all the autobiographies, and this still would require subjective decisions as to whether an occupation or an experience was central to the autobiography. Despite these problems, however, I believe my tabulation is worthwhile to present as it suggests further lines of research.

Many of the categories in table 1 are self-explanatory. Others, however, require a few words. I included in the category of social reformer those persons who told a story of active efforts to effect social change, for example, Socialists, Communists, abolitionists, suffragettes, Zionists, and union organizers. The category of adventurers consists of explorers, shark hunters, those who have sailed solo around the world, and so forth. In the category of frontier stories, I included the autobiographies of pioneers, cowboys, Indian fighters, scouts, gold miners, trappers, and those who told a story of residing with Indians. Within the table, I arranged the occupations (or experience) roughly in order of their chronological appearance as a type of American autobiography.

As we can see in this table, the number of published autobiographies grew rapidly in the nineteenth century as literacy rose, the number of circulating libraries increased, and improvements in publishing made it possible to mass produce affordable books. By my count, 325 American autobiographies were published from 1800 to 1849, 1,441 autobiographies from 1850 to 1899, 4,187 autobiographies from 1900 to 1949, and 2,477 autobiographies in the shorter span from 1950 to 1980.

Although women have written just over 19 percent of the American autobiographies that I coded, it is noteworthy that their proportion has increased substantially over time. Women wrote 10 percent of these published autobiographies from 1800 to 1849, 13 percent from 1850 to 1899, 19 percent from 1900 to 1949, and 24 percent from 1950 to 1980. The only categories in which women wrote most of the autobiographies were those of socialites (71 percent) and tales of domestic life (68 percent). Women also wrote a significant percentage of the stories of social workers (46 percent), childhood memoirs (43 percent), and stories of immigration (38 percent).

Religious autobiographies (either members of the clergy or persons telling of a religious experience) make up the largest category of American autobiographies from 1800 through the 1930s. They constitute just over 17 percent of the American autobiographies that I coded—ranging from 52 percent in the decade of 1800–1809 to a low of 6 percent in the 1960s. Since the 1930s, religious themes have been remarkably resilient—making up the second largest category in each decade except the 1960s.

The category of writers, constituting roughly 8 percent of all the autobiographers, began to equal the number of religious autobiographers beginning in the 1930s and predominated among autobiographers during the 1940s and 1950s. Furthermore, it is almost certainly the case that I have undercounted the number of writers, for many of the stories of childhood or a particular experience may have been written by professional writers (a fact that often is not mentioned in the annotations).

From 1960 to 1980, entertainers (including actors, singers, musicians, dancers, and those associated with the entertainment business such as producers, directors, and agents) became the largest category of autobiographers. This increase in entertainers' autobiographies supports the sociologist Leo Lowenthal's (1950) contention, in his well-known study of biographies in popular magazines from 1901 to 1941, that there has been a shift in public interest toward biographies of "idols of consumption"—particularly if one also includes sports figures, artists, and writers as Lowenthal did in a general category relating to leisure time interests. Explaining historical shifts in the occupations of autobiographers, however, is complex as many factors are involved, for example, changes in the total number of people participating in an occupation, memoir-worthy events such as wars, imitations spawned by a successful autobiography, the age at which persons choose to write their autobiographies, and publishers' and editors' decisions.

Other important categories among American autobiographies have been military memoirs (the second largest category from the 1860s through the 1910s), business career stories (generally popular from the 1870s through the 1930s), and frontier stories (especially popular in the 1850s but still prevalent through the 1930s). Over time, the occupations and experiences of autobiographers have become increasingly varied, so that the single largest category in a decade no longer accounts for up to one-half of the autobiographers as it has in the past, but instead does not exceed 15 percent.

Notes

Chapter One: Introduction

1. Quoted by John Lofland 1984, p. 21.

2. See Gecas 1982; Pratkanis and Greenwald 1985; and Hales 1985 for comments on this development. Elvi Whittaker (1992, p. 196) points out that we can see the considerable growth in academic interest by examining *The Social Science Index* where the number of items relating to the self more than tripled from 1974/1975 to 1990/1991.

3. See discussions of this change by Johnson 1985; Potter and Wetherell 1987; Collins 1988; and Bruner 1990.

4. See Rorty 1967 on the "linguistic turn"; and Hiley, Bohman, and Shusterman 1991 on the "interpretive turn."

5. It is easy to confuse these differing definitions of the self. Part of the problem relates to the dual nature of the self—the self as both knower ("I") and as known ("me"). As André Gide ([1927] 1951, p. 65) explained it, "I am constantly getting outside myself, and as I watch myself act I cannot understand how a person who

acts is the same as the person who is watching him act, and who wonders in astonishment and doubt how he can be actor and watcher at the same moment." Some uses of the term *self* relate to the notion of self as subject or knower (an essence or internal structure that persists over time), and some refer to the self as known (the object of one's reflections). "Self" as subject and initiator of action is not directly observable—as David Hume ([1739–40] 1978), among others, pointed out. In contrast, the self as object of one's reflections is something that we can investigate. In an attempt to clarify this distinction, some researchers have used the term *self-concept* to refer to the self-as-known. Morris Rosenberg (1979, p. ix), for example, defined *self-concept* as "the totality of the individual's thoughts and feelings with reference to himself or herself as an object." Others, however, argue that it is useless to distinguish between self and self-concept, since self as knower cannot be observed empirically (Damon and Hart 1988).

6. Geertz (1983, p. 59), for example, has made this often-quoted observation: "The Western conception of the person as a bounded, unique, more or less integrated motivational and cognitive universe, a dynamic center of awareness, emotion, judgment, and action organized into a distinctive whole and set contrastively both against other such wholes and against its social and natural background, is, however incorrigible it may seem to us, a rather peculiar idea within the context of the world's cultures." See also the work of Lee 1950; Read 1955; Hallowell 1955; Geertz 1973; Rosaldo 1980; and Fortes 1987. Additionally, there are comparisons of Asian and Western perspectives on the self (Smith 1983; Wu 1984; Marsella, De Vos, and Hsu 1985; Elvin 1985; and Roland 1988, 1991).

7. Much of the work has been speculative, for example, the well-known argument concerning the rise of individualism in the West (e.g., Burckhardt 1937; and Morris 1972).

8. Morris Rosenberg and Howard Kaplan (1982) found over 4,500 articles (including those by sociologists) dealing with the self-concept.

9. See Kihlstrom and Cantor 1984; and Pratkanis and Greenwald 1985.

10. See, for example, Harré 1984, 1987; Shotter 1984; and Gergen 1984, 1985, 1988, 1989.

11. Viktor Gecas (1985, p. 432) suggests that "the rise of 'self' and 'identity' to mainstream status in sociology has been contingent on the adoption and transformation of these concepts by . . . positivistic orientations."

12. See also Zurcher 1977; Benton 1981; Wood and Zurcher 1988.

13. See Crites 1971; Collins 1988; Becker and McCall 1990.

14. As we also learn "vocabularies of motives" (Mills 1940). The phrase "vocabulary of self" has been used by others such as James Benton (1981, p. 45); Kenneth Gergen (1989, p. 70); and Robert Perinbanayagam (1991, p. 12). Richard Rorty, too, uses the term "vocabularies." See, for example, *Contingency, Irony, and Solidarity* (1989).

15. For a review of psychological studies of the development of self-understanding, see Damon and Hart (1988).

16. In *Movements of Thought in the Nineteenth Century,* Mead (1936, pp. 59, 71)

does postulate that a "new self" arose during the Romantic period—defined by a type of self-reflexiveness new to human beings. As he wrote, "The self of this mode becomes the assured center of the universe, that out of which the world is to be built" (p. 83).

17. See Geertz 1973; Denzin 1991; and Maines 1993. B. F. Skinner used a similar argument, although he did so to attack the validity of data obtained from introspection. As Owen Flanagan (1984, p. 103) summarized it, "For Skinner, self-knowledge, when and where it exists, is a social product. How we categorize mental events, and how well we do so depends on the breadth, depth, and intricacy of the language we have learned, and on the contexts in which that language is introduced and subsequently utilized."

18. Ken Plummer (1983) has summarized the debate over the use of personal documents in research. To follow this debate, see Dollard 1935, 1938; Blumer 1939; Allport 1942; Gottschalk, Kluckhohn, and Angell 1945; Langness 1965; Becker 1966; Bukowski 1974; Bogdan and Taylor 1975; Mariampolski and Hughes 1978; Denzin 1978, 1989; Frank 1979; Langness and Frank 1981; Bertaux 1981; Bertaux and Kohli 1984; Crapanzano, Ergas, and Modell 1986; and Angrosino 1989.

19. See Kohli 1981; and McCall and Wittner 1990.

20. See McCall and Wittner 1990. The oral history movement, which has primarily developed since the 1940s, is a response to such a criticism. There have been hundreds of projects to tape-record the life histories of persons who would not otherwise write an autobiography (Plummer 1983). For a discussion of the Polish memoir competitions begun in 1921 by Florian Znaniecki to encourage workers to write their autobiographies, see Jacek Bukowski (1974).

21. Paul Delany (1969, p. 18) found in his study of British autobiography in the seventeenth century that "those [religious] sects which drew numbers from the lower and lower-middle classes produced many autobiographies; Anglicans, on the other hand, were more influenced by genteel inhibitions against self-revelation."

22. I am using *life history* and *life story* as synonymous with *autobiography*. Some scholars reserve *life history* for those stories "elicited or prompted by another person" (Watson and Watson-Franke 1985, p. 2).

23. As Margaret Mead has written in another context: "If one wants to know the grammatical structure of a language, it is sufficient to use very few informants about whom the necessary specified information has been collected; if one wants to know how many people use a certain locution . . . in preference to another, then sampling of the wider type is necessary" (Honigmann 1982, p. 83).

24. See, for example, Mehlman 1974; Jay 1987; Couser 1989; and Eakin 1992.

25. For complete details on method, see Appendix A.

26. Some commentators, for instance, have described the history of autobiography as a history of increasing self-awareness. An early example is the work of Georg Misch ([1907] 1951, p. 2), who was influenced by Goethe's belief that autobiographies could throw light upon "the great process of the liberation of human personality."

27. I am borrowing the term "components of the self" from the psychiatrist

Frank Johnson (1985). Many writers throughout history have used structural metaphors when describing the nature of the self or the soul. Aristotle (1907), for example, discussed "parts of the soul"—including a tripartite division into the reasoning, passionate, and concupiscent parts. And William James ([1890] 1950, 1:292) referred to "constituents of the Self."

Chapter Two: Autobiography as a Social Situation

1. As Goffman (1959, p. 35) explained, "When the individual presents himself before others, his performance will tend to incorporate and exemplify the officially accredited values of the society."

2. Dillon Johnston observed that "the autobiography, more than any literary genre, tends to talk about itself. . . . A discussion of the formation of autobiography almost always becomes part of the subject matter" (quoted by Francis Hart 1970, p. 490). In using the term *rhetoric,* I follow Geoffrey Leech's (1983, p. 15) general definition of it as "the effective use of language in communication." From this perspective, rhetoric is not the contrast case for rational or objective argument but is a type of action in which all persons engage.

3. See Michal McCall and Judith Wittner (1990) for a discussion of storytelling as a social act.

4. Literary critics who have discussed autobiography as a social act include Bruss 1976; Renza 1977; Gunn 1982; Jay 1984; and Abbott 1988. Bruss, for example, used the speech act theory of J. L. Austin and John Searle to analyze autobiographies. See also Maines 1993.

5. Rousseau ([1781] 1953, p. 606), however, did read his *Confessions* to others, and he included the reaction to his public reading in his conclusion: "Mme d'Egmont was the only person who seemed moved. She trembled visibly but quickly controlled herself, and remained quiet, as did the rest of the company."

6. As Terry Eagleton (1983, p. 84) noted, "Every literary text is built out of a sense of its potential audience, includes an image of whom it is written *for;* every work encodes within itself what [Wolfgang] Iser calls an 'implied reader,' intimates in its every gesture the kind of 'addressee' it anticipates." Iser (1978, pp. 32–33) also has discussed Erwin Wolff's concept of the *intended reader* who "can embody not only the concepts and conventions of the contemporary public but also the desire of the author both to link up with these concepts and to work on them—sometimes just portraying them, sometimes acting upon them."

7. For example, as Roy Pascal (1960, p. 73) observed, "The various drafts of Gibbon's *Memoir* differ primarily because of his uncertainty of purpose and, to some extent, his uncertainty of what public he was writing for—whether 'discreet and indulgent friends' or the 'public' at large."

8. When family members decide to publish such an autobiography posthumously, they sometimes "clean up" the story for a general audience. William Temple Franklin, while editing his grandfather's memoir, made roughly twelve

hundred changes—such as replacing Franklin's colloquialism "stared like a pig poisoned" to "stared with astonishment" (Franklin [1793] 1923, p. xxiii).

9. In contrast, Stendhal (1958, p. 6), in his autobiographical *The Life of Henry Brulard,* contemplated the response of future readers: "This is something new for me: to be talking to people about whose turn of mind, education, prejudices and religion one is wholly ignorant!"

10. Susan Allen Toth (1987) reported that after she published her memoir, she was contacted by persons from her past who wished to dispute her memory of specific events.

11. An autobiographer, nevertheless, can challenge the audience's "horizon of expectations" and play a part in developing new autobiographical conventions. See Hans Jauss's (1982) discussion of reception theory.

12. A publisher reportedly cancelled a contract for the autobiography of Marlene Dietrich because her manuscript left out an intimate discussion of her lovers (McDowell 1991).

13. The thirteenth edition of *The Chicago Manual of Style* (1982, p. 169), for example, advised writers that the use of quotation marks to highlight the ironical use of a word may "offend an intelligent reader who is quite capable of detecting the irony or the oddness of the expression without having it pointed out."

14. Currying favor, however, is not the only approach to the readers. The literary historian William L. Andrews (1986), for example, has pointed out that African-American autobiographers in the 1800s who wrote of slavery began to treat their readers as persons in need of enlightenment.

15. The autobiographer may also be trying to convince himself or herself of such virtues. As Mark Twain (1924, 2:312) mused, "This autobiography of mine is a mirror, and I am looking at myself in it all the time. Incidentally I notice the people that pass along at my back . . . and whenever they say or do anything that can help advertise me and flatter me and raise me in my own estimation, I set these things down in my autobiography."

16. Donald Stauffer (1941, pp. 28–29) noted that many eighteenth-century English memoirs, particularly those of actors, included an appendix of the author's witticisms.

17. The quotation is from Montaigne ([1580] 1946, p. 316). Patricia Spacks (1980, pp. 113–14) and others have argued that modesty is characteristic of female autobiographers: "To a striking degree they fail directly to emphasize their *own* importance, though writing in a genre which implies self-assertion and self-display." I found, however, that male autobiographers are also sensitive to cultural norms regarding conceit.

18. Benjamin Franklin ([1793] 1923, pp. 2–3) did so in his memoir: "And, lastly (I may as well confess it, since my denial of it will be believed by nobody), perhaps I shall a good deal gratify my own *vanity.* Indeed, I scarce ever heard or saw the introductory words, '*Without vanity I may say,*' etc., but some vain thing immediately followed" (his emphasis). Yet Franklin took some care not to appear excessively

vain. As Lemay and Zall (1981, p. lvi) have discovered, Franklin made corrections in his memoir such as the following: after first writing "having emerg'd from the Poverty and Obscurity in which I was born & bred, to a State of Affluence & some Degree of Fame in the World," he then changed the word "Fame" to the more unassuming "Reputation." His grandson, however, subsequently defeated his modesty by replacing the word "Reputation" with "Celebrity."

19. An exception in my sample of autobiographers was Samuel Boicourt (1857), whose boasting is so boundless that it appears to be a farce. He bragged that his parents kept his head bandaged as a child "until his skull became thick enough to stand the pressure of his intellect" (p. 38). And he opened with the proclamation that "the great spirit of philosophy that once appeared in Socrates, and afterwards in Sir Issac [sic] Newton, now breaks forth with renewed lustre in the genius of Doctor Boicourt" (p. 5).

20. Thanks to Ralph Turner for making this point.

21. See John Hazlett 1990. Contemporary readers also peruse fiction and poetry for the autobiographical element buried within. The writer Ludwig Lewisohn (1922, p. 1) commented in his autobiography that "both the novelist and the philosopher is only an autobiographer in disguise. Each writes a confession; each is a lyricist at bottom."

22. As James Olney (1985, p. 150) observed, the purpose of the autobiography also affects its truth claims. He illustrated this point in a discussion of slave narratives: "The writer of a slave narrative finds himself in an irresolvably tight bind as a result of the very intention and premise of his narrative, which is to give a picture of 'slavery as it is.' Thus it is the writer's claim, it *must* be his claim, that he is not emplotting, he is not fictionalizing, and he is not performing any act of *poiesis*."

23. See Jonathan Culler (1975) for a discussion of similar tactics used in fiction.

24. Probably the most famous self-proclaimed autobiographical attempt at frankness was Rousseau's ([1781] 1953, pp. 478–79) *Confessions:* "I decided to make it a work unique and unparalleled in its truthfulness, so that for once at least the world might behold a man as he was within."

25. There have been changing standards among biographers, as well, concerning the extent to which they report their subjects' defects, foibles, and misdeeds. Many observers have pointed out a twentieth-century trend in biography toward greater descriptions of private life and personal faults. Joyce Carol Oates (1988, p. 3) has referred to this type of biography as "pathography." During the years following World War I, "debunking" biographies became popular (Garraty 1964). In spirit, however, this is not a new trend. Donald Stauffer (1941, pp. 132–35) described eighteenth-century English biographers who demonstrated a "fondness for lowering exalted characters." And it was during the early eighteenth century that the author John Arbuthnot referred to a biographer as "one of the new terrors of Death" (Williams 1965, p. 101).

26. The spiritualist Andrew Jackson Davis (1857, p. 95) disclosed in his autobiography that he had been disguising his mother's and his own lack of education by recalling their conversation as "being more direct and less uncouth and bungling

than it was in fact." Davis might have gone back and amended his accounts of these conversations, but instead he let them stand along with his confession.

27. Geoffrey Leech (1983, pp. 146–47), in a discussion of pragmatics, or the relation of an utterance to its context, proposes that a principle of interpersonal rhetoric is the *Interest Principle,* which is evidenced by "the temptation we feel, when retelling a personal anecdote, to embroider on the anecdote various kinds of elaboration and exaggeration."

28. Robert Folkenflik (1993, p. 15) reports a parody of the usual author's query in the *Los Angeles Times Book Review:* "I am writing my autobiography and would appreciate hearing from anyone who can remember anything interesting or exciting about my life."

29. The Russian formalist critic Victor Shklovsky ([1917] 1965) used the concept "defamiliarization"—making the familiar seem unfamiliar—to analyze how everyday incidents can be made interesting. Wallace Martin (1986, p. 117) has summarized this idea: "Everyday incidents become interesting if complex characters participate in them, or if they are perceived by a consciousness remote from our own (the clown, the madman, the naif, the visitor from another culture)." Interesting stories may include those of travelers and adventurers who encounter the unfamiliar, persons from another social world, and persons who tell the reader about life during an earlier historical period.

30. See Donald Stauffer 1941. This idea can be found earlier, as in Dr. Samuel Johnson's ([1750] 1953, p. 133) comment in *The Rambler:* "I have often thought that there has rarely passed a life of which a judicious and faithful narrative would not be useful."

31. I also found few descriptions of the physical appearance of the autobiographers unless they differed markedly from others. As a turn-of-the century commentator noted, "We don't get a history of the body—primarily of the mind (Gill 1907, p. 77). This lack of attention to appearance may be to avoid appearing vain (Shumaker 1954) or indelicate, but it also may be that people don't describe themselves unless they differ from the norm (see McGuire and McGuire 1981). Paul John Eakin (1992, p. 184n.4) has observed, however, that a concern with the body does appear in the substantial number of memoirs focusing on illness, which began appearing in the latter half of the nineteenth century in the United States. See also Arthur Frank 1993.

32. As with most generalizations about human beings, there are exceptions to this. The self-styled poet Robert Coffin (1825, p. 200), who appeared to have run out of material in his autobiography, began to make comments such as "I often wash myself, and change my clothing on Saturdays."

33. Rousseau ([1781] 1953, p. 31), on the other hand, defensively avowed in his *Confessions* that he didn't care whether the readers found a particular detail of his life interesting: "I am well aware that the reader does not require information, but I, on the other hand, feel impelled to give it to him. Why should I not relate all the little incidents of that happy time, that still give me a flutter of pleasure to recall."

34. Quoted by Avrom Fleishman 1983, p. 18.

35. Cited by Thomas Cooley 1976, p. 28.

36. Goethe's (1848) subtitle for his memoir—*Dichtung und Wahrheit* or *Poetry and Truth*—shows his recognition of this tension between the "truth" and the imaginative construction of a life (Gusdorf [1956] 1980, p. 42).

37. See Brian Finney 1985.

38. See Jonathan Culler's (1975) similar point about fiction.

39. There are exceptions, of course, to the use of an overarching story line in an autobiography. Michel Leiris ([1939] 1984) and Roland Barthes (1977), for example, put together their autobiographies as discussions of various topics and images. Mark Twain (1924, 1:193) once argued that the "right way" to do an autobiography was to "start it at no particular time of your life; wander at your free will all over your life; talk only about the thing which interests you for the moment; drop it the moment its interest threatens to pale." Jorge Luis Borges (1964b, p. 137) also has suggested that "a history of a man's dreams is not inconceivable; or of the organs of his body; or of the mistakes he has made; or of all the moments when he imagined the Pyramids; or of his traffic with night and with dawn."

40. See also John Sturrock 1993.

41. Donald Stauffer (1941), among others, has discussed this aspect of the creation of autobiography. See also Frank Kermode 1967.

42. From Nietzsche's viewpoint, as Sturrock (1993, p. 5n.4) points out, *events* can be seen as "constructs of discourse, artificially isolated from out of the pure continuity of the life-process."

43. Wayne Shumaker (1954, p. 132) suggested that many autobiographers use a chronology to tell their life stories because of "a conscious or subconscious realization that the putting of first things first makes possible constantly deepening reference and richer reverberations."

44. In contrast, Dorothy Lee (1950, p. 543) found that when she asked a member of the Wintu tribe of Indians to tell her life story, "The first three quarters of this, approximately, are occupied with the lives of her grandfather, her uncle and her mother before her birth."

45. The autobiographer Andrew Jackson Davis (1857, p. 16) was uneasy about discussing his birth since it occurred before he "awaked into conscious memory." St. Augustine ([400] 1963, p. 25) made a similar comment about his recollections of infancy: "I am reluctant to count it as part of this present life of mine which I live in the world; for, so far as the darkness of forgetfulness is concerned, it is just the same as the period of life which I spent in my mother's womb."

46. Dorothy Lee (1959, p. 115), in comparison, found that a history for the Trobriand Islanders was "an aggregate of anecdotes, that is, unconnected points, told without respect to chronological sequence, or development, or causal relationship."

47. Cited by Avrom Fleishman 1983, p. 7.

48. George Lakoff and Mark Turner (1989) discuss metaphors that people have used to characterize life, death, and time.

49. Jorge Luis Borges (1964a, p. 63), in "Funes the Memorious," told the tale of

a man who could remember everything—including such details as "the mottled streaks on a book . . . he had seen only once." This man found that the task of reconstructing a whole day from his memory required an entire day's work. Mark Twain (1924, 1:283) made a similar point in his autobiography when he argued that a "full autobiography" would "consist of 365 double-size volumes per year."

50. Quoted by Leon Edel 1984, p. 15.

51. As Sartre (1964, p. 125) explained it, when reading about someone's life, "[T]hough you may try to put yourself in his place, to pretend to share his passions, his blunders, his prejudices, to revive bygone acts of resistance or a touch of impatience or apprehension, you will be unable to keep from evaluating his behavior in the light of results which were not foreseeable and of information which he did not possess or from giving particular weight to events whose effects left their mark on him at a later time but which he lived through casually."

52. Quoted by Stuart Charmé 1984, p. 14.

53. See Fleishman 1976; and Eakin 1985.

54. "Ghostwriters Materialize," *Sacramento Bee,* 28 July 1987.

Chapter Three: The Self as Morality Play

1. See Appendix B. Approximately one-third of American autobiographers from 1800 to 1899 were clergy or persons who concentrated on their religious experiences. Of the clergy, most were evangelical Protestants (e.g., Methodists, Baptists, or Presbyterians), and their stories were similar despite denominational differences. Few religious autobiographers during this period were Catholics or Jews. In 1826, Goethe suggested that "Protestants may be more prone to autobiography than Catholics who can turn to a confessor" (quoted in Egan 1984, p. 173).

2. See, for example, Shumaker 1954; Weintraub 1978; and Fleishman 1983.

3. Looking only at estimates of church membership in the United States during the mid-nineteenth century, we might doubt this conclusion. In 1855, according to the religious historian Timothy Smith (1957, p. 17), 4,088,675 persons (out of a total population of approximately 27,000,000) were members of Protestant churches. Nevertheless, as Richard Hofstadter (1963, p. 89) concluded, there were probably many more churchgoers than church members during this period because of the rigorous membership requirement of a conversion experience. These figures also do not include membership in the Roman Catholic Church, which had over one million adherents in 1850 (Finke and Stark 1992).

4. According to the autobiography of the evangelist Peter Cartwright (1856, p. 24), "A mighty revival of religion broke out" around 1799. Richard Hofstadter (1963, p. 64) maintained that "with the Awakenings, the Puritan age in American religion came to an end and the evangelical age began."

5. As part of the evangelical movement, the interdenominational American Tract Society, founded in the 1820s, had by 1860 blanketed settled areas of the country with almost two hundred million religious tracts and books (Griffin 1967, p. 83).

6. See Starr 1965; Shea 1968; Greven 1977; Westbrook 1979; and Peterson 1986.

7. See Fleming ([1933] 1969). In some Puritan churches, elders or ministers read the conversion accounts of women so that they need not speak in church (Dunn 1980).

8. See Appendix B.

9. Richard Altick (1957, p. 109) observed that the evangelical suspicion of fiction, which peaked in the early nineteenth century in England, "fatefully determined the reading experience of millions of people." Such a concern with the moral aspects of reading material also was reflected in children's literature published in the United States in the first half of the nineteenth century, where the purpose of such literature was moral education (MacLeod 1975).

10. Many nineteenth-century evangelical Protestant autobiographers were of working-class origin (Smith 1957; Greven 1977). Conceivably anyone could write such an autobiography, yet women wrote only between 9 and 10 percent of the religious autobiographies during the nineteenth century despite the fact that they outnumbered male church members by a ratio of about 2–1 (Kett 1977, p. 65). Few women were members of the clergy, and there also was a disparity between male and female literacy in the early nineteenth century (Soltow and Stevens 1981). Women's experiences in church, nevertheless, made them familiar with the standard conversion narrative.

11. During this same period, Newgate novels, which centered on criminals, were popular in England (Hollingsworth 1963).

12. Wayne Shumaker (1954), in his study of English autobiography, suggested that many of these rogues' confessions were ghostwritten.

13. Among the Protestants, of course, there was not universal agreement on theological issues. Philip Greven (1977, pp. 13ff.) found different levels of belief— "evangelicals, moderates, and genteels"—based on the degree of acceptance of ideas such as the sinful self, the need for a dramatic conversion, infant damnation, the necessity of self-denial, the role of reason in governing the passions, and the role of good works in salvation. But among the religious autobiographies produced in the nineteenth century, the proselytizing viewpoint of the evangelicals is predominant.

14. Merle Curti (1980, p. 71) noted that *human nature* is a term first commonly used in the eighteenth century.

15. Elaine Pagels (1988) argued that this viewpoint of universal original sin is rooted not in the Bible but in St. Augustine's personal interpretation of the letter of St. Paul to the Romans.

16. Quoted by Karl Menninger 1973, p. 230.

17. This concern about battling the passions was even evident in the earliest known board game in the United States—"Mansions of Happiness." In this game, developed in 1843, a player had to avoid pitfalls such as the passions in order to win the game (*The New York Times*, 9 September 1988).

18. Jay Wharton Fay ([1939] 1966, p. 45), in a survey of early American psychology, discussed how a two-part division of the faculties—reason and will—was

common before the 1820s. In this scheme, the faculty of will, referring to "inclination," included emotions and passions. A three-part division of the faculties, popularized by Asa Burton and Thomas Upham in the 1820s and 1830s, made a distinction between will and emotion. See also Cooley 1976.

19. See Misiak and Sexton 1966. Phrenology, the nineteenth-century belief that the shape of the skull was indicative of mental faculties, was a derivative of faculty psychology.

20. Charles Spearman (1937, p. 174) commented that "throughout history . . . there has been a see-saw on whether feeling and desire are basally the same . . . or separate."

21. This combination of feelings and passions also was illustrated in a nineteenth-century manual on pedagogy in which the author systematically diagrammed the categories of the human soul (White 1886, pp. 23ff.). The category of feeling included both "corporeal" and "psychical" feelings. Corporeal feelings included "sensations, appetites, and instincts of bodily origin" such as hunger and lust, while psychical feelings consisted of emotions, affections, and desires such as joy and sorrow that have their "origin in the soul."

22. Commentators have related this emphasis on the importance of emotion in religious experience to the stress on feelings promulgated by the romantic movement of the nineteenth century. For example, Perry Miller (1965, p. 60) argued that "the Revival was a romantic phenomenon . . . even while revivalists were denouncing almost all the imported literature of Romanticism." In Protestant preaching of this period, as in romantic literature, emotion had a higher value than intellect.

23. Richard Hofstadter (1963, p. 74) discussed this development in American religious history: "As later revivalism moved from New England and the Middle Colonies out into . . . the South and West, it became more primitive, more emotional, more given to 'ecstatic manifestations.'" Such sporadic revivals were necessary in pioneer communities that were served only by itinerant ministers (Marshall 1992).

24. Ernst Curtius (1953, p. 159) has called this the "inexpressibility topoi" and noted that persons have used it in all ages since the time of Homer.

25. George Landow (1979, pp. xix–xx) describes how the idea of a moral sense developed in the eighteenth century: "After Locke convinced Englishmen that man possesses no innate ideas, not even those of goodness, philosophers sought some replacement for them. Lord Shaftesbury, Francis Hutcheson, and Adam Smith postulated that men have an innate moral sense, and, according to Smith . . . the human being recognizes the moral value of his acts by vicariously experiencing their effect upon another, which he does by an instinctive projection or 'sympathy.'" See Charles Taylor (1989) for further discussion of the development of this idea.

26. Merle Curti (1980, p. 39), among others, has discussed how earlier Puritans did not take such a dim view of reason. The Puritans did see reason as "tainted by corruption," but they gave it more importance in daily life.

27. The autobiographer Andrew Jackson Davis (1857, p. 39) commented on the

"growing tendency [in the first half of the nineteenth century] to reduce the importance of reason in man's moral conduct."

28. Beginning approximately in the 1830s, the Methodist church began to encourage its preachers to get an education in order to gain respectability. During the period 1835–60, the Methodist church opened more than two hundred colleges (Hofstadter 1963). In general, religious denominations were responsible for the development of most of the 516 colleges and universities established in the United States before the Civil War (Hudson 1973).

29. See Vernon Bourke (1964) for an extended discussion of the various definitions of will.

30. Pei-Yi Wu (1984, p. 109) discussed what he called "one of the fundamental paradoxes of the self, a problem with which moral philosophy and religion perennially have had to grapple." He observed that "on the one hand the ego has to be restrained, denied, checked; on the other hand a strong will is required to accomplish these ends, as well as to resist temptations, and to redeem past wrongs that the self has committed. Self-effacement has to go hand in hand with firm resolution."

31. They seemed to agree with St. Augustine who argued that bodily pain, suffering, aging, and involuntary sexual arousal prove the impotence of the will in controlling the body (Pagels 1988).

32. See Norman Pettit (1966) for a discussion of conflicting attitudes among the Puritans in the seventeenth century about the role of will and personal responsibility.

33. See also the discussion of will in Chapter 4.

34. Commentators have found anywhere from two to at least eleven stages in a conversion (Dorsey 1993). Many secular autobiographers also have adopted the form of the conversion narrative to describe an identity transformation. For detailed studies of conversion narratives, see, for example, Starr 1965; Shea 1968; King 1983; and Brereton 1991.

35. Joseph Kett (1977, p. 64) noted that the Puritans expected conversion in maturity or young adulthood, but by the time of the revivals in the early 1800s, the idea of teenage conversions developed and became common.

36. An influential model for a description of the sins of childhood is St. Augustine's ([400] 1963, p. 45) account in his *Confessions* of how he and "some other wretched youths" set out late at night and stole all the pears that they could carry from a tree.

37. Susan Harding (1987), in an analysis of this process, argued that a spiritual crisis or "coming under conviction" is necessary. Individuals must acutely realize their own impurities and yearn for a change.

38. See Arlie Hochschild (1979) for a discussion of "emotion work."

39. As Charles Taylor (1989, p. 184) observed, "The Protestant culture of introspection becomes secularized as a form of confessional autobiography." See also Peter Dorsey 1993.

40. See John Lofland (1966) for a sociological analysis of the conversion process.

41. This quotation from Shepard's *Parable of the Ten Virgins* is used by David Leverenz (1980, p. 1).

42. In contrast, Ruth Bloch (1978, p. 101), in her study of the development of the concept of the "moral mother," found that "in seventeenth- and early eighteenth-century literature written and read in America, motherhood was singularly un-idealized, usually disregarded as a subject, and even at times actually denigrated."

43. According to Joseph Kett (1977, p. 79), there were many tracts and pamphlets after 1820 on "the principles and duties of Christian motherhood." Barbara Welter (1972, p. 245), in her analysis of the "cult of true womanhood" from 1820 to 1860, described the four "cardinal virtues" for women during this period as "piety, purity, submissiveness and domesticity."

44. Kett (1977, p. 79), in his study of adolescence in America, also found that family ideology in the nineteenth century gave a preeminent position to motherhood, and "if fathers figured at all in the literature, it was merely as remote chairmen of the board."

45. In popular religious literature from 1875 to 1955, according to Louis Schneider and Sanford Dornbusch (1958, p. 23), "The world of society has no influence upon the individual and is not to be reckoned as important in any sense in the question of his religious destiny." Schneider and Dornbusch viewed this as a "crucially important gap" in this literature (p. 24).

46. This quotation from Richard Sibbes in *The Saints Cordials* (1637) is used by Taylor (1989, p. 222).

47. David Brion Davis (1957, p. 5), in his study of homicide in American fiction, noted that early nineteenth-century indictments in the United States for murder included this statement: "Not having the fear of God before his eyes, but being moved and seduced by the instigations of the devil."

48. In a much later religious autobiography, Bishop Fulton Sheen (1980, p. 1) made this comment about biblical stories of men's lives: "Carlyle was wrong in saying that 'there is no life of a man faithfully recorded.' Mine was!"

49. See John Barbour (1992) for an insightful discussion of the relationship of conscience and autobiography.

50. The autobiographer Ansel Nickerson (1888, p. 13), listing things that Civil War soldiers carried with them, mentioned *Pilgrim's Progress,* bibles, prayer books, and dictionaries. Lee Soltow and Edward Stevens (1981, p. 80), in a survey of 338 estate inventories from two Ohio counties from 1790 to 1859, found that 74 percent owned religious books.

51. See James R. Moore (1979) for a discussion of the continuities between religious ideas and Darwinism.

52. Sheen (1980, p. 334) explained that one of the offers that the devil made to Jesus was to "satisfy every 'id' of fallen nature."

Chapter Four: Masters of Fate

1. Rex Burns (1976, p. 63) claims that the label *self-made man,* which originated in the United States, first appeared in print in 1828 in a magazine for youth. I found, however, that Benjamin Rush, a signer of the Declaration of Independence, used

this term as if it were common parlance when he was writing his autobiography around 1800 (although it was not published until much later).

2. The laudatory adjective *self-made* apparently was reserved for men. As Mrs. Rachel Watson (1871, p. 92) wrote in her autobiography of domestic life in the wilderness, "The province for female endeavor seems constricted and ungenerous, and beset with snares and temptations on every side." The model established for women was that of the industrious, thrifty, angelic mother. Female autobiographers in the latter half of the nineteenth century, nevertheless, did use ideas such as self-development and self-cultivation. Some women even told of their business successes—although this wasn't typically the theme of their autobiographies, and they did not do so to provide evidence that they were "self-made." In the 1800s, women wrote roughly 4 percent of the autobiographies that focused on business careers.

3. Only the first segment of Franklin's autobiography appeared in English in 1793 (Cremin 1980). The second and third segments were not widely known in the United States until 1818, and the last part was not available until 1868 (Lemay and Zall 1986).

4. McGuffey's readers, first published in 1836, reputedly sold over 122 million copies and were most popular in the 1870s and 1880s (Huber 1971, p. 24). See Ruth Elson (1964) for a study of nineteenth-century American schoolbooks.

5. The development of the *bildungsroman* is usually traced to works such as Goethe's *Wilhelm Meister's Apprenticeship,* translated into English in 1824 (Bruford 1975). Jerome Buckley (1970, p. 94), however, notes that the term was not in common usage until the 1870s. Mill ([1873] 1969, p. 151) himself attributed a general interest in "the right and duty of self-development" to German authors such as Goethe.

6. Among the clergy, Unitarian ministers were most responsible for popularizing the "theology of self-culture" (Robinson 1982, p. 30).

7. In 1891, an American dictionary first included the "gaining of money" as a definition of success (Weiss 1969, p. 98).

8. See Appendix B.

9. Tocqueville ([1835] 1966, 2:35) commented that "aristocratic nations are naturally too liable to narrow the scope of human perfectibility; democratic nations, to expand it beyond reason."

10. By many reports, the American reaction to Charles Darwin's publication of *On the Origin of Species* in 1859 was delayed until the end of the Civil War.

11. Irvin Wyllie (1954, pp. 83–84) argued that the success cult did not use Darwin and Spencer: "It preached no warfare of each against all, but rather a warfare of each man against his baser self. The problem of success was not that of grinding down one's competitors, but of elevating one's self—and the two were not equivalent." I also found that advocates of the self-made man did not discuss a war of all against all when they told their life stories, but, nonetheless, they did make use of ideas of evolution and development to explain their own lives.

12. Precursors of Darwin included his grandfather, Erasmus Darwin, and Sir Charles Lyell who published *Principles of Geology* in 1832.

13. Spencer's books, such as the *Principles of Psychology*, sold over 350,000 copies in the United States from the 1860s until the early 1900s (Hofstadter [1944] 1955, p. 34).

14. Frederick Jackson Turner's (1976) frontier thesis, first published in 1893, argued for the importance of the physical environment in producing American individualism.

15. Donald Stauffer (1941, p. 340) found this idea a century earlier in English biographies: "In the interpretation of human life, the greatest single conception which gained wide currency in eighteenth century biography was the idea that in most mortals good and evil, strength and frailty, were inextricably tangled."

16. Benjamin Franklin ([1793] 1923, pp. 134–35) expressed such a notion in his memoir: "I concluded . . . that the contrary habits must be broken, and good ones acquired and established, before we can have any dependence on a steady, uniform rectitude of conduct." Andrew Delbanco (1995, p. 76) has noted that Franklin "eliminated entirely from his *Autobiography* the word 'sin' and, borrowing a term from the print shop, substituted 'erratum' whenever he spoke of betrayal or other actions that he wished to excise from the public record of his life."

17. See Charles Camic (1986) for a discussion of the use of the idea of habit by Western social theorists in the nineteenth and early twentieth centuries. Camic describes the transformation of the concept of habit in light of the development of evolutionary theory and the growth of psychology as a science. The autobiographer James Fagan (1912, pp. 167–68) attempted such an explanation of his "bad habit" of beer drinking: "With my first glass of beer I deliberately went to work and hired a . . . tiny quantity of gray matter in my brain and devoted it to the interests of the saloon. As time went on . . . the avenue of nerves between my mind and the little bed of gray matter in my brain devoted to beer-drinking interests became a well-beaten thoroughfare."

18. Ernest Hilgard (1987, p. 218) has pointed out that psychologists, beginning with William James, came to define learning as "the formation of habitual responses appropriate to recurrent stimuli."

19. According to David Brion Davis (1957, p. 22), there was a "flood of books" in the 1840s and 1850s about moral culture—particularly the nurture of such feelings in women.

20. In an 1852 self-help book in which the epigraph was "self-made or never made," the author specifically defined intellectual improvement as mental discipline (Fowler 1852, p. ix).

21. Carnegie endowed libraries as a place where people could engage in such self-development. As Lawrence Cremin (1980, p. 307) noted, "The arguments for public libraries, which began to gain currency after 1850, tended to combine all the assertions in favor of widespread reading—self-culture, moral improvement, and vocational advancement."

22. Even John Stuart Mill ([1873] 1969, pp. 19–20), while detailing his precocious development, claimed that he was "rather below than above par" in quickness of apprehension and in the retentiveness of his memory.

23. Mill ([1873] 1969, p. 86) emphasized how, in his own education, the faculty of reason had been developed at the expense of the cultivation of feelings.

24. Around the turn of the twentieth century, the most popular success manual, with sales around 750,000 copies, was a book entitled *Power of Will: A Practical Companion-Book for Unfoldment of Selfhood through Direct Personal Culture* (Weiss 1969).

25. Joseph Kett (1977) traced this change in the meaning of *character,* in part, to an influential essay on "decision of character" published in 1805 by the English Baptist minister John Foster.

26. This quotation is from White (1886, p. 319). When psychologists began devising mental tests at the end of the nineteenth century, they included tests to measure character ("orexis"). See Pittel and Mendelsohn 1966.

27. William James ([1890] 1950, 1:125) attempted a scientific explanation of the development of character: Will is "an aggregate of tendencies to act in a firm and prompt and definite way upon all the principal emergencies of life. A tendency to act only becomes effectively ingrained in us in proportion to the uninterrupted frequency with which the actions actually occur, and the brain 'grows' to their use."

28. I found this quotation in Sheringham (1993, p. 10). In a book on interpretive biography, the sociologist Norman Denzin (1989, p. 7) defined biography in general as "life documents . . . which describe turning-point moments in individuals' lives." But this definition does not take into account historical or cultural variations in biographical techniques. As David Brumble (1988, p. 15) observed in his study of American Indian autobiography, "When Eagle-ribs and White Bull tell tales of their war deeds, we do not find turning points; the stories do not work in connected fashion toward a climactic moment."

29. A famous example of such a life story was that of John Stuart Mill ([1873] 1969, pp. 41–42), who discussed his "mental progress" and the formation of an intellectual creed: "The reading of this book [about Bentham] was an epoch in my life; one of the turning points in my mental history." Mill added, "I now had opinions; a creed, a doctrine, a philosophy; in one among the best senses of the word, a religion; the inculcation and diffusion of which could be made the principal outward purpose of a life."

30. A nineteenth-century self-help author argued that work is good because it "consumes those energies created by food, breath, etc., which must be expended on something, in muscular action; but when this door of escape is closed by fashionable idleness, its next egress is through . . . the PROPENSITIES" (Fowler 1852, p. 51).

31. Richard Huber (1971) examined the use of this idea in the success literature in the nineteenth century.

32. The belief in positive environmental influences on human behavior played a part in the movement during the 1880s and 1890s for public parks, which were be-

lieved to "encourage the virtues associated with country living" (Curti 1980, p. 229).

33. C. Wright Mills (1940) argued that pecuniary motives have become more acceptable in the United States to explain business enterprise.

34. Robert Wuthnow (1976, pp. 101–2) has made a similar observation: "Society was merely the land of opportunity in which the individual functioned. Above all, it posed no barriers to the individual who wished to succeed."

35. Early nineteenth-century romanticism celebrated the hero (Perry 1989).

36. Not all nineteenth-century autobiographers, however, spent their entire childhood with their parents. The experience of the manufacturer Ichabod Washburn (1878, pp. 17–18) was not unusual: "The time arrived when my mother felt the necessity of being relieved from the expense of my support, and before I was nine years of age I was 'put out to live,' as the term was." Or, instead of being farmed out to earn their keep, others reported being sent to live with relatives such as grandparents or uncles.

37. John Stuart Mill ([1873] 1969), in contrast, described his father's active participation in his own mental development, and he did not even mention his mother in the final version of his autobiography.

38. Morse Peckham (1959, p. 29) argued that "the grand thesis of metaphysical evolutionism—from simple to complex means from good to better . . . —not only received no support from the *Origin* but, if the book were properly understood . . . was positively demolished."

39. Other commentators have proposed that "the emphasis on control and self-sacrifice attending the concept of character ill served an economy that required continual spending on proliferating goods" (Rubin 1992, p. 24).

Chapter Five: The Uncertain Self

1. Quoted by Robert Farr 1981, p. 307.

2. The sociologist Benjamin Nelson (1957, p. 9) once asked this question: "Will the Twentieth Century go down in history as the *Freudian Century?*"

3. A. R. Luria (1976, p. 147) found in his studies of Russian illiterate peasants from remote villages in the 1930s that the "task of analyzing one's own psychological features or subjective qualities went beyond the capabilities of a considerable proportion of our subjects." One woman, for example, when queried about her "personal shortcomings," responded that she needed more clothes. She still did not understand what the researcher meant when he rephrased the question as "Tell me what kind of person you are now."

4. This is not a one-way relationship, of course. Psychologists draw upon conventional understandings of human action. Jerome Bruner (1990, p. 14), however, has argued that folk wisdom is not simply supplanted by psychology since the latter often dismisses as subjective that which is crucial to folk psychology: intentions and beliefs.

5. We can find additional evidence for the spread of a psychological approach by

examining published reviews of autobiographies. By the early twentieth century, some critics began to fault autobiographers who did not adopt such a perspective. Louis Kronenberger (1930, p. 10), for example, groused that a particular autobiographer's "recollections of life . . . have no structure and no psychology."

6. Many of these psychological concepts and theories intertwined with sociological ideas developing during the same period. In this chapter, however, I attempt to isolate the psychological ideas to look more closely at attempts to explain the nature of the "inner" self—particularly internal forces or dynamics such as drives and instincts that help explain human behavior.

7. The first American textbook to use *psychology* in the title, Friedrich Rauch's *Psychology: or, a View of the Human Soul, Including Anthropology,* appeared in 1840 (Hilgard 1987).

8. See James Benton (1981) for a related study of middle-class magazines from 1920 to 1978.

9. The idea of motive "in its modern psychological sense" came into use at the end of the eighteenth century (McReynolds 1990, p. 156). The term *motivation* was introduced into the English language in 1873.

10. Jerome Kagan (1983, p. 544) found a similar change in developmental psychology textbooks: "In those published before 1920, *will* bears the burden of explaining acts chosen by the child; in modern texts, *motivation* assumes that responsibility." In 1968, the American Psychological Association held a symposium entitled, "Whatever Happened to Will in American Psychology?" (Woodward 1984, p. 148).

11. Vernon Bourke (1964, p. 229) cites this quotation from N. L. Munn's *Psychology, the Fundamentals of Human Adjustment.*

12. This all-inclusive concept of motivation, however, has been the subject of definitional disputes within psychology. In his textbook on motivation, John Atkinson (1964, p. 273) made this point: "The term [motivation] has no fixed technical meaning in contemporary psychology. It is often used in reference to the conscious feeling of desire and the whole complex of ideas and feelings which together seem to constitute the conscious antecedents of behavior according to traditional wisdom. Just as often, 'motivation' is used to refer to the unconscious determinants of behavior which Freud emphasized."

13. Lincoln Steffens (1931, p. 149) recalled that during his sojourn as a student at Wilhelm Wundt's laboratory, Wundt made this comment about William James's work: "It is literature, it is beautiful, but it is not psychology."

14. See Hamilton Cravens (1978) for a detailed study of this controversy during the years 1900–1941. The literary movements of realism and naturalism, developing in the latter half of the nineteenth century, also attended to issues of heredity and environment.

15. The debate between the Weismannists and Lamarckians lasted from roughly 1890 to 1910 (Stocking 1982).

16. A few empirical studies of infants had already appeared—Dietrich Tiedemann published one of the earliest in Germany in 1787 (Riley 1983). The first

American journal devoted to the study of childhood as a stage of life, the *Pedagogical Seminary,* was founded in 1891 by the psychologist G. Stanley Hall.

17. As Frank Johnson (1985, p. 111) makes clear, terms such as *instinct, motivation, drive, need,* and *libido* often rely on "metaphorical or analogical references to physical, biological, or physiological systems."

18. R. S. Woodworth added the concept of *drive* to the vocabulary of psychology in 1918 (McReynolds 1990), and theorists like John Dewey substituted the old idea of *impulse* for the concept of instinct (House 1936).

19. Quoted by Gerth and Mills ([1946] 1980, p. 143).

20. Although it is possible to trace the idea of the unconscious back to at least G. W. Leibnitz, it was Freud who thoroughly developed this idea (Ellenberger 1970). William James proclaimed that this "discovery that memories, thoughts, and feelings exist outside the primary consciousness is the most important step forward that has occurred in psychology since I have been a student of that science" (Humphrey 1954, p. 1).

21. The nature of the relationship between emotion and motivation is unclear. In a dictionary of psychology, James Chaplin (1985, p. 152) noted that "a problem of definition that has loomed large in recent psychological discussion of the emotions is that of the relationship between feeling and emotion on the one hand and motivation on the other . . . Indeed, so close is the relationship between motives and emotions that some psychologists believe we do not need both terms." Atkinson (1964, p. 23), discussing the difficulty of separating *instinct* from *emotion,* noted that Darwin and Spencer described emotions as "a revival in weakened, residual form of reactions that were at one time useful in more violent dealings with the object inspiring them." Part of the problem is that the concept of emotion itself is nebulous (Sarbin 1986a).

22. For example, the James-Lange theory of emotions.

23. The psychologist Edwin Boring (1950, p. 274) wrote that he agreed with John Dewey that "the psychology of individual differences flourishes in democracies" because it is contrary to the idea of inherited class distinctions. One manifestation of this interest in individual differences, for example, was the development of intelligence tests such as the Binet test first published in 1905.

24. "Personality" became a topic in psychology textbooks in the United States during the decade of 1910–19 (Davis and Gould 1929). Around the time of World War I, psychologists also began to develop personality tests—precursors of tests such as the Minnesota Multiphasic Personality Inventory.

25. The autobiographer Georgiana Kirby (1887, p. 6), for example, used *personality* in this sense when she referred to an occasion when others had forgotten her presence: "When my small [she was short in stature] personality was remembered."

26. Freud critiqued the concept of personality, however, by arguing that "'personality' . . . is a loosely defined term from surface psychology that does nothing in particular to increase understanding of the real processes, that is to say, *metapsychologically* it says nothing" (quoted by Russell Jacoby 1975, pp. 30–31).

27. Susman, however, as well as Irvin Wyllie (1954), stressed a sociological defi-

nition of personality, that is, getting along with others. Susman suggests that such a switch related to the increasing number of bureaucratic jobs in the early twentieth century in which such social skills would be useful. But it was the definition of personality as a unique set of behavioral characteristics that these early twentieth-century autobiographers initially took up.

28. See Merle Curti (1980) for a discussion of the development of a scientific conception of human nature in the nineteenth century.

29. See B. F. Skinner's (1971) *Beyond Freedom and Dignity.*

30. In the latter half of the nineteenth century, Cesare Lombroso developed his theory that criminals were throwbacks to an earlier evolutionary stage in human history.

31. Quoted by Jerome Kagan 1983, p. 545.

32. This article became part of William James's *Principles of Psychology* ([1890] 1950, 1:104), which became the standard psychology textbook for college courses in the United States during that time.

33. Nathan Hale (1971, p. 267) found that Havelock Ellis was more widely read than Freud in the United States before 1920. In his memoirs, H. L. Mencken ([1940] 1955, pp. 186–87) claimed that "the great science of sex hygiene which eventually developed into a major American industry" began in 1897 with the publication of a book by Reverend Sylvanus Stall entitled *What a Young Boy Ought to Know.*

34. In his 1940 article on "vocabularies of motives," C. Wright Mills observed that it had become common in the United States to discuss sex as a motive. For a recent discussion of this trend, see Ken Plummer's *Telling Sexual Stories* (1995).

35. A good contrast case is Clifford Geertz's (1983, p. 62) description of Balinese beliefs: "There is in Bali a persistent and systematic attempt to stylize all aspects of personal expression to the point where anything idiosyncratic, anything characteristic of the individual merely because he is who he is physically, psychologically, or biographically, is muted in favor of his assigned place in the continuing and, so it is thought, never-changing pageant that is Balinese life."

36. The English writer Edmund Gosse (1907, p. 134) complained in the early years of this century that "the rage for what is called 'originality' is pushed to such a length in these days that even children are not considered promising, unless they attempt things preposterous and unparalleled. From his earliest hour, the ambitious person is told that to make a road where none has walked before, to do easily what it is impossible for others to do at all, to create new forms of thought and expression, are the only recipes for genius."

37. In this sense of an "accumulation of particulars," we might understand William James's interest in autobiographies, which he revealed in a letter to Henry Adams in 1907: "I may add that autobiographies are my particular line of literature, the only books I let myself buy outside of metaphysical treatises" (Ford 1938, p. 485n.1). I originally found this quotation in Olney (1972, p. x).

38. This reflexive concern with the self can be found in many words coined in the latter half of the nineteenth century: self-analysis (1862), self-questioning

(1862), self-identity (1866), self-reflective (1875), self-awareness (1880), and self-expression (1892).

39. Raymond Williams (1983, p. 162) observed that in the nineteenth century "there was a remarkable efflorescence of the word [individual]. Increasingly the phrase 'an individual'—a single example of a group—was joined and overtaken by 'the individual': a fundamental order of being."

40. Some of the words previously used to note individual differences (that also carried the connotation that such differences are inborn) included disposition, temperament, streaks, gifts, constitution, and makeup.

41. The effect of psychoanalysis on autobiography has been discussed by Mazlish 1970; Downing 1977; Sturrock 1977; and Eakin 1985, among others. The writer James Atlas (1988, p. 42) has stressed the importance of psychoanalytic ideas for twentieth-century biographers as well: "Any biographer setting up shop these days is virtually required to draw upon the discoveries of Freud, to analyze his subject's unconscious life with the same zeal that his counterpart of an earlier time brought to the assembling of documents." If one adopts this perspective, then a comparison of autobiographies with biographies can be instructive. Conversely, some psychoanalysts also began to write biographies, for example, Erik Erikson's *Young Man Luther* (1958). The term *psychobiography* was coined in 1931.

42. Paul John Eakin (1992, p. 84) has argued that "beyond a general acceptance that frankness is a desideratum, however, and that sexuality ought to be included in the story of a life, the impact of the Freudian concept of the unconscious on autobiography has not been very substantial." I would agree that most autobiographers have not wholeheartedly adopted a Freudian perspective, but this does not mean they have ignored most of its tenets. I think Richard Rorty's (1986, p. 3) comment is more fitting: "Freud *did* change our self-image. Finding out about our unconscious motives is not just an intriguing exercise, but more like a moral obligation."

43. For a related study of how psychoanalytic ideas were used and transformed in France, see Serge Moscovici's study of social representations, *La Psychanalyse, Son Image et Son Public* (1961).

44. Pierre Janet introduced the idea of the *subconscious* in 1889 as part of the theory of dissociation developed to explain the phenomena of multiple personalities and hypnosis (Hilgard 1987). Ernest Jones (1953, p. 403) observed that Freud never used the term *subconscious* because it misleadingly connotes something that is "slightly less conscious." In the 1920s, Emile Coué helped to popularize the idea of the subconscious with his advice that useful suggestions aimed at the subconscious mind can improve a person's behavior and outlook, for example, "Day by day, in every way, I'm getting better and better" (Burnham 1988).

45. I found some of these autobiographers beginning to use "character" to refer to an unusual or eccentric person as did Yogi Berra (Berra and Fitzgerald 1961, p. 110) when he commented in his autobiography, "No wonder I got the reputation of being a character."

46. As Raymond Williams (1983, pp. 246–47) pointed out, the term *psychological* has even come to refer in contemporary everyday use to "an area of the mind

(unconscious), which is primarily that of 'feeling' rather than of 'reason' or 'intellect' or 'knowledge.'"

47. Daniel Bell (1976, p. 19) observed a trend in Western society that he labeled the "dialectic of release and restraint." He argued that "the shift to release occurs with the breakup of religious authority in the mid-nineteenth century. In effect, the culture—particularly modernist culture—took over the relation with the demonic. But instead of taming it, as religion tried to do, the secular culture (art and literature) began to accept it, explore it, and revel in it, coming to see it as a source of creativity."

48. In a survey of university students, Ralph Turner (1975, p. 153) discovered that an "overwhelming majority . . . acknowledge a personal quest for identity." He did not, however, find this to be the case among the general adult population at that time.

49. An interesting contrast with Meyer's interpretation of her dream is that of Abigail Bailey's (1815, p. 23): "I have no idea that dreams are generally much to be noticed. But when I reflect upon what I then experienced of this nature, and compare it with trains of subsequent facts, I am constrained to believe, that God did see fit to afford me some solemn premonitions in sleep."

50. See Appendix B. Richard Coe (1984, p. 40) has pointed out that the autobiography of childhood was becoming a "clearly defined literary form" in Europe by the 1830s—a development that some commentators have also related to romanticism.

51. The median percentage of pages devoted to childhood in my sample of autobiographers from the first half of the twentieth century was more than double what it had been a century earlier (14 percent as compared to 6 percent). This calculation, furthermore, does not include those autobiographies devoted solely to memories of childhood. Any count of pages, however, must be only a rough guide since autobiographers usually do not announce the end of childhood. Nevertheless, they do often make it apparent what they see as divisions in their lives, for example, by chapter divisions and titles and by no further references to themselves as children. The end of childhood might be demarcated by marriage (for women), leaving home, one's first job, beginning college, or a religious conversion.

52. The title of a popular self-help book in the 1920s was *The Caveman within Us.* Its author, William J. Fielding, argued that "beginning with the age of one or one and one-half years, the mind of the civilized child is an outline, crude but unmistakable, of the prehistoric evolution of the human race" (p. 28).

53. See Curti 1980; and Hilgard 1987. The word *adolescence,* however, had originally appeared in English as early as the fifteenth century.

54. Andrew Delbanco (1995, p. 144) reports that "the line between fortune and providence was breaking down in public discourse as early as the 1820s, when the idea of chance first crept into the language of the clergy." See also Ian Hacking's (1990, p. 10) discussion of how the idea of chance became "the centerpiece of natural and social science" in the nineteenth century.

55. Jerome Kagan (1983, p. 540), in a review of child development textbooks, re-

ported that "prior to 1910, it was unusual for a text to devote more than a few paragraphs to the direct influence of the family on the child. After 1920, it was impossible to find a text that did not devote a long section or whole chapters to parents, siblings, and the social class of the family as formative factors." See also Peggy Rosenthal's (1984) discussion of changes in the connotations of the word *relationship*.

56. In a study of more recent books for children, Anne Scott MacLeod (1985, p. 107) discovered "an astonishing hostility toward parents, making parental inadequacies a central theme, especially (though not exclusively) in books written for the teen market."

57. The behaviorist John Watson (1928) included a chapter in his advice manual *Psychological Care of Infant and Child* entitled "The Dangers of Too Much Mother Love." Considerably earlier, Rousseau ([1762] 1974, p. 14), had argued in *Émile* that "the mother may lavish excessive care on her child instead of neglecting him; she may make an idol of him; she may develop and increase his weakness." Rousseau maintained that the education of the child must be by the father or a male tutor. For a well-known article that followed Wylie's book ([1942] 1955), see Arnold Green's (1946) "The Middle-Class Male Child and Neurosis."

58. See Strout (1981) for a discussion of the fate of the hero in a "psychological age."

59. As Domna Stanton (1984, p. 6) observed, *autobiographical* sometimes has served as a term of reproach when applied to women's writings ("to affirm that women could not transcend, but only record, the concerns of the private self"). But even in this writing that reflects such a self-focus, most of these autobiographers have been men.

60. Elizabeth Bruss (1976, p. 18) pointed out that the biographer James Boswell recognized this difficulty in the eighteenth century when he "no longer [found] the distinction between 'fact' and 'fiction' sufficient; a new opposition must be made between competing kinds of fact—between the objective fact and affective psychology of observation associated with biography and the more arbitrary and capricious realm of subjective fact and private sensibility that is the domain of autobiography."

61. As the writer André Maurois expressed it: "Memory is a great artist" (cited by Pascal 1960, p. 70).

62. Some commentators suggest that autobiographers such as Adams wrote in the third person in an attempt to gain some objectivity on their lives through distance (Lejeune 1989). Stephen Shapiro (1968, pp. 443–44), however, adds that such distance can be used for the purposes of ironic contrast, to praise oneself less directly, or to defend one's self-image by adopting a supposedly more objective standpoint.

63. In his *Anti-Memoirs,* André Malraux (1968, pp. 4–5) commented that "introspective autobiography has changed its character, because the confessions of the most provocative memorialist seem puerile by comparison with the monsters conjured up by psychoanalytical exploration, even to those who contest its conclusions."

206 Notes to Pages 118–123

64. In 1907, W.A. Gill published an article in *Atlantic Monthly* noting the trend toward the "nude in autobiography," that is, a discussion of personal faults and blemishes.

65. Thomas De Quincey ([1821] 1966, p. 22), in his *Confessions of an English Opium-Eater*, wrote that "nothing, indeed, is more revolting to English feelings than the spectacle of a human being obtruding on our notice his moral ulcers or scars and tearing away that 'decent drapery' which time or indulgence to human frailty may have drawn over them."

66. Bruce Mazlish (1970, p. 33) gave such a reading to Freud's brief autobiography of his career—noting an attribution on Freud's part that readers may interpret as a matter of self-deception. Freud (1925, pp. 24–25) asserted that it was his wife's "fault" that he was not known as the discoverer of the anesthetizing properties of cocaine because he paused in his work to visit her. He concluded his discussion of this event with the statement, "I bore my fiancée no grudge for her interruption of my work."

67. Leon Edel (1984, pp. 28–29) insisted that biographers should take this approach: "I mean the kind of analysis which enables us to see through the rationalizations, the postures, the self-delusions and self-deceptions of our subjects—in a word the manifestations of the unconscious as they are projected in conscious forms of action within whatever walks of life our subject has chosen." A writer from the 1920s complained that "the worst foe of biography that has yet appeared is the disciple of Freud, who crawls like a snail over all that is comely in life and Art" (quoted by Garraty 1964, p. 142).

68. Novelists, of course, also have borrowed biographical techniques. Donald Stauffer (1941, p. 66), among others, has discussed how novelists, in an attempt to be more realistic, have "imitated the exact details, the matter-of-fact tone, the enumeration of dates and places, the unconscious personal biases, the meditations and apologies, even the ineptnesses, which they found in earlier biographers."

69. According to Wayne Booth (1983, p. 191), fiction writers in the 1920s adopted the idea that telling a story chronologically was less realistic than telling a story in a more disjointed style using flashbacks and so forth. As Ford Madox Ford ([1927] 1983, p. 183) once observed, when one discusses one's life with others, "one goes back, one goes forward. One remembers points that one has forgotten, and one explains them all the more minutely since one recognizes that one has forgotten to mention them in their proper places."

70. Some nineteenth-century commentators, too, worried about a "cult of individuality." Emile Durkheim ([1893] 1964, p. 172) was troubled over the extent to which "the individual becomes the object of a sort of religion. We erect a cult in behalf of personal dignity . . . It is still from society that it takes all its force, but it is not to society that it attaches us; it is to ourselves." Laura Marcus (1994), in her history of autobiographical criticism, has pointed out the prominence of the debate over the proper amount of attention to be focused on self.

71. The interest in motivation eventually declined among psychologists (except among psychoanalysts) with the advent of cognitive psychology in the late 1950s.

This shift reintroduced the importance of *action* in contrast to *behavior,* which connotes passivity (Hilgard 1987).

72. Ralph Turner used the phrase "the uncertain self" in his 1975 article, "Is There a Quest for Identity?"

Chapter Six: The Beleaguered Self

1. The historian Merle Curti (1980, p. 217) also has described such a change: "In the last decades of the nineteenth century . . . a quite different conception of human nature emerged. It viewed man's makeup in terms of the social forces and interpersonal relationships that molded both individual and social behavior." Many observers have noted such a shift toward a sociocultural explanation of human behavior. See, for example, Gerth and Mills 1953; Hale 1971; Cravens 1978; Finkelstein 1982; and Baumeister 1986, 1987. John R. Seeley (1967) deemed this change a "sociological revolution" in the twentieth century.

2. In contrast, Michelle Rosaldo (1980, p. 224) found in her study of the Ilongot in the Philippines that "the 'self,' for them, is not an entity whose 'nature,' either good or bad, must then be tainted, tamed, or otherwise perplexed by the demands of its society . . . Nor will they, in their early years, be taught responsibility, individuality, and an independent 'sense of self' with which to criticize and resist the corrupting claims of sociality."

3. According to Charles H. Cooley, those Americans who became interested in sociology during the years between 1870 and 1890 were influenced by the work of Spencer (Hofstadter [1944] 1955).

4. Jerome Kagan (1983, p. 531) has described a related change in child development textbooks: "Most nineteenth-century writers classified the onset of reliable imitation in the infant . . . as a sign that the child was now capable of volitional action. Many twentieth-century observers used the same event to index the emergence of social behavior. It is likely that this change in categorization is due, in part, to the increasing importance assigned to social interaction by modern observers."

5. Albion Small (1916, p. 755) referred to Lester Ward's introduction of the concept of "social forces" in 1883 as the "foundation of American sociology."

6. As Richard Hofstadter (1963, p. 398) and other commentators have argued, industrialization and the development of the "new bourgeois world" played an important part in "romantic assertions of the individual against society."

7. Psychologists in the twentieth century who accepted the importance of social influences included behaviorists, who looked to the environment rather than heredity in explaining human behavior; the neo-Freudians, such as Harry Stack Sullivan and Karen Horney, who placed greater emphasis than Freud on sociocultural factors in the explanation of human behavior; and humanistic psychologists, such as Carl Rogers, who picked up the theme of the individual versus society. One also might include the culture-and-personality theorists during the 1930s, 1940s, and 1950s, who considered the relation between personality variables and culture.

8. George W. Stocking, Jr. (1982, p. 203), argued that although many anthro-

pologists have credited Edward B. Tylor with coming up with the idea of "culture" in 1871, Tylor's definition referred to culture as "a singular phenomenon, present to a higher or lower degree in all peoples."

9. Such a division of the self is used with varying degrees of forgetfulness of the metaphorical nature of such an idea. As Rom Harré (1981) has observed, people often lump together the ideas of *private, inner,* and *personal* as well as the ideas of *social, outer,* and *public.* Harré argues that "the distinction between individual and social states should not be confused with that between public and private states, nor with that between inner and outer states" (p. 80).

10. Dorothy Ross (1991, pp. 236–37), in her survey of the development of the social sciences, noted that the earliest usage she found of the concept of *social control* was by Mill.

11. The question of how human beings differ from other animals had been the concern of late-nineteenth-century theorists such as Chauncey Wright, who published an essay on "The Evolution of Self-Consciousness" in 1873 (Russett 1976).

12. Another way to consider this division of the self, as the psychiatrist Frank Johnson (1985, p. 97) has done, is "self-as-state" versus "self-as-process"—one "emphasizing internal, structural, and biological factors" with the latter "accentuating transactional, situational, and contextual variables."

13. Freud ([1920] 1938, p. 252) specified these blows: Copernicus let us know that the earth is not the center of the universe, Darwin informed us that human beings have descended from animals, and Freud made us realize that we know little about what is going on unconsciously in our own minds.

14. The educator William Alcott (1839, pp. 293–94), for instance, made this observation: "In the school room [pupils] may be more or less disguised [sic]; but in their sports, they are sometimes, incautiously, off their guard; and they then show themselves out in their true naked character."

15. Geertz made this comment in a colloquy of culture theorists—the transcripts of which were published in Shweder and LeVine (1984, p. 15).

16. This is also the case for writers like Robert Louis Stevenson in *Dr. Jekyll and Mr. Hyde* ([1886] 1980, p. 104) where he wrote, "Man is not truly one, but truly two. I say two, because the state of my own knowledge does not pass beyond that point . . . I hazard the guess that man will be ultimately known for a mere polity of multifarious, incongruous and independent denizens." In addition, there was the literary device of "the double" to discuss divided selves (Miyoshi 1969; Robert Rogers 1970).

17. Robert Hogan and Jonathan Cheek (1983, p. 341) have commented on the wide appeal of this metaphor of "inner" and "outer" among personality theorists and social psychologists.

18. Clifford Geertz made this relevant observation: "Let's imagine that the Western concept of a centered, highly continuous self really suppresses a natural fact—the fact that we're playing roles throughout our lives. That it creates a myth of continuity that has overcome the actual experience of the fact that we behave so radically different in radically different contexts" (Shweder and LeVine 1984, p. 15).

19. An example of the nineteenth-century literary use of this concept was Matthew Arnold's (1979) "genuine self" in his poem, "The Buried Life," published in 1852.

20. Humanistic psychologists such as Carl Rogers have focused on the internal, "real" self. Rogers (1961, p. 109) urged his clients "to drop the false fronts, or the masks, or the roles with which [they have] faced life."

21. A British autobiographer, Aubrey Menen (1970, pp. 10–11), used the metaphor of peeling an onion when describing his search for the inner self: "One by one, you strip away those parts of your personality which consist of the things that you do because the world taught you to do them, or made you do them. Layer by layer—your parents' advice, your schooling, your job, your social position—all go.

"Then, one evening, after a long day of thought . . . , I saw that everything had gone and there was no more to discard."

22. The sociologist Peter Berger (1965, pp. 40–41) has argued that "psychologism . . . brings about a strange reversal of the disenchantment and demythologization of modern consciousness. The other world, which religion located in a transcendental reality, is now introjected within human consciousness itself. It becomes the other self (the more real, or the healthier, or the more mature self) which is the goal of the psychological quest."

23. Gordon Allport (1937, p. 39) cites this definition from E. W. Burgess.

24. Critics such as C. Wright Mills (1951, p. 263) decried such advice: "Now the stress is on agility rather than ability, on 'getting along' in a context of associates, superiors, and rules, rather than 'getting ahead' across an open market; on who you know rather than what you know; on techniques of self-display and the generalized knack of handling people, rather than on moral integrity, substantive accomplishments, and solidity of person."

25. Jerome Kagan (1983, p. 538), in his study of child development textbooks, quotes an author in 1930 who explained that "play is neither demanded nor imposed, but bubbles up spontaneously."

26. In his memoir, Sartre (1964, pp. 142, 139) used recollections of his schooldays to illustrate his point that "children are conformists": "Far from wanting to shine, I laughed in chorus with the others, I repeated their catchwords and phrases, I kept quiet, I obeyed, I imitated my neighbors' gestures, I had only one desire: to be integrated."

27. In an article on identity and maturity, psychologists Robert Hogan and Jonathan Cheek (1983, p. 341) offer just such a definition of maturity: "Playing one's organizational or social roles with detachment and role distance."

28. As Paul Zweig (1968, p. 245) commented, "There is a paradox in this notion of a 'cultural' voice whose energies are directed against the institutions of 'public life.'"

29. From roughly 1910 to the end of World War II, the literary movement *modernism* included a theme of opposition to bourgeois society (Beckson and Ganz 1989). The literary critic Alan Kennedy (1974, p. 7) claimed that "the central assertion of modern literature might be put as . . . 'I exist in spite of God and in defiance of Society.'"

30. David Leverenz (1980, p. 278n.43) noted that both Ludwig Lewisohn and H. L. Mencken were among those who helped popularize the idea that Puritanism equated repressiveness.

31. Richard Hofstadter (1963, p. 368) found a similar viewpoint in theories of education: "The notion of education advanced at the turn of the century by . . . pedagogical reformers was romantic in the sense that they set up an antithesis between the development of the individual—his sensibility, the scope of his fancy, the urgency of his personal growth—and the imperatives of the social order, with its demands for specified bodies of knowledge, prescribed manners and morals, and a personal equipment suited to traditions and institutions. Theirs was a commitment to the natural child against artificial society."

32. William James ([1890] 1950, 1:310), in contrast, defined self-esteem with less reference to the viewpoint of others. He claimed self-esteem could be characterized as success divided by pretensions or as "the ratio of our actualities to our supposed potentiality."

33. Michelle Rosaldo (1984, p. 138) observed that some psychologists have come to believe that a consideration of "face" has become "a central motive for the psyche."

34. Some nineteenth-century doctors postulated that the pace of contemporary life led to nervous diseases. In the 1860s, for example, the physician George M. Beard introduced the diagnosis of "neurasthenia" as "exhausted nerves due to the fast-paced American life" (Burnham 1968, p. 60; Ellenberger 1970, p. 242). Earlier in the century, the educational reformer William Alcott (1839, p. 111) grumbled that he lived "in a day when parents have too much to do to find time for bringing up their children." And Sophia Wyatt (1854, p. iii) longed for the good old 1790s when "'slow and sure' was the watchword."

35. As the sociologist Robert Perinbanayagam (1991, p. 153) has pointed out, "[Obscenities and blasphemies] are peerless in their capacity to evoke cultural anxieties and signify defiance of conventionalities."

36. Josephine Hendin (1990, p. 49) notes a similar change in fiction: "The comparable fiction of the 1980s seems to be giving up the countercultural attack on adulthood, authority, and repression. There is in progress a quiet but sharp recoil from the concepts of self and society, from the quest for authentic emotion, from the visions of individualism and possibility that have been animating forces in our literature."

37. See Philip Dodd (1987) for a discussion of this point. He distinguishes between the "coexistence of autobiography as an elite/literary form affiliated to fiction and autobiography as a popular/nonfiction form affiliated to history" (p. 62).

38. In my data, I also found an increase in the number of autobiographies written by members of minority groups beginning roughly in the years after World War II—but most notably increasing in the 1960s. A concomitant trend since the early 1970s has been critical analyses of such autobiographies. See, for example, Cooke 1973; Butterfield 1974; Smith 1974; Boelhower 1982; Krupat 1985; Andrews 1986, 1993; Braxton 1989; Payne 1992; and Padilla 1993.

39. In this regard, Gleason (1992, p. 134) observed that a "primordialist argument inevitably suggests the conclusion that, if ethnicity is bound to persist anyhow, there is no great need for new social policies designed to foster or protect it."

40. Werner Sollors (1989, p. xiii) reports that the first use of "ethnicity" in this sense in print was by W. Lloyd Warner in his 1941 book *The Social Life of a Modern Community.*

41. For a discussion of the varying definitions of cultural pluralism, see Philip Gleason (1992).

42. Early slave narratives emphasized a shared humanity—the way in which the slave was "a man and a brother" to whites (Andrews 1986, pp. 1–2).

43. Psychologists Jerald Jellison and Jane Green (1981) argue that there is a general preference in American society for explanations of behavior based on internal rather than external factors.

44. They may show a particular sensitivity to how racism and sexism are built into our language. Charlayne Hunter-Gault (1992, p. iv), for example, put this notice in the front of her autobiography: "In referring to people of color, I have used terms that were in current usage at the time of the events described." And Ruben Navarrette (1993, p. xvii), on a page entitled "Author's Note on Terminology," offered this explanation: "I have refrained from using the term *people of color,* which I find offensive, preferring instead the more relative term *minority.* I have not often used the word *chicano*—a political remnant of an earlier time. I have also been reluctant to use the more contemporary term *Hispanic,* choosing *Latino* instead, though not for the same reasons that the ethnic left finds the label *Hispanic* objectionable."

Chapter Seven: Conclusion

1. I am indebted to Bruner's (1990, p. 51) discussion of storytelling as a moral stance. See also Robert Wuthnow (1987) on moral codes, Charles Taylor's (1989) *Sources of the Self,* and Richard Rorty (1986) on a "vocabulary of moral reflection."

Appendix A: Method

1. Thomas Cooley (1976, p. 3) reports that the term "autobiography" was coined in 1797. More recently, Robert Folkenflik (1993, p. 1) found the term "autobiographical" used in 1786. Earlier terms included confession, memoir, and life.

2. Among literary scholars, there has been a substantial debate over the definition of autobiography. For example, there is the question of how much fiction (if any) can be included in such a story without it losing its classification as an autobiography. For an extended discussion, see Philippe Lejeune (1989). To study vocabularies of the self, I believe Delany's definition to be sufficient, although some critics would question his requirement that the narrative be unified and his use of the male pronoun to refer to the autobiographer.

3. I find that a distinction between autobiography and memoir is difficult to sustain in close analysis. Memoirists focus on the external world, but they often discuss their thoughts and feelings as well.

4. See Michael Wood and Louis Zurcher (1988) for a content analysis of American diaries.

5. For comparison purposes, I also read French, British, German, and Japanese autobiographies as well as American autobiographies published before 1800.

6. See, for example, Jelinek 1980, 1986; Mason 1980; Stanton 1984; Heilbrun 1985, 1988; Peterson 1986, 1993; Smith 1987; Brodzki and Schenck 1988; Benstock 1988; Nussbaum 1989; Bell and Yalom 1990; Fowler and Fowler 1990; Conway 1992; Smith and Watson 1992.

7. Literary critic Alan Kennedy (1974, p. 4) used this phrase when characterizing sociologists who study literature.

8. See Jane Tompkins 1980; and Wallace Martin 1986.

9. See, for example, Wendy Griswold 1987.

Primary Sources

Abrey, Daniel. 1903. *Reminiscences.* Corunna, Mich.: Louis Sheardy.

Adams, Henry. [1906] 1918. *The Education of Henry Adams: An Autobiography.* Boston: Houghton Mifflin.

Alcott, William A. 1839. *Confessions of a School Master.* New York: Gould, Newman and Saxton.

Alden, Timothy. 1827. *An Account of Sundry Missions Performed Among the Senecas and Munsees.* New York: J. Seymour.

Anderson, Sherwood. [1924] 1969. *A Story Teller's Story.* New York: Penguin Books.

Anzaldúa, Gloria. 1987. *Borderlands/La Frontera.* San Francisco: Aunt Lute Books.

Arbuckle, J. W. 1942. *In the Midst of the Years: Being a Revision of Yesterday and To-morrow.* Waterloo, Iowa: By the author.

Atherton, Gertrude. 1932. *Adventures of a Novelist.* New York: Liveright.

Bailey, Abigail. 1815. *Memoirs of Mrs. Abigail Bailey, Who Had Been The Wife of Major Asa Bailey, Formerly of Landaff, (N.H.). Written By Herself.* Edited by Ethan Smith. Boston: Samuel T. Armstrong.

Bailey, Robert. 1822. *The Life and Adventures of Robert Bailey, From his Infancy up to December 1821 Interspersed with Anecdotes, and Religious and Moral Admonitions.* New York: By the author.

Beecher, Lyman. 1865. *Autobiography, Correspondence, Etc.* Edited by Charles Beecher. New York: Harper and Brothers.

Benton, Thomas Hart. 1937. *An Artist in America.* New York: Robert M. McBride and Company.

Berra, Lawrence P. (Yogi), and Ed Fitzgerald. 1961. *Yogi: The Autobiography of a Professional Baseball Player.* Garden City, N.Y.: Doubleday and Company.

Binns, John. 1854. *Recollections of the Life of John Binns: Twenty-Nine Years in Europe and Fifty-Three in the United States. Written By Himself, with Anecdotes, Political, Historical, and Miscellaneous. With a Portrait.* Philadelphia: By the author.

Boicourt, Samuel L. 1857. *Life of Dr. Samuel L. Boicourt, of Louisville, Kentucky.* Louisville: By the author.

Bok, Edward. 1920. *The Americanization of Edward Bok: An Autobiography.* Philadelphia: Drake Press.

Brinkerhoff, Roeliff. 1900. *Recollections of a Lifetime.* Cincinnati: Robert Clarke Co.

Bruell, James D. 1886. *Sea Memories: Personal Experiences in the U.S. Navy in Peace and War by an Old Salt.* Biddeford Pool, Maine: By the author.

Burroughs, Stephen. [1804] 1924. *Memoirs of the Notorious Stephen Burroughs of New Hampshire.* New York: Dial Press.

Carnegie, Andrew. 1920. *Autobiography of Andrew Carnegie.* Boston: Houghton Mifflin.

Cartwright, Peter. 1856. *Autobiography of Peter Cartwright: The Backwoods Preacher.* Edited by W. P. Strickland. New York: Phillips and Hunt.

Cary, Lorene. 1991. *Black Ice.* New York: Vintage Books.

Chase, Ilka. 1941. *Past Imperfect.* Garden City, N.Y.: Blue Ribbon Books.

Cleaver, Eldridge. 1968. *Soul on Ice.* New York: Delta.

Cobb, Enos. 1846. *An Exposition of Dr. Cobb's Art of Discovering the Faculties of the Human Mind and Bodily Infirmities; To Which is Added an Auto-Biographical Sketch of the Author and a Poetic Description of Several Cities, Towns, and Villages Which He Has Visited.* Montpelier, Vt.: n.p.

Coffin, Robert Stevenson. 1825. *The Life of the Boston Bard Written by Himself.* Mount Pleasant, N.Y.: Steven Marshall Roscoe.

Colson, Charles. 1976. *Born Again.* Old Tappan, N.J.: Chosen Books.

Darrow, Clarence. 1932. *The Story of My Life.* New York: Scribner's Sons.

Davis, Andrew Jackson. 1857. *The Magic Staff.* New York: J. S. Brown.

Davis, Rebecca Harding. 1904. *Bits of Gossip.* Boston: Houghton Mifflin.

Dumond, Annie. 1868. *Annie Nelles; or, The Life of a Book Agent. An Autobiography.* Cincinnati: By the author.

Fagan, James O. 1912. *The Autobiography of an Individualist.* Boston: Houghton Mifflin.

Fairbank, Calvin. 1890. *Reverend Calvin Fairbank During Slavery Times. "How He 'Fought the Good Fight' to Prepare 'the Way.'"* Chicago: R. R. McCabe.

Flipper, Henry Ossian. [1878] 1968. *The Colored Cadet at West Point. The Autobiography of Lieut. Henry Ossian Flipper, U.S.A., First Graduate of Color from the U.S. Military Academy.* New York: Homer Lee.

Fong-Torres, Ben. 1994. *The Rice Room: Growing Up Chinese-American: From Number Two Son to Rock 'n' Roll.* New York: Penguin.

Fox, Ebenezer. 1838. *The Revolutionary Adventures of Ebenezer Fox of Roxbury, Massachusetts.* Boston: Monroe and Francis.

Fulton, David [Jack Thorne, pseud.]. 1892. *Recollections of a Sleeping Car Porter.* Jersey City, N.J.: Doan and Pilson.

Gano, John. 1806. *Biographical Memoirs of the Late Reverend John Gano of Frankfort (Kentucky). Formerly of the City of New York. Written Principally by Himself.* New York: Southwick and Hardcastle.

Gates, Henry Louis, Jr. 1994. *Colored People.* New York: Vintage Books.

Glasgow, Ellen. [1954] 1980. *The Woman Within.* New York: Hill and Wang.

Goldstein, Andrew. 1973. *Becoming: An American Odyssey.* New York: Saturday Review Press.

Graydon, Alexander. 1811. *Memoirs of A Life, Chiefly Passed in Pennsylvania, Within the Last Sixty Years With Occasional Remarks Upon the General Occurrences, Character, and Spirit of that Eventful Period.* Harrisburgh, Pa.: John Wyeth.

Harding, Chester. 1866. *My Egotistography.* Cambridge: John Wilson and Son.

Hawkes, Clarence. [1915] 1946. *Hitting the Dark Trail: Starshine through Thirty Years of Night.* Holyoke, Mass.: Sunshine Press.

Hemingway, Ernest. 1964. *A Moveable Feast.* New York: Charles Scribner's Sons.

Hess, Joseph. 1888. *The Autobiography of Joseph F. Hess, The Converted Prize-Fighter. A Book of Thrilling Experiences and Timely Warnings to Young Men.* 2d ed. Rochester, N.Y.: E. R. Andrews.

Hewitt, Edward Ringwood. 1943. *Those Were the Days: Tales of a Long Life.* New York: Duell, Sloan and Pearce.

Hochschild, Adam. 1986. *Half the Way Home: A Memoir of Father and Son.* New York: Viking.

Hunter-Gault, Charlayne. 1992. *In My Place.* New York: Vintage Books.

Iacocca, Lee [with William Novak]. 1984. *Iacocca: An Autobiography.* New York: Bantam Books.

Jarratt, Devereux. 1806. *The Life of the Reverend Devereux Jarratt, Rector of Bath Parish, Dinwiddie County, Virginia. Written By Himself, In a Series of Letters Addressed to the Rev. John Coleman, One of the Ministers of the Protestant Episcopal Church in Maryland.* Baltimore: Warner and Hanna.

Kazin, Alfred. 1951. *A Walker in the City.* New York: Harcourt, Brace, and World.

Keeler, Ralph. 1870. *Vagabond Adventures.* Boston: Fields, Osgood and Company.

Kendrick, Elder Ariel. 1847. *Sketches of the Life and Times of Elder Ariel Kendrick. Being a Short Account of His Birth, Conversion, Call to the Ministry, and His*

Labors as a Gospel Minister, With Other Incidents Occurring Under His Notice. Written by Himself. Ludlow, Vt.: Barton and Tower.

King, Alexander. 1958. *Mine Enemy Grows Older.* New York: Simon and Schuster.

Kirby, Georgiana. 1887. *Years of Experience: An Autobiographical Narrative.* New York: G. P. Putnam's Sons.

Leland, John. [1838] 1845. *The Writings of the Late Elder John Leland, Including Some Events in His Life, Written By Himself, With Additional Sketches, &c., by Miss L. F. Greene, Lanesboro, Mass.* New York: G. W. Wood.

Lewis, Faye C. 1971. *Nothing to Make a Shadow.* Ames, Iowa: Iowa State University Press.

Lewis, Joseph Vance. 1910. *Out of the Ditch: A True Story of An Ex-Slave.* Houston: Rein and Sons.

Lewis, Wilmarth Sheldon. 1967. *One Man's Education.* New York: Alfred A. Knopf.

Lewisohn, Ludwig. 1922. *Up Stream: An American Chronicle.* London: Boni and Liveright.

McAllister, Ward. 1890. *Society as I Have Found It.* New York: Cassell.

McBride, James. 1996. *The Color of Water: A Black Man's Tribute to His White Mother.* New York: Riverhead Books.

McCall, Nathan. 1994. *Makes Me Wanna Holler. A Young Black Man in America.* New York: Random House.

McCarthy, Mary. 1957. *Memories of a Catholic Girlhood.* New York: Harcourt Brace Jovanovich.

McDonald, Worden. 1978. *An Old Guy Who Feels Good: The Autobiography of a Free-Spirited Working Man.* Berkeley, Calif.: By the author.

Malcolm X. 1964. *The Autobiography of Malcolm X.* New York: Grove Press.

Martin, Joseph Plumb. 1830. *A Narrative of Some of the Adventures, Dangers, and Sufferings of a Revolutionary Soldier, Interspersed with Anecdotes of Incidents that Occurred Within His Own Observation.* Hallowell, Maine: Glazier, Masters and Company.

Mencken, Henry Louis. [1940] 1955. *Happy Days, 1880–1892.* New York: Alfred A. Knopf.

Meyer, Agnes Ernst. 1953. *Out of These Roots: The Autobiography of an American Woman.* Boston: Little, Brown.

Monette, Paul. 1992. *Becoming a Man: Half a Life Story.* San Francisco: HarperSanFrancisco.

Moody, John. [1933] 1946. *The Long Road Home.* New York: Macmillan.

Morgan, Henry. 1874. *Shadowy Hand; or Life Struggles: A Story of Real Life.* Boston: By the author.

Murray, Lindley. 1827. *Memoirs of the Life and Writings of Lindley Murray: In a Series of Letters, Written By Himself.* Philadelphia: Samuel Wood and Sons.

Nabokov, Vladimir. [1951] 1966. *Speak, Memory.* New York: Pyramid Books.

Navarrette, Ruben, Jr. 1993. *A Darker Shade of Crimson: Odyssey of a Harvard Chicano.* New York: Bantam Books.

Nickerson, Ansel D. 1888. *A Raw Recruit's War Experiences.* Providence, R.I.: Press Company.

Nock, Albert Jay. 1943. *Memoirs of a Superfluous Man.* New York: Harper and Brothers.

Patterson, Samuel. [1817] 1825. *A Narrative of the Adventures, Sufferings and Privations of Samuel Patterson, a Native of Rhode Island, Experienced by Him in Several Voyages to Various Parts of the World, Embracing a Short Account of the Numerous Places Visited by Him in his Eventful Life, And a Particular Description of the Manners, Customs, etc. of the People of the Sandwich and Fejee [sic] Islands. Published with a Design of Enabling the Subject of this Narrative to Obtain some Alleviation of his Misfortunes from a Generous Publick.* 2d ed. Providence, R.I.: The Journal.

Perera, Victor. 1986. *Rites: A Guatemalan Boyhood.* New York: Harcourt Brace Jovanovich.

Powdermaker, Hortense. 1966. *Stranger and Friend: The Way of An Anthropologist.* New York: W. W. Norton and Company.

Quincy, Eliza S. M. [1821] 1861. *Memoir of the Life of Eliza S. M. Quincy.* Boston: John Wilson and Son.

Quinn, Anthony. 1972. *The Original Sin: A Self-Portrait.* Boston: Little, Brown.

Richards, Linda. [1911] 1915. *Reminiscences of Linda Richards, America's First Trained Nurse.* Boston: Whitcomb and Barrows.

Richards, Lucy. 1842. *Memoirs of the Late Miss Lucy Richards of Paris, Oneida County, N.Y. Written by Herself.* New York: G. Lane and P. P. Sandford.

Ritter, Jacob. 1844. *Memoirs of Jacob Ritter, a Faithful Minister in the Society of Friends.* Edited by Joseph Foulke. Philadelphia: Chapman and Jones.

Rockefeller, John D. 1913. *Random Reminiscences of Men and Events.* Garden City, N.Y.: Doubleday, Page and Company.

Rodriguez, Richard. 1982. *Hunger of Memory: The Education of Richard Rodriguez.* New York: Bantam.

Rush, Benjamin. 1948. *The Autobiography of Benjamin Rush: His "Travels through Life" together with his* Commonplace Book *for 1789–1813.* Edited by George W. Corner. Princeton: Princeton University Press.

Sheen, Fulton J. 1980. *Treasure in Clay.* Garden City, N.Y.: Doubleday and Company.

Shepard, Elihu. 1869. *Autobiography of Elihu H. Shepard, Formerly Professor of Languages in St. Louis College.* St. Louis: Knapp.

Sims, J. Marion, M.D., LL.D. 1884. *The Story of My Life.* Edited by H. Marion-Sims. New York: D. Appleton and Company.

Solomon, Hannah. [1946] 1974. *Fabric of My Life: The Autobiography of Hannah G. Solomon.* New York: Bloch.

Southwick, Sarah H. 1893. *Reminiscences of Early Anti-Slavery Days.* Cambridge, Mass.: By the author.

Steffens, Joseph Lincoln. 1931. *The Autobiography of Lincoln Steffens.* New York: Harcourt, Bracc, and Company.

Sugimoto, Etsu Inagaki. 1925. *A Daughter of the Samurai: How a Daughter of Feudal Japan, Living Hundreds of Years in One Generation, Became a Modern American.* Garden City, N.Y.: Doubleday, Page and Company.

Thomas, Ebenezer S. 1840. *Reminiscences of the Last Sixty-Five Years, Commencing with the Battle of Lexington. Also, Sketches of His Own Life and Times.* Hartford, Conn.: By the author.

Towle, Nancy. 1832. *Vicissitudes Illustrated, in the Experience of Nancy Towle, in Europe and America. Written by Herself.* Charleston, S.C.: By the author.

Train, George Francis. 1902. *My Life in Many States and in Foreign Lands: Dictated in My Seventy-Fourth Year.* New York: D. Appleton and Company.

Twain, Mark. 1924. *Mark Twain's Autobiography.* 2 vols. Edited by Albert Bigelow Paine. New York: Harper and Brothers.

Van Cott, Maggie N. 1883. *The Harvest and the Reaper.* New York: George A. Sparks.

Viscardi, Henry, Jr. 1952. *A Man's Stature.* New York: Paul S. Eriksson.

Walling, George. 1887. *Recollections of a New York Chief of Police: An Official Record of Thirty Eight Years as Patrolman, Detective, Captain, Inspector and Chief of the New York Police.* New York: Caxton Book Concern Limited.

Washburn, Ichabod. 1878. *Autobiography and Memorials of Ichabod Washburn.* Edited by Henry Cheever. Boston: D. Lothrop and Co.

Watson, Rachel Mrs. 1871. *The Life of My Family; Or, The Log-House in the Wilderness. A True Story.* New York: By the author.

Wells, William Charles. 1818. *A Memoir of the Life of William Charles Wells, M.D. Written by Himself.* London: Archibald Constable.

White, K. 1809. *A Narrative of the Life, Occurrences, Vicissitudes and Present Situation of K. White.* Schenectady, N.Y.: By the author.

Williams, R. G. 1896. *Thrilling Experience of the Welsh Evangelist R. G. Williams, Reformed Drunkard and Gambler or Forty-Eight Years in Darkness and Sin and Eleven Years in the Light and Love of Christ Jesus.* Chicago: Mark and Williams.

Wyatt, Sophia Hayes. 1854. *The Autobiography of a Landlady of the Old School With Personal Sketches of Eminent Characters, Places, and Miscellaneous Items.* Boston: By the author.

Young, Peter. 1817. *A Brief Account of the Life and Experience, Call to the Ministry, Travels and Afflictions of Peter Young, Preacher of the Gospel. Written by himself. In two parts.* Portsmouth, N.H.: Beck and Foster.

Bibliography

Abbott, H. Porter. 1988. "Autobiography, autography, fiction: groundwork for a taxonomy of textual categories." *New Literary History* 19:597–615.

Aboulafia, Mitchell. 1986. *The Mediating Self: Mead, Sartre, and Self-Determination.* New Haven: Yale University Press.

Allport, Gordon W. 1937. *Personality: A Psychological Interpretation.* New York: Henry Holt and Company.

_____. 1942. *The Use of Personal Documents in Psychological Science.* New York: Social Science Research Council.

Alter, Robert. 1989. *The Pleasures of Reading in an Ideological Age.* New York: Simon and Schuster.

Altick, Richard D. 1957. *The English Common Reader: A Social History of the Mass Reading Public.* Chicago: University of Chicago Press.

Anderson, Norman. 1968. "Likableness ratings of 555 personality-trait words." *Journal of Personality and Social Psychology* 9:272–79.

Andrews, William L. 1986. *To Tell a Free Story: The First Century of Afro-American Autobiography, 1760–1865.* Urbana: University of Illinois Press.

Andrews, William L., ed. 1993. *African American Autobiography.* Englewood Cliffs, N.J.: Prentice-Hall.

Angrosino, Michael V. 1989. *Documents of Interaction: Biography, Autobiography, and Life History in Social Science Perspective.* Gainsville: University of Florida Press.

Appiah, K. Anthony. 1994. "Identity, authenticity, survival." In *Multiculturalism,* edited by Amy Gutmann, 149–63. Princeton: Princeton University Press.

Aristotle. 1907. *De Anima.* Translated by R. D. Hicks. Cambridge: Cambridge University Press.

————. 1962. *Nichomachean Ethics.* Translated by Martin Ostwald. Indianapolis: Bobbs-Merrill.

Arnold, Matthew. 1979. *The Poems of Matthew Arnold.* Edited by Miriam Allott. New York: Longman.

Aron, Arthur, and Elaine N. Aron. 1986. *The Heart of Social Psychology.* Lexington, Mass.: D. C. Heath and Company.

Atkinson, John W. 1964. *An Introduction to Motivation.* New York: Van Nostrand Reinhold.

Atlas, James. 1988. "Speaking ill of the dead." *The New York Times Magazine,* 6 November.

Augustine, Saint. [400] 1963. *The Confessions.* New York: Mentor Books.

Austin, J. L. [1961] 1979. *Philosophical Papers.* 3d ed. Edited by J. O. Urmson and G. J. Warnock. Oxford: Oxford University Press.

Averill, James. 1986. "The acquisition of emotions during adulthood." In *The Social Construction of Emotions,* edited by Rom Harré, 98–118. Oxford: Basil Blackwell.

Baker, Therese L. 1994. *Doing Social Research.* 2d ed. New York: McGraw-Hill.

Baldwin, James Mark. [1894] 1968. *Mental Development in the Child and the Race.* New York: Augustus M. Kelley.

Barbour, John D. 1992. *The Conscience of the Autobiographer: Ethical and Religious Dimensions of Autobiography.* New York: St. Martin's Press.

Barnes, Julian. 1984. *Flaubert's Parrot.* New York: McGraw-Hill.

Barth, Fredrik. 1969. *Ethnic Groups and Boundaries.* London: George Allen and Unwin.

Barthes, Roland. 1977. *Roland Barthes.* Translated by Richard Howard. New York: Hill and Wang.

Baumeister, Roy F. 1986. *Identity: Cultural Change and the Struggle for Self.* New York: Oxford University Press.

————. 1987. "How the self became a problem: a psychological review of historical research." *Journal of Personality and Social Psychology* 52:163–76.

Becker, Carl. [1932] 1965. *The Heavenly City of the Eighteenth-Century Philosophers.* New Haven: Yale University Press.

Becker, Howard. 1966. Introduction to *The Jack Roller* by Clifford R. Shaw. Chicago: University of Chicago Press.

_____. 1982. "Culture: a sociological view." *Yale Review* 71:513–27.

Becker, Howard S., and Michal M. McCall, eds. 1990. *Symbolic Interaction and Cultural Studies.* Chicago: University of Chicago Press.

Beckson, Karl, and Arthur Ganz. 1989. *Literary Terms: A Dictionary.* 3d ed. New York: Farrar, Straus and Giroux.

Bell, Daniel. 1976. *The Cultural Contradictions of Capitalism.* New York: Basic Books.

Bell, Susan Groag, and Marilyn Yalom, eds. 1990. *Revealing Lives: Autobiography, Biography, and Gender.* Albany: State University of New York Press.

Bellamy, Edward. [1888] 1967. *Looking Backward, 2000–1887.* Cambridge: Harvard University Press.

Benstock, Shari. 1988. *The Private Self: Theory and Practice of Women's Autobiographical Writings.* Chapel Hill: University of North Carolina Press.

Benton, James S. 1981. "The new sensibility: self and society in the post-industrial age." Ph.D. diss., University of California at Los Angeles.

Berger, Peter. 1963. *Invitation to Sociology.* Garden City, N.Y.: Doubleday and Company.

_____. 1965. "Toward a sociological understanding of psychoanalysis." *Social Research* 32:26–41.

Berger, Peter, and Thomas Luckmann. 1966. *The Social Construction of Reality: A Treatise in the Sociology of Knowledge.* Garden City, N.Y.: Doubleday and Company.

Bernard, L. L. 1909. "The teaching of sociology in the United States." *American Journal of Sociology* 15:164–213.

_____. 1924. *Instinct: A Study in Social Psychology.* New York: Henry Holt.

Bertaux, D. 1981. *Biography and Society: The Life History Approach in the Social Sciences.* Beverly Hills, Calif.: Sage.

Bertaux, D., and Martin Kohli. 1984. "The life story approach: a continental view." *Annual Review of Sociology* 10:215–37.

Blackie, John Stuart. n.d. *On Self-Culture: Intellectual, Physical, and Moral.* New York: Charles Scribner's Sons.

Blassingame, John W. 1979. *The Slave Community.* Rev. ed. New York: Oxford University Press.

Bloch, Ruth H. 1978. "American feminine ideals in transition: the rise of the moral mother, 1785–1815." *Feminist Studies* 4: 101–26.

Bloom, Lynn Z., and Ning Yu. 1994. "American autobiography: the changing critical canon." *a/b: Auto/Biography Studies* 9:167–80.

Blumer, Herbert. 1939. *Critiques of Research in the Social Sciences. I: An Appraisal of Thomas and Znaniecki's The Polish Peasant in Europe and America.* New York: Social Science Research Council.

_____. 1969. *Symbolic Interactionism: Perspective and Method.* Englewood Cliffs, N.J.: Prentice-Hall.

Bode, Carl. 1956. *The American Lyceum: Town Meeting of the Mind.* New York: Oxford University Press.

Boelhower, William Q. 1982. *Immigrant Autobiography in the United States: (Four Versions of the Italian American Self)*. Verona: Essedue Edizioni.

Bogdan, Robert, and Steven J. Taylor. 1975. *Introduction to Qualitative Research Methods*. New York: John Wiley and Sons.

Bohman, James F. 1991. "Holism without skepticism." In *The Interpretive Turn: Philosophy, Science, Culture,* edited by David R. Hiley, James F. Bohman, and Richard Shusterman, 129–54. Ithaca: Cornell University Press.

Booth, Wayne C. 1983. *The Rhetoric of Fiction*. 2d ed. Chicago: University of Chicago Press.

Borges, Jorge Luis. 1964a. *Labyrinths: Selected Stories and Other Writings*. New York: New Directions.

_____. 1964b. *Other Inquisitions 1937–1952*. Translated by Ruth L. C. Sims. Austin: University of Texas Press.

Boring, Edwin G. 1950. "The influence of evolutionary theory upon psychological thought." In *Evolutionary Thought in America,* edited by Stow Persons, 268–98. New Haven: Yale University Press.

Boswell, James. 1934. *Life of Johnson*. Vol. 3. Edited by George Hill. Revised by L. F. Powell. Oxford: Clarendon Press.

Bourke, Vernon J. 1964. *Will in Western Thought: An Historico-Critical Survey*. New York: Sheed and Ward.

Bourdieu, Pierre. 1977. *Outline of a Theory of Practice*. Cambridge: Cambridge University Press.

Braxton, Joanne M. 1989. *Black Women Writing Autobiography: A Tradition within a Tradition*. Philadelphia: Temple University Press.

Brereton, Virginia Lieson. 1991. *From Sin to Salvation: Stories of Women's Conversions, 1800 to the Present*. Bloomington: Indiana University Press.

Briscoe, Mary Louise. 1982. *American Autobiography 1945–1980*. Madison: University of Wisconsin Press.

Brodzki, Bella, and Celeste Schenck, eds. 1988. *Life/Lines: Theorizing Women's Autobiography*. Ithaca: Cornell University Press.

Bromwich, David. 1989. "The future of tradition: notes on the crisis of the humanities." *Dissent* (Fall): 541–57.

Bruford, Walter H. 1975. *The German Tradition of Self- Cultivation*. Cambridge: Cambridge University Press.

Brumble, H. David, III. 1988. *American Indian Autobiography*. Berkeley: University of California Press.

Bruner, Edward M., ed. 1984. *Text, Play, and Story: The Construction and Reconstruction of Self and Society*. Washington, D.C.: American Ethnological Society.

Bruner, Jerome. 1987. "Life as narrative." *Social Research* 54:11–32.

_____. 1990. *Acts of Meaning*. Cambridge, Mass.: Harvard University Press.

_____. 1994. "The 'remembered' self." In *The Remembering Self,* edited by Ulric Neisser and Robyn Fivush, 41–54. Cambridge: Cambridge University Press.

Bruss, Elizabeth W. 1976. *Autobiographical Acts: The Changing Situation of a Literary Genre.* Baltimore: Johns Hopkins University Press.

Buckley, Jerome H. 1970. "Autobiography in the English *bildungsroman.*" In *The Interpretation of Narrative,* edited by Morton Bloomfield, 93–104. Cambridge, Mass.: Harvard University Press.

Bukowski, Jacek. 1974. "Biographical method in Polish sociology." *Zeitschrift für Soziologie* 3:18–30.

Bunyan, John. [1666] 1987. *Grace Abounding to the Chief of Sinners.* New York: Penguin Books.

Burckhardt, Jacob. 1937. *The Civilization of the Renaissance in Italy.* New York: Oxford University Press.

Burke, Kenneth. 1939. "Freud and the analysis of poetry." *American Journal of Sociology* 45:391–417.

———. 1945. *A Grammar of Motives.* Berkeley: University of California Press.

Burnham, John C. 1968. "Historical background for the study of personality." In *Handbook of Personality Theory and Research,* edited by E. Borgatta and W. Lambert, 3–81. Chicago: Rand McNally.

———. 1988. *Paths into American Culture: Psychology, Medicine, and Morals.* Philadelphia: Temple University Press.

Burns, Rex. 1976. *Success in America: The Yeoman Dream and the Industrial Revolution.* Amherst: University of Massachusetts Press.

Bushnell, Horace. [1847] 1975. *Views of Christian Nurture and of Subjects Adjacent Thereto.* Delmar, N.Y.: Scholars' Facsimiles and Reprints.

Butterfield, Herbert. 1965. *The Whig Interpretation of History.* New York: W. W. Norton and Company.

Butterfield, Stephen. 1974. *Black Autobiography in America.* Amherst: University of Massachusetts Press.

Camic, Charles. 1986. "The matter of habit." *American Journal of Sociology* 91:1039–87.

Carroll, Lewis. 1866. *Alice's Adventures in Wonderland.* New York: D. Appleton and Company.

Cawelti, John G. 1965. *Apostles of the Self-Made Man.* Chicago: University of Chicago Press.

Caws, Peter. 1994. "Identity: cultural, transcultural, and multicultural." In *Multiculturalism: A Critical Reader,* edited by David Theo Goldberg, 371–87. Oxford: Basil Blackwell.

Cervantes, Miguel de. [1604] 1950. *The Adventures of Don Quixote.* Translated by J. M. Cohen. Baltimore: Penguin Books.

Channing, William Ellery. 1838. *Self-Culture.* Boston: Dutton and Wentworth.

Chaplin, J. P. 1985. *Dictionary of Psychology.* New York: Dell Publishing.

Charmé, Stuart L. 1984. *Meaning and Myth in the Study of Lives: A Sartrean Perspective.* Philadelphia: University of Pennsylvania Press.

Charvat, William. 1959. *Literary Publishing in America 1790–1850.* Philadelphia: University of Pennsylvania Press.

Chicago Manual of Style, The. 1982. 13th ed. Chicago: University of Chicago Press.

Chin, Frank. 1985. "This is not an autobiography." *Genre* 18:109–30.

Coe, Richard N. 1984. *When the Grass Was Taller: Autobiography and the Experience of Childhood.* New Haven: Yale University Press.

Cohen, Anthony P. 1993. "Culture as identity: an anthropologist's view." *New Literary History* 24:195–209.

Collins, Randall. 1988. *Theoretical Sociology.* New York: Harcourt Brace Jovanovich.

Conway, Jill. 1992. *Written by Herself. Autobiographies of American Women: An Anthology.* New York: Vintage Books.

Cooke, Michael G. 1973. "Modern black autobiography in the tradition." In *Romanticism: Vistas, Instances, Continuities,* edited by David Thorburn and Geoffrey Hartman, 255–80. Ithaca: Cornell University Press.

Cooley, Charles Horton. [1902] 1956. *Human Nature and the Social Order.* Rev. ed. Glencoe, Ill.: Free Press.

Cooley, Charles Horton, Robert Angell, and Lowell Carr. 1933. *Introductory Sociology.* New York: Charles Scribner's Sons.

Cooley, Thomas. 1976. *Educated Lives: The Rise of Modern Autobiography in America.* Columbus: Ohio State University Press.

Corrigan, Philip. 1975. "Dichotomy is contradiction: on 'society' as constraint and construction." *The Sociological Review* 23:211–43.

Couser, G. Thomas. 1979. *American Autobiography: The Prophetic Mode.* Amherst: University of Massachusetts Press.

_____. 1989. *Altered Egos: Authority in American Autobiography.* New York: Oxford University Press.

Cowley, Malcolm. 1950. "Naturalism in American literature." In *Evolutionary Thought in America,* edited by Stow Persons, 300–333. New Haven: Yale University Press.

Crapanzano, Vincent, Yasmine Ergas, and Judith Modell. 1986. "Personal testimony: narratives of the self in the social sciences and the humanities." *SSRC Items* 40:25–30.

Cravens, Hamilton. 1978. *The Triumph of Evolution: American Scientists and the Heredity-Environment Controversy 1900–1941.* Philadelphia: University of Pennsylvania Press.

Crawford, Christina. 1978. *Mommie Dearest.* New York: Willian Morrow and Company.

Cremin, Lawrence A. 1980. *American Education: The National Experience 1783–1876.* New York: Harper and Row.

Crites, Stephen. 1971. "The narrative quality of experience." *Journal of the American Academy of Religion* 39:291–311.

Culler, Jonathan. 1975. *Structuralist Poetics: Structuralism, Linguistics and the Study of Literature.* Ithaca: Cornell University Press.

Curti, Merle. 1980. *Human Nature in American Thought.* Madison: University of Wisconsin Press.

Curtis, Susan. 1991. *A Consuming Faith: The Social Gospel and Modern American Culture*. Baltimore: Johns Hopkins University Press.

Curtius, Ernst R. 1953. *European Literature and the Latin Middle Ages*. Princeton: Princeton University Press.

Damon, William, and Daniel Hart. 1988. *Self-Understanding in Childhood and Adolescence*. Cambridge: Cambridge University Press.

Darwin, Charles. [1871] 1981. *Descent of Man, and Selection in Relation to Sex*. Princeton: Princeton University Press.

Davis, David Brion. 1957. *Homicide in American Fiction, 1798–1860*. Ithaca: Cornell University Press.

Davis, David Brion, ed. 1967. *Ante-bellum Reform*. New York: Harper and Row.

Davis, Robert A., and Silas E. Gould. 1929. "Changing tendencies in general psychology." *The Psychological Review* 36:320–31.

Degler, Carl N. 1991. *In Search of Human Nature: The Decline and Revival of Darwinism in American Social Thought*. New York: Oxford University Press.

Delany, Paul. 1969. *British Autobiography in the Seventeenth Century*. London: Routledge and Kegan Paul.

Delbanco, Andrew. 1995. *The Death of Satan*. New York: Farrar, Straus and Giroux.

de Man, Paul. 1979. "Autobiography as De-facement." *MLN* 94:919–30.

Denzin, Norman. 1978. *The Research Act*. Chicago: Aldine.

———. 1989. *Interpretive Biography*. Sage University Paper Series on Qualitative Research Methods. Vol. 17. Beverly Hills: Sage.

———. 1991. "Representing lived experiences in ethnographic texts." In *Studies in Symbolic Interaction*. Vol. 12, 59–70.

De Quincey, Thomas. [1821] 1966. *Confessions of An English Opium-Eater*. New York: New American Library.

De Vos, George. 1975. "Ethnic pluralism: conflict and accommodation." In *Ethnic Identity: Cultural Continuities and Change*, edited by G. De Vos and Lola Romanuccis-Ross, 5–41. Palo Alto: Mayfield.

Dillon, George L. 1986. *Rhetoric as Social Imagination*. Bloomington: Indiana University Press.

Dodd, Philip. 1987. "History or fiction: balancing contemporary autobiography's claims." *Mosaic* 20:61–70.

Dollard, J. 1935. *Criteria for the Life History: With Analyses of Six Notable Documents*. New Haven: Yale University Press.

———. 1938. "The life history in community studies." *American Sociological Review* 3:724–37.

Dorsey, Peter A. 1993. *Sacred Estrangement: The Rhetoric of Conversion in Modern American Autobiography*. University Park: Pennsylvania State University Press.

Downing, Christine. 1977. "Re-visioning autobiography: the bequest of Freud and Jung." *Soundings* 15:210–28.

Du Bois, W. E. B. [1903] 1961. *The Souls of Black Folk*. Greenwich, Conn.: Fawcett.

Dumont, Louis. 1985. "A modified view of our origins: the Christian beginnings of modern individualism." In *The Category of the Person,* edited by M. Carrithers, S. Collins, and S. Lukes, 93–122. Cambridge: Cambridge University Press.

Dunn, Mary Maples. 1980. "Saints and sisters: Congregational and Quaker women in the early colonial period." In *Women in American Religion,* edited by Janet Wilson James, 27–46. Philadelphia: University of Pennsylvania Press.

Durkheim, Emile. [1893] 1964. *The Division of Labor in Society.* New York: Free Press.

_____. [1912] 1961. *The Elementary Forms of the Religious Life.* New York: Collier.

Eagleton, Terry. 1983. *Literary Theory: An Introduction.* Minneapolis: University of Minnesota Press.

Eakin, Paul John. 1985. *Fictions in Autobiography: Studies in the Art of Self-Invention.* Princeton: Princeton University Press.

_____. 1992. *Touching the World: Reference in Autobiography.* Princeton: Princeton University Press.

_____, ed. 1991. *American Autobiography: Retrospect and Prospect.* Madison: University of Wisconsin Press.

Edel, Leon. 1984. *Writing Lives: Principia Biographica.* New York: W. W. Norton and Company.

Egan, Susanna. 1984. *Patterns of Experience in Autobiography.* Chapel Hill: University of North Carolina Press.

Ellenberger, Henri. 1970. *The Discovery of the Unconscious: The History and Evolution of Dynamic Psychiatry.* New York: Basic Books.

Elson, Ruth M. 1964. *Guardians of Tradition: American School Books of the Nineteenth Century.* Lincoln: University of Nebraska Press.

Elvin, Mark. 1985. "Between the earth and heaven: conceptions of the self in China." In *The Category of the Person,* edited by M. Carrithers, S. Collins, and S. Lukes, 156–89. Cambridge: Cambridge University Press.

Emerson, Ralph Waldo. [1841] 1949. *Selected Essays.* Chicago: Peoples Book Club.

Erikson, Erik H. [1950] 1963. *Childhood and Society.* New York: W. W. Norton and Company.

_____. 1958. *Young Man Luther: A Study in Psychoanalysis and History.* New York: W. W. Norton and Company.

_____. 1975. *Life History and the Historical Moment.* New York: W. W. Norton and Company.

Evans, Rand B. 1984. "The origins of American academic psychology." In *Explorations in the History of Psychology in the United States,* edited by Josef Brozek, 17–60. Lewisburg, Pa.: Bucknell University Press.

Fancher, Raymond E. 1979. "A note on the terms 'nature and nurture.'" *Journal of the History of the Behavioral Sciences* 15:321–22.

Faris, Ellsworth. 1921. "Are instincts data or hypotheses?" *American Journal of Sociology* 27:184–96.

Farr, Robert M. 1981. "On the nature of human nature and the science of behavior." In *Indigenous Psychologies: The Anthropology of the Self,* edited by Paul Heelas and Andrew Lock, 303–17. London: Academic Press.

Fay, Jay Wharton. [1939] 1966. *American Psychology before William James.* New York: Octagon Books.

Fielding, William J. 1922. *The Caveman within Us: His Peculiarities and Powers; How We Can Enlist His Aid for Health and Efficiency.* New York: E. P. Dutton and Company.

Finke, Roger, and Rodney Stark. 1992. *The Churching of America, 1776–1990: Winners and Losers in Our Religious Economy.* New Brunswick, N.J.: Rutgers University Press.

Finkelstein, Joanne. 1982. "Self and civility: the politics of social psychology." In *Studies in Symbolic Interaction.* Vol. 4, 107–13. Greenwich, Conn.: JAI Press.

Finney, Brian. 1985. *The Inner I: British Literary Autobiography of the Twentieth Century.* New York: Oxford University Press.

Fischer, David Hackett. 1970. *Historians' Fallacies: Toward a Logic of Historical Thought.* New York: Harper and Row.

Flanagan, Owen. 1984. *The Science of the Mind.* Cambridge, Mass.: MIT Press.

Flaubert, Gustave. [1857] 1981. *Madame Bovary.* Translated by Lowell Bair. New York: Bantam Books.

Fleishman, Avrom. 1976. "The fictions of autobiographical fiction." *Genre* 9:73–86.

———. 1983. *Figures of Autobiography: The Language of Self-Writing in Victorian and Modern England.* Berkeley: University of California Press.

Fleming, Donald. 1967. "Attitude: the history of a concept." *Perspectives in American History* 1:287–365.

Fleming, Sanford. [1933] 1969. *Children and Puritanism.* New York: Arno Press.

Flugel, J. C. 1933. *A Hundred Years of Psychology.* London: Duckworth.

Folkenflik, Robert, ed. 1993. *The Culture of Autobiography: Constructions of Self-Representation.* Stanford: Stanford University Press.

Ford, Ford Madox. [1927] 1983. *The Good Soldier: A Tale of Passion.* New York: Vintage Books.

Ford, Worthington C., ed. 1938. *Letters of Henry Adams.* Vol. 2. Boston: Houghton Mifflin Company.

Fortes, Meyer. 1987. *Religion, Morality and the Person.* New York: Cambridge University Press.

Fosdick, Harry Emerson. 1923. *Twelve Tests of Character.* New York: George H. Doran Co.

Foucault, Michel. 1980. *Power/Knowledge: Selected Interviews and Other Writings, 1972–1977.* Edited by Colin Gordon. New York: Pantheon.

Fowler, Lois J., and David H. Fowler. 1990. *Revelations of Self: American Women in Autobiography.* Albany: State University of New York Press.

Fowler, O. S. 1852. *Self-Culture and Perfection of Character.* New York: Fowler and Well.

Frank, Arthur. 1993. "The rhetoric of self-change: illness experience as narrative." *The Sociological Quarterly* 34:39–52.

Frank, Gelya. 1979. "Finding the common denominator: a phenomenological critique of life history method." *Ethos* 7:68–94.

Franklin, Benjamin. [1793] 1923. *The Autobiography of Benjamin Franklin.* Boston: Houghton Mifflin Company.

Freud, Sigmund. [1905] 1960. *Jokes and Their Relation to the Unconscious.* Edited by James Strachey. New York: W. W. Norton and Company.

_____. [1920] 1938. *A General Introduction to Psychoanalysis.* New York: Garden City Publishing Co.

_____. 1925. *An Autobiographical Study.* London: Hogarth Press.

_____. [1930] 1961. *Civilization and Its Discontents.* Translated by James Strachey. New York: W. W. Norton and Company.

_____. 1975. *Letters of Sigmund Freud.* Edited by Ernst L. Freud. New York: Basic Books.

Frye, Northrop. 1970. *The Stubborn Structure: Essays on Criticism and Society.* Ithaca: Cornell University Press.

Furst, Lilian R. 1970. *Romanticism in Perspective.* New York: Humanities Press.

Gagnier, Regenia. 1991. *Subjectivities: A History of Self-Representation in Britain, 1832–1920.* New York: Oxford University Press.

Gans, Herbert. 1979. "Symbolic ethnicity: the future of ethnic groups and cultures in America." *Ethnic and Racial Studies* 2:1–20.

Garfinkel, Harold. 1967. *Studies in Ethnomethodology.* Englewood Cliffs, N.J.: Prentice-Hall.

Garraty, John A. 1964. *The Nature of Biography.* New York: Vintage Books.

Gecas, Viktor. 1982. "The self-concept." *Annual Review of Sociology* 8:1–33.

_____. 1985. "Self and identity beyond mainstream social psychology." *Contemporary Sociology* 14:432–34.

Geertz, Clifford. 1973. *The Interpretation of Cultures.* New York: Basic Books.

_____. 1983. *Local Knowledge: Further Essays in Interpretive Anthropology.* New York: Basic Books.

Gergen, Kenneth J. 1971. *The Concept of Self.* New York: Holt, Rinehart and Winston.

_____. 1984. "Theory of the self: impasse and evolution." *Advances in Experimental Social Psychology* 17:49–115.

_____. 1985. "The social constructionist movement in modern psychology." *American Psychologist* 40:266–75.

_____. 1988. "If persons are texts." In *Hermeneutics and Psychological Theory,* edited by Stanley Messer, Louis Sass, and Robert Woolfolk, 28–51. New Brunswick, N.J.: Rutgers University Press.

_____. 1989. "Warranting voice and the elaboration of the self." In *Texts of Identity,* edited by John Shotter and Kenneth Gergen, 70–81. Newbury Park, Calif.: Sage.

Gergen, Kenneth J., and Keith E. Davis, eds. 1985. *The Social Construction of the Person*. New York: Springer-Verlag.

Gergen, Kenneth J., and Mary M. Gergen. 1983. "Narratives of the self." In *Studies in Social Identity*, edited by Theodore Sarbin and Karl Scheibe, 254–73. New York: Praeger.

_____. 1988. "Narrative and the self as relationship." *Advances in Experimental Social Psychology* 21:17–56.

Gerth, H., and C. Wright Mills, eds. [1946] 1980. *From Max Weber: Essays in Sociology*. New York: Oxford University Press.

_____. 1953. *Character and Social Structure: The Psychology of Social Institutions*. New York: Harcourt, Brace and World.

Gibbon, Edward. [1796] 1984. *Memoirs of My Life*. New York: Penguin Books.

Giddens, Anthony. 1979. *Central Problems in Social Theory*. Berkeley: University of California Press.

Gide, André. [1927] 1951. *The Counterfeiters*. New York: Alfred A. Knopf.

_____. 1935. *If It Die*. New York: Vintage Books.

Gill, W. A. 1907. "The nude in autobiography." *Atlantic Monthly* 99:71–79.

Glazer, Nathan. 1975. *Affirmative Discrimination: Ethnic Inequality and Public Policy*. New York: Basic Books.

Gleason, Philip. 1992. *Speaking of Diversity: Language and Ethnicity in Twentieth-Century America*. Baltimore: Johns Hopkins University Press.

Goethe, Johann Wolfgang von. 1848. *Dichtung und Wahrheit*. London: Bohn.

_____. 1984. *Faust I & II*. Edited and translated by Stuart Atkins. Princeton: Princeton University Press.

Goffman, Erving. 1959. *The Presentation of Self in Everyday Life*. Garden City, N.Y.: Doubleday and Company.

_____. 1961. *Encounters*. Indianapolis: Bobbs-Merrill.

_____. 1983. "Felicity's condition." *American Journal of Sociology* 89:1–53.

Goldberg, S. L. 1993. *Agents and Lives: Moral Thinking in Literature*. Cambridge: Cambridge University Press.

Gosse, Edmund. 1907. *Father and Son: A Study of Two Temperaments*. New York: W. W. Norton and Company.

Gottschalk, Louis, Clyde Kluckhohn, and Robert Angell. 1945. *The Use of Personal Documents in History, Anthropology, and Sociology*. New York: Social Science Research Council.

Gould, Stephen Jay. 1977. *Ontogeny and Phylogeny*. Cambridge, Mass.: Harvard University Press.

Green, Arnold W. 1946. "The middle class male child and neurosis." *American Sociological Review* 11:31–41.

Greven, Philip. 1977. *The Protestant Temperament: Patterns of Child-Rearing, Religious Experience, and the Self in Early America*. New York: Alfred A. Knopf.

Griffin, Clifford S. 1967. "Religious benevolence as social control." In *Ante-*

bellum Reform, edited by David Brion Davis, 81–96. New York: Harper and Row.

Griswold, Wendy. 1981. "American character and the American novel: an expansion of reflection theory in the sociology of literature." *American Journal of Sociology* 86:740–65.

————. 1987. "The fabrication of meaning: literary interpretation in the United States, Great Britain, and the West Indies." *American Journal of Sociology* 92:1077–1117.

Gunn, Janet Varner. 1982. *Autobiography: Toward a Poetics of Experience.* Philadelphia: University of Pennsylvania Press.

Gusdorf, Georges. [1956] 1980. "Conditions and limits of autobiography." In *Autobiography: Essays Theoretical and Critical,* edited by James Olney, 28–48. Princeton: Princeton University Press.

Hacking, Ian. 1990. *The Taming of Chance.* Cambridge: Cambridge University Press.

Hale, Nathan G., Jr. 1971. *Freud and the Americans: The Beginnings of Psychoanalysis in the United States, 1876–1917.* New York: Oxford University Press.

Hales, Susan. 1985. "The inadvertent rediscovery of self in social psychology." *Journal for the Theory of Social Behavior* 15:237–81.

Hall, G. Stanley. 1904. *Adolescence: Its Psychology and Its Relations to Physiology, Anthropology, Sociology, Sex, Crime, Religion and Education.* New York: D. Appleton and Company.

Hallowell, A. Irving. 1955. *Culture and Experience.* Philadelphia: University of Pennsylvania Press.

Harding, Susan F. 1987. "Convicted by the holy spirit: the rhetoric of fundamental Baptist conversion." *American Ethnologist* 14:167–81.

Harré, Rom. 1981. "Psychological variety." In *Indigenous Psychologies: The Anthropology of the Self.* London: Academic Press.

————. 1984. *Personal Being: A Theory for Individual Psychology.* Cambridge, Mass.: Harvard University Press.

————. 1987. "Persons and selves." In *Persons and Personality: A Contemporary Inquiry,* edited by Arthur Peacocke and Grant Gillett, 99–115. Oxford: Basil Blackwell.

Hart, Francis R. 1970. "Notes for an anatomy of modern autobiography." *New Literary History* 1:485–511.

Hazlett, John Downton. 1990. "The situation of American autobiography: generic blurring in 'contemporary' historiography." *Prose Studies* 13:261–77.

Hearnshaw, L. S. 1987. *The Shaping of Modern Psychology.* London: Routledge and Kegan Paul.

Heilbrun, Carolyn G. 1985. "Women's autobiographical writings: new forms." *Prose Studies* 8:14–28.

————. 1988. *Writing a Woman's Life.* New York: Ballantine Books.

Heine, Patricke J. 1971. *Personality in Social Theory.* Chicago: Aldine.

Hendin, Josephine. 1990. "A material difference: notes on the newness of 1980s fiction." *Dissent* (Winter): 49–57.

Hewitt, John P. 1989. *Dilemmas of the American Self.* Philadelphia: Temple University Press.

Hewitt, John P., and Randall Stokes. 1975. "Disclaimers." *American Sociological Review* 40:1–11.

Hiley, David R., James F. Bohman, and Richard Shusterman, eds. 1991. *The Interpretive Turn: Philosophy, Science, Culture.* Ithaca: Cornell University Press.

Hilgard, Ernest R. 1987. *Psychology in America: A Historical Survey.* New York: Harcourt Brace Jovanovich.

Hochschild, Arlie Russell. 1979. "Emotion work, feeling rules and social structure." *American Journal of Sociology* 85:551–75.

Hofstadter, Richard. [1944] 1955. *Social Darwinism in American Thought.* Rev. ed. New York: George Braziller.

―――――. 1963. *Anti-Intellectualism in American Life.* New York: Vintage Books.

Hogan, Robert, and Jonathan M. Cheek. 1983. "Identity, authenticity, and maturity." In *Studies in Social Identity,* edited by Theodore Sarbin and Karl Scheibe, 339–57. New York: Praeger.

Hollingsworth, Keith. 1963. *The Newgate Novel 1830–1847.* Detroit: Wayne State University Press.

Honigmann, John J. 1982. "Sampling in ethnographic fieldwork." In *Field Research: A Sourcebook and Field Manual,* edited by Robert G. Burgess, 79–90. London: George Allen and Unwin.

House, Floyd Nelson. 1936. *The Development of Sociology.* New York: McGraw-Hill.

Howarth, William L. 1974. "Some principles of autobiography." *New Literary History* 5:363–81.

Howells, William Dean. 1909. "Autobiography, a new form of literature." *Harper's Monthly Magazine* 119:795–98.

Huber, Richard M. 1971. *The American Idea of Success.* New York: McGraw-Hill.

Hudson, Winthrop S. 1973. *Religion in America.* 2d ed. New York: Charles Scribner's Sons.

Hugo, Victor. 1937. *The Hunchback of Notre Dame.* New York: Book League of America.

Hume, David. [1739–40] 1978. *A Treatise of Human Nature.* 2d ed. Edited by L. A. Selby-Bigge. Oxford: Clarendon Press.

Humphrey, Robert. 1954. *Stream of Consciousness in the Modern Novel.* Berkeley: University of California Press.

Hunt, Freeman. [1856] 1969. *Lives of American Merchants.* New York: Augustus Kelley.

Iser, Wolfgang. 1978. *The Act of Reading: A Theory of Aesthetic Response.* Baltimore: Johns Hopkins University Press.

Jacoby, Russell. 1975. *Social Amnesia: A Critique of Conformist Psychology from Adler to Laing.* Boston: Beacon Press.

James, Henry. 1987. *The Complete Notebooks of Henry James.* Edited by Leon Edel and Lyall H. Powers. New York: Oxford University Press.

James, William. 1887. "The laws of habit." *The Popular Science Monthly* 30:433–51.

_____. [1890] 1950. *Principles of Psychology.* New York: Dover Publications.

_____. [1902] 1939. *The Varieties of Religious Experience, A Study in Human Nature.* New York: Modern Library.

_____. 1920. *The Letters of William James.* Vol. 2. Edited by Henry James. Boston: Atlantic Monthly Press.

Jauss, Hans R. 1982. *Toward an Aesthetic of Reception.* Translated by Timothy Bahti. Minneapolis: University of Minnesota Press.

Jay, Paul. 1984. *Being in the Text: Self-Representation from Wordsworth to Roland Barthes.* Ithaca: Cornell University Press.

_____. 1987. "What's the use? Critical theory and the study of autobiography." *Biography* 10:39–54.

Jelinek, Estelle C. 1986. *The Tradition of Women's Autobiography: from Antiquity to the Present.* Boston: Twayne Publishers.

_____, ed. 1980. *Women's Autobiography: Essays in Criticism.* Bloomington: Indiana University Press.

Jellison, Jerald M., and Jane Green. 1981. "A self-presentation approach to the fundamental attribution error: the norm of internality." *Journal of Personality and Social Psychology* 40:643–49.

Johnson, Frank. 1985. "The western concept of self." In *Culture and Self: Asian and Western Perspectives,* edited by Anthony Marsella, George De Vos, and Francis Hsu, 91–138. New York: Tavistock.

Johnson, Samuel. [1750] 1953. *The Rambler.* New York: Everyman's Library.

Jones, Ernest. 1953. *The Life and Work of Sigmund Freud.* Vol. 1. New York: Basic Books.

Jordanova, L. J. 1984. *Lamarck.* New York: Oxford University Press.

Juhasz, Joseph B. 1983. "Social identity in the context of human and personal identity." In *Studies in Social Identity,* edited by Theodore Sarbin and Karl Scheibe, 289–318. New York: Praeger.

Jung, Carl. 1923. *Psychological Types, or: The Psychology of Individuation.* London: Pantheon.

Kagan, Jerome. 1983. "Classifications of the child." In *Handbook of Child Psychology,* edited by Paul Mussen, 527–60. 4th ed. New York: John Wiley and Sons.

Kaplan, Louis. 1961. *A Bibliography of American Autobiographies.* Madison: University of Wisconsin Press.

Kazin, Alfred. 1959. "The alone generation." *Harper's Magazine* 219:127–31.

_____. 1964. "Autobiography as narrative." *The Michigan Quarterly Review* 3:210–16.

Kennedy, Alan. 1974. *The Protean Self: Dramatic Action in Contemporary Fiction.* New York: Columbia University Press.

Kermode, Frank. 1967. *The Sense of an Ending: Studies in the Theory of Fiction.* New York: Oxford University Press.

Kett, Joseph F. 1977. *Rites of Passage: Adolescence in America 1790 to the Present.* New York: Basic Books.

Kihlstrom, John F., and Nancy Cantor. 1984. "Mental representations of the self." *Advances in Experimental Social Psychology* 17:1–47.

King, John Owen. 1983. *The Iron of Melancholy: Structures of Spiritual Conversion in America from the Puritan Conscience to Victorian Neurosis.* Middletown, Conn.: Wesleyan University Press.

Kingston, Maxine Hong. 1976. *The Woman Warrior.* New York: Alfred A. Knopf.

Koestler, Arthur. [1952] 1969. *Arrow in the Blue.* New York: Macmillan Company.

Kohli, Martin. 1981. "Biography: account, text, method." In *Biography and Society,* edited by D. Bertaux, 61–75. Beverly Hills, Calif.: Sage.

Kronenberger, Louis. 1930. Review of *Kiki's Memoirs. New York Times Book Review,* 28 September.

Krupat, Arnold. 1985. *For Those Who Come After: A Study of Native American Autobiography.* Berkeley: University of California Press.

Kuhn, Manford H., and Thomas S. McPartland. 1954. "An empirical investigation of self-attitudes." *American Sociological Review* 19:68–76.

Lakoff, George, and Mark Turner. 1989. *More than Cool Reason: A Field Guide to Poetic Metaphor.* Chicago: University of Chicago Press.

Landow, George P. 1979. *Approaches to Victorian Autobiography.* Athens: Ohio University Press.

Langness, Lewis L. 1965. *The Life History in Anthropological Science.* New York: Holt, Rinehart and Winston.

Langness, L. L., and Gelya Frank. 1981. *Lives: An Anthropological Approach to Biography.* Novato, Calif.: Chandler and Sharp.

Lasch, Christopher. 1977. *Haven in a Heartless World: The Family Besieged.* New York: Basic Books.

Lears, T. J. Jackson. 1981. *No Place of Grace: Antimodernism and the Transformation of American Culture 1880–1920.* New York: Pantheon.

Lebra, Takie Sugiyama. 1984. *Japanese Women: Constraint and Fulfillment.* Honolulu: University of Hawaii Press.

Lee, Dorothy. 1950. "Notes on the conception of the self among the Wintu Indians." *Journal of Abnormal and Social Psychology* 45:538–43.

———. 1959. "Codifications of reality: lineal and nonlineal." In *Freedom and Culture,* 105–20. Englewood Cliffs, N.J.: Prentice-Hall.

Leech, Geoffrey N. 1983. *Principles of Pragmatics.* London: Longman.

Leiris, Michel. [1939] 1984. *Manhood: A Journey from Childhood into the Fierce Order of Virility.* San Francisco: North Point Press.

Lejeune, Philippe. 1989. *On Autobiography.* Minneapolis: University of Minnesota Press.

Lemay, J. A., and P. M. Zall, eds. 1981. *The Autobiography of Benjamin Franklin: A Genetic Text.* Knoxville: University of Tennessee Press.

_____. 1986. *Benjamin Franklin's Autobiography.* New York: W. W. Norton and Company.

Lesser, Wendy. 1988. "Autobiography and the 'I' of the beholder." *The New York Times Book Review,* 27 November.

Leverenz, David. 1980. *The Language of Puritan Feeling.* New Brunswick, N.J.: Rutgers University Press.

Lofland, John. 1966. *Doomsday Cult: A Study of Conversion, Proselytization, and Maintenance of Faith.* Englewood Cliffs, N.J.: Prentice-Hall.

_____. 1984. "Erving Goffman's sociological legacies." *Urban Life* 13:7–34.

Lowenthal, Leo. 1950. "Biographies in popular magazines." In *Reader in Public Opinion and Communication,* edited by Bernard Berelson and Morris Janowitz, 289–98. Glencoe, Ill.: Free Press.

Luria, A. R. 1976. *Cognitive Development.* Cambridge, Mass.: Harvard University Press.

Lutz, Catherine A. 1988. *Unnatural Emotions: Everyday Sentiments on a Micronesian Atoll and Their Challenge to Western Theory.* Chicago: University of Chicago Press.

Lyman, Stanford. 1994. *Color, Culture, Civilization.* Urbana: University of Illinois Press.

Lyman, Stanford M., and William A. Douglass. 1973. "Ethnicity: strategies of collective and individual impression management." *Social Research* 40:344–65.

McCall, Michal M., and Judith Wittner. 1990. "The good news about life history." In *Symbolic Interaction and Cultural Studies,* edited by Howard S. Becker and Michal M. McCall, 46–89. Chicago: University of Chicago Press.

MacCunn, John. 1912. *The Making of Character: Some Educational Aspects of Ethics.* New York: Macmillan Company.

McDowell, Edwin. 1991. "More books revealing lusts, especially for sales." *The New York Times,* 14 January.

McGuire, William J., and Claire V. McGuire. 1981. "The spontaneous self-concept as affected by personal distinctiveness." In *Self-Concept: Advances in Theory and Research,* edited by Mervin Lynch, Ardyth Norem-Hebeisen, and Kenneth Gergen, 147–71. Cambridge, Mass.: Ballinger.

MacLeod, Anne Scott. 1975. *A Moral Tale: Children's Fiction and American Culture 1820–1860.* Hamden, Conn.: Archon.

_____. 1985. "An end to innocence: the transformation of childhood in twentieth-century children's literature." In *Opening Texts: Psychoanalysis and the Culture of the Child,* edited by Joseph H. Smith and William Kerrigan, 100–117. Baltimore: Johns Hopkins University Press.

McLoughlin, William G., ed. 1968. *The American Evangelicals, 1800–1900.* New York: Harper and Row.

McReynolds, Paul. 1990. "Motives and metaphors: a study in scientific creativity." In *Metaphors in the History of Psychology,* edited by David Leary, 133–72. Cambridge: Cambridge University Press.

Maines, David R. 1993. "Narrative's moment and sociology's phenomena: toward a narrative sociology." *The Sociological Quarterly* 34:17–38.

Malraux, André. 1968. *Anti-Memoirs*. New York: Holt, Rinehart and Winston.

Mannheim, Karl. 1952. "The problem of generations." In *Essays on the Sociology of Knowledge,* 276–322. New York: Oxford University Press.

Marcus, Laura. 1994. *Auto/biographical Discourses.* New York: St. Martin's Press.

Marden, Orison Swett. 1895. *Architects of Fate; or, Steps to Success and Power, a Book Designed to Inspire Youth to Character-Building, Self-Culture, and Noble Achievement.* New York: Houghton Mifflin Company.

Mariampolski, Hyman, and Dana Hughes. 1978. "The use of personal documents in historical sociology." *The American Sociologist* 13:104–13.

Marsella, Anthony, George De Vos, and Francis Hsu, eds. 1985. *Culture and Self: Asian and Western Perspectives.* New York: Tavistock.

Marshall, David B. 1992. *Secularizing the Faith: Canadian Protestant Clergy and the Crisis of Belief, 1850–1940.* Toronto: University of Toronto Press.

Martin, Wallace. 1986. *Recent Theories of Narrative.* Ithaca, N.Y.: Cornell University Press.

Marty, Martin E. 1972. *Protestantism.* New York: Holt, Rinehart and Winston.

Mason, Mary. 1980. "The other voice: autobiographies of women writers." In *Autobiography: Essays Theoretical and Critical,* edited by James Olney, 207–35. Princeton: Princeton University Press.

Mathews, Donald G. 1978. "The second great awakening as an organizing process, 1780–1830." In *Religion in American History,* edited by John Mulder and John Wilson, 199–217. Englewood Cliffs, N.J.: Prentice-Hall.

Mauss, Marcel. [1938] 1979. "A category of the human mind: the notion of person, the notion of 'self.'" In *Sociology and Psychology,* 59–94. Translated by Ben Brewster. London: Routledge and Kegan Paul.

Mazlish, Bruce. 1970. "Autobiography and psycho-analysis: between truth and self-deception." *Encounter* 35:28–37.

Mead, George Herbert. 1932. *The Philosophy of the Present.* Chicago: University of Chicago Press.

———. 1934. *Mind, Self and Society.* Edited by Charles Morris. Chicago: University of Chicago Press.

———. 1936. *Movements of Thought in the Nineteenth Century.* Chicago: University of Chicago Press.

Mehlman, Jeffrey. 1974. *A Structural Study of Autobiography: Proust, Leiris, Sartre, Lévi-Strauss.* Ithaca: Cornell University Press.

Menen, Aubrey. 1970. *The Space within the Heart.* New York: McGraw-Hill.

Menninger, Karl. 1973. *Whatever Became of Sin?* New York: Hawthorn Books.

Mill, John Stuart. [1859] 1991. *On Liberty and Other Essays.* Edited by John Gray. New York: Oxford University Press.

———. [1873] 1969. *Autobiography.* Boston: Houghton Mifflin Company.

Miller, J. Hillis. 1995. "Narrative." In *Critical Terms for Literary Study,* edited by

Frank Lentricchia and Thomas McLaughlin, 66–79. 2d ed. Chicago: University of Chicago Press.

Miller, Joan G. 1984. "Culture and the development of everyday social explanation." *Journal of Personality and Social Psychology* 46:961–78.

Miller, Perry. 1965. *The Life of the Mind in America: From the Revolution to the Civil War.* New York: Harcourt, Brace, and World.

Mills, C. Wright. 1940. "Situated actions and vocabularies of motives." *American Sociological Review* 5:904–13.

_____. 1951. *White Collar: The American Middle Classes.* New York: Oxford University Press.

_____. 1959. *The Sociological Imagination.* New York: Oxford University Press.

Misch, Georg. [1907] 1951. *A History of Autobiography in Antiquity.* Cambridge, Mass.: Harvard University Press.

Misiak, Henryk, and Virginia S. Sexton. 1966. *A History of Psychology.* New York: Grune and Stratton.

Miyoshi, Masao. 1969. *The Divided Self: A Perspective on the Literature of the Victorians.* New York: New York University Press.

Moberg, George. 1983. "Tips on how—and why—to write your autobiography." *Writers Digest* (May): 32–33.

Montaigne, Michel de. [1580] 1946. *The Essays of Montaigne.* Translated by E. J. Trechmann. New York: Random House.

Moore, James R. 1979. *The Post-Darwinian Controversies.* Cambridge: Cambridge University Press.

Morgan, Edmund S. 1963. *Visible Saints: The History of a Puritan Idea.* Ithaca: Cornell University Press.

Morris, Colin. 1972. *The Discovery of the Individual 1050–1200.* New York: Harper and Row.

Morss, John R. 1990. *The Biologizing of Childhood: Developmental Psychology and the Darwinian Myth.* London: Lawrence Erlbaum Associates.

Moscovici, Serge. 1961. *La Psychanalyse, Son Image et Son Public: Etude sur la Representation Sociale de la Psychanalyse.* Paris: Presses Universitaires de France.

Mosier, Richard D. 1965. *Making the American Mind: Social and Moral Ideas in the McGuffey Readers.* New York: Russell and Russell.

Nadel, Ira B. 1987. "Narrative and the popularity of biography." *Mosaic* 20:131–42.

Nash, Manning. 1989. *The Cauldron of Ethnicity in the Modern World.* Chicago: University of Chicago Press.

Nelson, Benjamin, ed. 1957. *Freud and the 20th Century.* New York: Meridian Books.

Nichols, Ashton. 1987. *The Poetics of Epiphany: Nineteenth-Century Origins of the Modern Literary Movement.* Tuscaloosa: University of Alabama Press.

Nichols, J. L. 1904. *The Business Guide . . . or . . . Safe Methods of Business.* Naperville, Ill.: J. L. Nichols and Co.

Nietzsche, Friedrich. 1968. *The Portable Nietzsche.* Selected and translated by Walter Kaufmann. New York: Viking Press.

Nussbaum, Felicity A. 1989. *The Autobiographical Subject: Gender and Ideology in Eighteenth-Century England.* Baltimore: Johns Hopkins University Press.

Nyberg, David. 1993. *The Varnished Truth: Truth Telling and Deceiving in Ordinary Life.* Chicago: University of Chicago Press.

Oates, Joyce Carol. 1988. Review of *Jean Stafford: A Biography,* by David Roberts. *The New York Times Book Review,* 28 August.

Olney, James. 1972. *Metaphors of Self: The Meaning of Autobiography.* Princeton: Princeton University Press.

_____. 1980. *Autobiography: Essays Theoretical and Critical.* Princeton: Princeton University Press.

_____. 1985. "'I was born': slave narratives, their status as autobiography and as literature." In *The Slave's Narrative,* edited by Charles Davis and Henry Louis Gates, Jr., 148–75. New York: Oxford University Press.

Omi, Michael, and Howard Winant. 1986. *Racial Formation in the United States from the 1960s to the 1980s.* New York: Routledge and Kegan Paul.

Ortner, Sherry B. 1984. "Theory in anthropology since the sixties." *Comparative Studies in Society and History* 26:126–66.

Orwell, George. 1954. "Such, such were the joys. . . . " In *A Collection of Essays,* 9–55. Garden City, N.Y.: Doubleday and Company.

Padilla, Genaro M. 1993. *My History, Not Yours: The Formation of Mexican American Autobiography.* Madison: University of Wisconsin Press.

Pagels, Elaine. 1988. *Adam, Eve, and the Serpent.* New York: Random House.

Pascal, Roy. 1960. *Design and Truth in Autobiography.* Cambridge, Mass.: Harvard University Press.

Payne, James Robert, ed. 1992. *Multicultural Autobiography: American Lives.* Knoxville: University of Tennessee Press.

Peckham, Morse. 1959. "Darwinism and Darwinisticism." *Victorian Studies* 3:19–40.

Perinbanayagam, R. S. 1991. *Discursive Acts.* New York: Aldine De Gruyter.

Perry, Lewis. 1989. *Intellectual Life in America: A History.* Chicago: University of Chicago Press.

Personal Narratives Group, eds. 1989. *Interpreting Women's Lives.* Bloomington: Indiana University Press.

Peterson, Linda H. 1986. *Victorian Autobiography: The Tradition of Self-Interpretation.* New Haven: Yale University Press.

_____. 1993. "Institutionalizing women's autobiography: nineteenth-century editors and the shaping of an autobiographical tradition." In *The Culture of Autobiography,* edited by Robert Folkenflik, 80–103. Stanford: Stanford University Press.

Pettit, Norman. 1966. *The Heart Prepared: Grace and Conversion in Puritan Spiritual Life.* New Haven: Yale University Press.

Pittel, Stephen M., and Gerald A. Mendelsohn. 1966. "Measurement of moral values: a review and critique." *Psychological Bulletin* 66:22–35.

Plato. 1973. *Phaedrus and the Seventh and Eighth Letters.* Translated by Walter Hamilton. New York: Penguin Books.

Plummer, Ken. 1983. *Documents of Life: An Introduction to the Problems and Literature of a Humanistic Method.* London: George Allen and Unwin.

————. 1995. *Telling Sexual Stories.* London: Routledge.

Plutarch. 1905. *Plutarch's Essays and Miscellanies.* Vol. 2. Edited by A. Clough and W. Goodwin. New York: Colonial Company.

Pope, Alexander. [1734] 1969. *An Essay on Man.* Menston, England: Scolar Press Limited.

Potter, Jonathan, and Margaret Wetherell. 1987. *Discourse and Social Psychology: Beyond Attitudes and Behavior.* London: Sage Publications.

Potter, Robert. 1975. *The English Morality Play: Origins, History and Influence of a Dramatic Tradition.* London: Routledge and Kegan Paul.

Pratkanis, Anthony, and Anthony Greenwald. 1985. "How shall the self be conceived?" *Journal for the Theory of Social Behavior* 15:311–29.

Pratt, Mary Louise. 1977. *Toward a Speech Act Theory of Literary Discourse.* Bloomington: Indiana University Press.

Rattansi, Ali. 1995. "Just framing: ethnicities and racisms in a 'postmodern' framework." In *Social Postmodernism: Beyond Identity Politics,* edited by Linda Nicholson and Steven Seidman, 250–86. Cambridge: Cambridge University Press.

Rauch, Friedrich A. 1840. *Psychology: or, a View of the Human Soul, Including Anthropology.* New York: M. W. Dodd.

Raval, Suresh. 1987. "Recent books on narrative theory: an essay-review." *Modern Fiction Studies* 33:559–70.

Read, K. E. 1955. "Morality and the concept of the person among the Gahuku-Gama." *Oceania* 25:233–82.

Renza, Louis. 1977. "The veto of the imagination: a theory of autobiography." *New Literary History* 9:1–26.

Richards, Robert J. 1987. *Darwin and the Emergence of Evolutionary Theories of Mind and Behavior.* Chicago: University of Chicago Press.

Rieff, Philip. 1959. *Freud: The Mind of a Moralist.* New York: Viking Press.

Riesman, David, Nathan Glazer, and Reuel Denney. 1950. *The Lonely Crowd: A Study of the Changing American Character.* New Haven: Yale University Press.

Riley, Denise. 1983. *War in the Nursery: Theories of the Child and Mother.* London: Virago.

Ritzer, George. 1988. *Contemporary Sociological Theory.* 2d ed. New York: Alfred A. Knopf.

Robinson, David. 1982. *Apostle of Culture: Emerson as Preacher and Lecturer.* Philadelphia: University of Pennsylvania Press.

Rodriguez, Richard. 1989. "An American writer." In *The Invention of Ethnicity,* edited by Werner Sollors, 3–13. New York: Oxford University Press.

Rogers, Carl. 1961. *On Becoming a Person: A Therapist's View of Psychotherapy.* Boston: Houghton Mifflin Company.

————. 1970. *Carl Rogers on Encounter Groups.* New York: Harper and Row.

Rogers, Robert. 1970. *The Double in Literature.* Detroit: Wayne State University Press.

Roland, Alan. 1988. *In Search of Self in India and Japan: Toward a Cross-Cultural Psychology.* Princeton: Princeton University Press.

————. 1991. "The self in cross-civilizational perspective: an Indian-Japanese-American comparison." In *The Relational Self: Theoretical Convergences in Psychoanalysis and Social Psychology,* edited by Rebecca C. Curtis, 160–80. New York: Guilford Press.

Roosevelt, Theodore. 1900. "Character and success." *Outlook* 64:725–27.

Rorty, Amélie Oksenberg, ed. 1976. *The Identities of Persons.* Berkeley: University of California Press.

Rorty, Richard. 1967. *The Linguistic Turn: Recent Essays in Philosophical Method.* Chicago: University of Chicago Press.

————. 1986. "Freud and moral reflection." In *Pragmatism's Freud: The Moral Disposition of Psychoanalysis,* edited by Joseph H. Smith and William Kerrigan, 1–27. Baltimore: Johns Hopkins University Press.

————. 1989. *Contingency, Irony, and Solidarity.* Cambridge: Cambridge University Press.

Rosaldo, Michelle Z. 1980. *Knowledge and Passion: Ilongot Notions of Self and Social Life.* Cambridge: Cambridge University Press.

————. 1984. "Toward an anthropology of self and feeling." In *Culture Theory: Essays on Mind, Self, and Emotion,* edited by Richard A. Shweder and Robert A. LeVine, 137–57. Cambridge: Cambridge University Press.

Rosenberg, Morris. 1979. *Conceiving the Self.* New York: Basic Books.

————. 1981. "The self-concept: social product and social force." In *Social Psychology: Sociological Perspectives,* edited by Morris Rosenberg and Ralph H. Turner, 593–624. New York: Basic Books.

Rosenberg, Morris, and Howard B. Kaplan, eds. 1982. *Social Psychology of the Self-Concept.* Arlington Heights, Ill.: Harlan Davidson.

Rosenthal, Peggy. 1984. *Words and Values: Some Leading Words and Where They Lead Us.* New York: Oxford University Press.

Ross, Dorothy. 1972. *G. Stanley Hall: The Psychologist as Prophet.* Chicago: University of Chicago Press.

————. 1991. *The Origins of American Social Science.* Cambridge: Cambridge University Press.

Roth, Philip. 1988. *The Facts: A Novelist's Autobiography.* New York: Farrar, Straus and Giroux.

Rotundo, E. Anthony. 1993. *American Manhood: Transformations in Masculinity from the Revolution to the Modern Era.* New York: Basic Books.

Rousseau, Jean-Jacques. [1762] 1974. *Émile.* London: J. M. Dent and Sons.

————. [1781] 1953. *The Confessions.* New York: Penguin Books.

Rubin, Joan Shelley. 1992. *The Making of Middlebrow Culture.* Chapel Hill: University of North Carolina Press.

Russett, Cynthia Eagle. 1976. *Darwin in America: The Intellectual Response 1865–1912.* San Francisco: W. H. Freeman and Company.

Safire, William. 1987. Review of *Man of the House,* by Tip O'Neill with William Novak. *The New York Times Book Review,* 6 September.

Sarbin, Theodore R. 1986a. "Emotion and act: roles and rhetoric." In *The Social Construction of Emotions,* edited by Rom Harré, 83–97. Oxford: Basil Blackwell.

Sarbin, Theodore R,, ed. 1986b. *Narrative Psychology: The Storied Nature of Human Conduct.* New York: Praeger.

Sartre, Jean-Paul. 1964. *The Words.* Greenwich, Conn: Fawcett Publications.

Sass, Louis A. 1988. "The self and its vicissitudes: an 'archaeological' study of the psychoanalytic avant-garde." *Social Research* 55:551–607.

Sayre, Robert F. 1981. "The proper study: autobiographies in American studies." In *The American Autobiography,* edited by Albert E. Stone, 11–30. Englewood Cliffs, N.J.: Prentice-Hall.

Schafer, Roy. 1980. "Narration in the psychoanalytic dialogue." *Critical Inquiry* 7:29–53.

Schlenker, Barry R. 1986. "Self-identification: toward an integration of the private and public self." In *Public Self and Private Self,* edited by Roy Baumeister, 21–62. New York: Springer-Verlag.

Schlenker, Barry R., and Mark R. Leary. 1982. "Audiences' reactions to self-enhancing, self-denigrating, and accurate self-presentations." *Journal of Experimental Social Psychology* 18:89–104.

Schneider, Louis, and Sanford M. Dornbusch. 1958. *Popular Religion: Inspirational Books in America.* Chicago: University of Chicago Press.

Schwartz, Howard, and Jerry Jacobs. 1979. *Qualitative Sociology: A Method to the Madness.* New York: Free Press.

Scott, Marvin B., and Stanford M. Lyman. 1968. "Accounts." *American Sociological Review* 33:46–62.

Searle, John R. 1969. *Speech Acts.* Cambridge: Cambridge University Press.

Seeley, John R. 1967. *The Americanization of the Unconscious.* New York: J. B. Lippincott Company.

Semmel, Bernard. 1973. *The Methodist Revolution.* New York: Basic Books.

Seymour, Charles C. B. 1858. *Self-Made Men.* New York: Harper and Brothers.

Shapiro, Stephen A. 1968. "The dark continent of literature: autobiography." *Comparative Literature Studies* 5:421–54.

Shaw, George Bernard. [1921] 1947. *Back to Methuselah: A Metabiological Pentateuch.* Rev. ed. New York: Oxford University Press.

Shea, Daniel B. 1968. *Spiritual Autobiography in Early America.* Princeton: Princeton University Press.

Sheed, Wilfrid. 1987. "Her youth observed." *The New York Times Book Review,* 19 April.

Shepard, Thomas. 1660. *The Parable of the Ten Virgins Open and Applied.* London: John Rothwell and Samuel Thomson.

Sheringham, Michael. 1993. *French Autobiography: Devices and Desires.* Oxford: Clarendon Press.

Shields, Stephanie A., and Beth Koster. 1989. "Emotional stereotyping of parents in child rearing manuals 1915–1980." *Social Psychology Quarterly* 52:44–55.

Shklovsky, Victor. [1917] 1965. "Art as technique." In *Russian Formalist Criticism: Four Essays,* edited by Lee Lemon and Marion Reis, 3–24. Lincoln: University of Nebraska Press.

Shotter, John. 1984. *Social Accountability and Selfhood.* New York: Basil Blackwell.

Shotter, John, and Kenneth Gergen, eds. 1989. *Texts of Identity.* Newbury Park, Calif.: Sage.

Shumaker, Wayne. 1954. *English Autobiography: Its Emergence, Materials, and Form.* Berkeley: University of California Press.

Shweder, Richard A., and Robert A. LeVine, eds. 1984. *Culture Theory: Essays on Mind, Self, and Emotion.* Cambridge: Cambridge University Press.

Simmel, Georg. [1917] 1950. "Individual and society in eighteenth- and nineteenth-century views of life." In *The Sociology of Georg Simmel,* edited by Kurt Wolff, 58–84. New York: Free Press.

Skinner, B. F. 1971. *Beyond Freedom and Dignity.* New York: Alfred A. Knopf.

————. 1974. *About Behaviorism.* New York: Vintage Books.

Skinner, Quentin. 1969. "Meaning and understanding in the history of ideas." *History and Theory* 8:3–53.

Small, Albion W. 1895. "The era of sociology." *American Journal of Sociology* 1:1 15.

————. 1916. "Fifty years of sociology in the United States." *American Journal of Sociology* 21:721–864.

Smelstor, Marjorie. 1984. "A hall of mirrors: modern autobiography and the process of creating the self." *Prose Studies* 7: 240–49.

Smilgis, Martha. 1989. "The celebs' golden mouthpiece." *Time Magazine,* 27 November, 82.

Smith, Jean. 1981. "Self and experience in Maori culture." In *Indigenous Psychologies: The Anthropology of the Self,* edited by Paul Heelas and Andrew Lock, 145–59. London: Academic Press.

Smith, M. Brewster. 1985. "The metaphorical basis of selfhood." In *Culture and Self: Asian and Western Perspectives,* edited by Anthony Marsella, George De Vos, and Francis Hsu, 56–88. New York: Tavistock.

Smith, Robert J. 1983. *Japanese Society: Tradition, Self, and the Social Order.* Cambridge: Cambridge University Press.

Smith, Sidonie. 1974. *Where I'm Bound: Patterns of Slavery and Freedom in Black American Autobiography.* Westport, Conn.: Greenwood Press.

————. 1987. *A Poetics of Women's Autobiography: Marginality and the Fictions of Self-Representation.* Bloomington: Indiana University Press.

Smith, Sidonie, and Julia Watson, eds. 1992. *De/Colonizing the Subject: The Poli-*

    tics of Gender in Women's Autobiography. Minneapolis: University of Minnesota
    Press.

_____. 1996. *Getting a Life: Everyday Uses of Autobiography.* Minneapolis:
    University of Minnesota Press.

Smith, Timothy L. 1957. *Revivalism and Social Reform in Mid-Nineteenth-Century
    America.* New York: Abingdon Press.

Sollors, Werner, ed. 1989. *The Invention of Ethnicity.* New York: Oxford Univer-
    sity Press.

Soltow, Lee, and Edward Stevens. 1981. *The Rise of Literacy and the Common
    School in the United States: A Socioeconomic Analysis to 1870.* Chicago: Univer-
    sity of Chicago Press.

Solzhenitsyn, Alexander. 1975. *The Gulag Archipelago 1918–1956.* Vol. 2. New York:
    Harper & Row.

Spacks, Patricia Meyer. 1976. *Imagining a Self: Autobiography and the Novel in
    Eighteenth-Century England.* Cambridge, Mass.: Harvard University Press.

_____. 1980. "Selves in hiding." In *Women's Autobiography: Essays in Criti-
    cism,* edited by Estelle C. Jelinek, 112–32. Bloomington: Indiana University
    Press.

Spearman, Charles E. 1937. *Psychology Down the Ages.* London: Macmillan and
    Co.

Spence, Donald P. 1982. *Narrative Truth and Historical Truth: Meaning and Inter-
    pretation in Psychoanalysis.* New York: W. W. Norton and Company.

Spencer, Herbert. [1855] 1899. *The Principles of Psychology.* 4th ed. London:
    Williams and Norgate.

_____. 1904. *An Autobiography.* 2 vols. New York: D. Appleton and Com-
    pany.

Spender, Stephen. 1951. *World within World: The Autobiography of Stephen
    Spender.* London: Faber and Faber.

Spengemann, William C., and L. R. Lundquist. 1965. "Autobiography and the
    American myth." *American Quarterly* 17:501–19.

Stanton, Domna C., ed. 1984. *The Female Autograph.* New York: New York Liter-
    ary Forum.

Starr, G. A. 1965. *Defoe and Spiritual Autobiography.* Princeton: Princeton Univer-
    sity Press.

Stauffer, Donald A. 1941. *The Art of Biography in Eighteenth Century England.*
    Princeton: Princeton University Press.

Steele, Shelby. 1988. "On being black and middle class." *Commentary* 85:42–47.

Stendhal [Marie Henry Beyle]. 1958. *The Life of Henry Brulard.* Translated by Jean
    Stewart and B. C. J. G. Knight. Chicago: University of Chicago Press.

Stevenson, Robert Louis. [1884] 1948. "A humble remonstrance." In *Henry James
    and Robert Louis Stevenson: A Record of Friendship and Criticism,* edited by
    Janet Adam Smith, 86–100. London: Rupert Hart-Davis.

_____. [1886] 1980. *Dr. Jekyll and Mr. Hyde.* New York: Signet.

Stocking, George W., Jr. 1982. *Race, Culture, and Evolution.* Chicago: University of Chicago Press.

Streitfeld, David. 1996. "Advertisements for themselves." *Vogue* (May): 161–64.

Strout, Cushing. 1981. "The historical hero in a psychological age." *Yale Review* 70:206–20.

Sturrock, John. 1977. "The new model autobiographer." *New Literary History* 9:51–63.

————. 1993. *The Language of Autobiography.* Cambridge: Cambridge University Press.

Susman, Warren I. 1984. *Culture as History: The Transformation of American Society in the Twentieth Century.* New York: Pantheon Books.

Sykes, Charles J. 1992. *A Nation of Victims: The Decay of American Character.* New York: St. Martin's Press.

Taylor, Charles. 1988. "The moral topography of the self." In *Hermeneutics and Psychological Theory,* edited by Stanley Messer, Louis Sass, and Robert Woolfolk, 298–320. New Brunswick, N.J.: Rutgers University Press.

————. 1989. *Sources of the Self: The Making of the Modern Identity.* Cambridge, Mass.: Harvard University Press.

Thomas, W. I. 1923. *The Unadjusted Girl.* Boston: Little, Brown, and Co.

Thomas, W. I., and Dorothy Swaine Thomas. 1928. *The Child in America.* New York: Alfred A. Knopf.

Thomas, W. I., and Florian Znaniecki. [1918–20] 1958. *The Polish Peasant in Europe and America.* New York: Dover Publications.

Thompson, E. P. 1966. *The Making of the English Working Class.* New York: Vintage Books.

Tocqueville, Alexis de. [1835] 1966. *Democracy in America.* New York: Harper and Row.

Tompkins, Jane P., ed. 1980. *Reader-Response Criticism: From Formalism to Post-Structuralism.* Baltimore: Johns Hopkins University Press.

Toth, Susan Allen. 1987. "The importance of being remembered." *The New York Times Book Review,* 28 June.

Trinh, T. Minh-ha. 1989. *Woman, Native, Other.* Bloomington: Indiana University Press.

Turner, Frederick Jackson. 1976. *The Frontier in American History.* Huntington, N.Y.: Robert E. Krieger Publishing Company.

Turner, Ralph H. 1975. "Is there a quest for identity?" *The Sociological Quarterly* 16:148–61.

————. 1976. "The real self: from institution to impulse." *American Journal of Sociology* 81:989–1016.

Twain, Mark. 1935. *Mark Twain's Notebook.* Edited by Albert Bigelow Paine. New York: Harper and Brothers.

Van den Berg, J. H. 1974. *Divided Existence and Complex Society: An Historical Approach.* Pittsburgh: Duquesne University Press.

Veroff, Joseph, Elizabeth Douvan, and Richard Kulka. 1981. *The Inner American: A Self-Portrait from 1957 to 1976.* New York: Basic Books.

Vincent, David. 1981. *Bread, Knowledge and Freedom: A Study of Nineteenth-Century Working Class Autobiography.* London: Methuen.

Ward, Lester Frank. [1897] 1926. *Dynamic Sociology, Or Applied Social Science, as Based upon Statical Sociology and the Less Complex Sciences.* New York: D. Appleton and Company.

Waters, Mary C. 1990. *Ethnic Options.* Berkeley: University of California Press.

Watson, John. 1928. *Psychological Care of Infant and Child.* New York: W. W. Norton and Company.

Watson, Lawrence, and Maria-Barbara Watson-Franke. 1985. *Interpreting Life Histories: An Anthropological Inquiry.* New Brunswick, N.J.: Rutgers University Press.

Weber, Max. [1904] 1958. *The Protestant Ethic and the Spirit of Capitalism.* New York: Charles Scribner's Sons.

_____. 1949. *The Methodology of the Social Sciences.* Edited by Edward Shils and Henry Finch. New York: Free Press.

Weintraub, Karl J. 1978. *The Value of the Individual: Self and Circumstance in Autobiography.* Chicago: University of Chicago Press.

Weiss, Richard. 1969. *The American Myth of Success: From Horatio Alger to Norman Vincent Peale.* New York: Basic Books.

Welter, Barbara. 1972. "The cult of true womanhood: 1820–1860." In *The American Sisterhood,* edited by Wendy Martin, 243–56. New York: Harper and Row.

Westbrook, Perry D. 1979. *Free Will and Determinism in American Literature.* Teaneck, N.J.: Fairleigh Dickinson University Press.

White, Emerson E. 1886. *The Elements of Pedagogy.* New York: Van Antwerp, Bragg.

Whittaker, Elvi. 1992. "The birth of the anthropological self and its career." *Ethos* 20: 191–219.

Whyte, William H., Jr. 1956. *The Organization Man.* Garden City, N.Y.: Doubleday.

Williams, Harold, ed. 1965. *The Correspondence of Jonathan Swift.* Vol. 4. London: Oxford University Press.

Williams, Raymond. 1983. *Keywords.* Rev. ed. New York: Oxford University Press.

Wishy, Bernard. 1968. *The Child and the Republic: The Dawn of American Child Nurture.* Philadelphia: University of Pennsylvania Press.

Wolfe, Tom. 1986. "Snob's progress." *The New York Times Book Review,* 15 June.

Wood, Michael R., and Louis A. Zurcher, Jr. 1988. *The Development of a Postmodern Self: A Computer-Assisted Comparative Analysis of Personal Documents.* New York: Greenwood Press.

Woodward, William R. 1984. "William James's psychology of will: its revolutionary impact on American psychology." In *Explorations in the History of Psychology in the United States,* edited by Josef Brozek, 148–95. Lewisburg, Pa.: Bucknell University Press.

Woolf, Virginia. [1939] 1976. *Moments of Being: Unpublished Autobiographical Writings*. Edited by Jeanne Schulkind. New York: Harcourt Brace Jovanovich.

Wright, Chauncey. 1873. "The evolution of self-consciousness." *North American Review* 116:251–73.

Wrong, Dennis H. 1961. "The oversocialized conception of man in modern sociology." *American Sociological Review* 26:183–93.

_____. 1990. "The influence of sociological ideas on American culture." In *Sociology in America,* edited by Herbert J. Gans, 19–30. Newbury Park, Calif.: Sage.

Wu, Pei-Yi. 1984. "Varieties of the Chinese self." In *Designs of Selfhood,* edited by Vytautas Kavolis, 107–31. Teaneck, N.J.: Fairleigh Dickinson University Press.

Wuthnow, Robert. 1976. *The Consciousness Reformation*. Berkeley: University of California Press.

_____. 1987. *Meaning and Moral Order*. Berkeley: University of California Press.

Wylie, Philip. [1942] 1955. *Generation of Vipers*. New York; Rinehart.

Wyllie, Irvin. 1954. *The Self-Made Man in America: The Myth of Rags to Riches*. New Brunswick, N.J.: Rutgers University Press.

Zurcher, Louis. 1977. *The Mutable Self*. Beverly Hills, Calif.: Sage.

Zweig, Paul. 1968. *The Heresy of Self-Love*. Princeton: Princeton University Press.

Index